D1445054

The house that Giacomo built

The house that Giacomo built

History of an Italian family, 1898–1978

Donald S. Pitkin

Amherst College

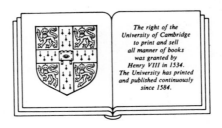

The right of the
University of Cambridge
to print and sell
all manner of books
was granted by
Henry VIII in 1534.
The University has printed
and published continuously
since 1584.

Cambridge University Press

Cambridge

London   New York   New Rochelle
Melbourne   Sydney

Published by the Press Syndicate of the University of Cambridge
The Pitt Building, Trumpington Street, Cambridge CB2 1RP
32 East 57th Street, New York, NY 10022, USA
10 Stamford Road, Oakleigh, Melbourne 3166, Australia

© Cambridge University Press 1985

First published 1985

Printed in the United States of America

Library of Congress Cataloging in Publication Data
Pitkin, Donald S. (Donald Stevenson), 1922–
The house that Giacomo built.
Bibliography: p.
Includes index.
1. Family – Italy – History – 20th century.   2. Labor
and laboring classes – Italy – History – 20th century.
I. Title.
HQ629.P53   1985   306.8'5'0945   84–29368
ISBN 0 521 30168 8

JUN 2 7 1007

For Steve and Roxie

Contents

Photographs appear between pages 17 and 18

Foreword

There are many Italies. There is the Italy of proud cities and provincial towns, surveyed by church towers and guarded by ancient battlements. There is the Italy of the senses discovered by the grand travelers of the Augustan Age and the Italy of the flowering lemon trees beloved of the German Romantics. There is the Italy of the Renaissance celebrated by Jacob Burckhardt and the somber Italy of the Counter-Reformation, the young Italy of the springtide of nations, the Italy of operatic passions. There is also the Italy of Gramsci's "failed revolution," the "cursed Italy" of the embittered emigrants, the "proletarian nation" of the Fascists, and the Italy of the Resistance with its 44,720 partisan dead. And there is the Italy of the "Economic Miracle" after the Second World War.

But there is still another and very different Italy, the Italy of the anthropologists, most of them working in small towns and villages after World War II. Donald Pitkin has been in the forefront of this band of researchers, writing his doctoral thesis on a village in the Pontine Marshes in 1954. He has since returned many times. His work, together with that of his colleagues, set the agenda of anthropology in Italy: the interplay of land tenure and family structure; the construction of gender and the sexual division of labor; the significance of dowry; the coding of honor and shame; the interaction of kinsmen and strangers, of patrons and clients; the counterpoint of formal Catholicism and popular religiosity; the antagonistic relationship of gentry and notables with people on the land; the conduct of local politics. This was not the grand Italy of poetic or political vision but an Italy of humbler folk, engaged in the actions and reactions of daily life, evaluating their own behavior and that of others, enacting cultural forms to create the dense network of reciprocities that lies at the base of those other Italies of art and history, power and wealth.

These agenda and themes are sounded again in Donald Pitkin's present book, but with a difference – for this is a different anthropological account. It is a tale of generations: Giovanni and Giulia, their daughter Maria and her husband Giacomo, and their friends and descendants. We are invited to witness their fierce and heroic struggles against grinding poverty, as well as their laborious ascent toward conditions of greater ease. We are shown how time and again they marshaled economic resources and social relationships to maintain the values of family within the orbit of the household, and to win dignity and respect in the public arena without.

In telling the story of these simple yet extraordinary people, and in having them tell it to us in their own words, Pitkin also speaks to three enduring anthropological issues. First, he addresses the issue of how the world of meaning and value is related to the sphere of material determinants. He shows us in detail how the extended family of the Rossis served them as a resource to enlarge and stabilize opportunities and yet also constituted for them a set of human relations valued in their own right. Unremitting labor was needed to sustain these values and goals. Second, he speaks to the issue of gender relations, an old concern given new prominence by feminist critique in recent decades. He shows us how much of the material provisioning of households and the marshaling of their social energy depends upon the labor of women. This labor is at once a site of exploitation and pain, a labor of commitment and love, and a source of personal reward and merit. And, third, he returns to the important question of whether different kinds of society and culture do not demand different distributions and organization of psychic energy within people. This was an important concern in American anthropology until the 1950s, when culture-and-personality studies fell into disfavor because their theories and methods could not fulfill the overly ambitious claims made for them. Yet the queries about the possible cultural channeling of emotion and cognition remain some of the most interesting questions that anthropology has asked. Pitkin has returned to some of these concerns in exploring the role of mutual dependency within extended Italian families and in asking what dependence training or independence training may do for the shaping of personalities. Thus Donald Pitkin's book shows us how Giacomo's house was put together with cement and love; but it also demonstrates how anthropology, a discipline devoted to observing and understanding "the imponderabilia of actual life," uncovers new and unsuspected chains of causation and implication in the shaping of human life.

Eric R. Wolf

Herbert Lehman College
City University of New York

Acknowledgments

I first wish to give thanks within my own circle of family for this book about another family: to my late wife Emily, whose love of Italy and the people of Valmonte helped make our field experience there the revelation that it was; to my mother, author Dorothy Pitkin, who taught me an appreciation for observation; and to my maternal grandfather, George Horton, whose writings on Greece provoked a fascination with the Mediterranean. I wish to recognize too the formative experience of the Noble and Greenough School, which kindled a respect for learning and a sense for a familial community as well. My principal mentors in anthropology were Clyde Kluckhohn, who taught his students the importance of seeing connections, and Conrad Arensberg, who insisted upon the ethnological importance of Europe.

I am especially indebted to Manlio Rossi-Doria, scholar of the Italian south, ardent fighter of Fascism, and exemplar of all that is most worthy in the Italian character. I also wish to thank Renata and Eugenio Gaddini, who have always provided me with every encouragement from 1951 to the present. And thanks too for the gentle but wise advice of the eminent Italian anthropologist Tullio Tentori.

I wish, also, to recognize one book that made all the difference, Carlo Levi's *Christ Stopped at Eboli*. I read it for the first time in 1948. It drew me like a magnet to that Italy which he described so beautifully.

In the final preparation of the manuscript I found perceptive the comments of my colleagues at Amherst College, Peter Czap, Jan Dizard, Robert May, Rose Olver and Kim Townsend, as well as my friend Ruth Backes. I owe much to Susan Urquhart, who adroitly transformed the manuscript from its earliest to final manifestation, and I am profoundly grateful to my prescient editor at Cambridge University Press, Sue Allen-Mills.

But finally it is to those people I have written about here to whom I

xi

am most deeply indebted. I count our friendship as one of the treasures of my life. Out of respect for their actual historical identities I have changed all family names and most Christian names. Valmonte, as well as several other places mentioned, are known by other appellations.

Prologue

I was unprepared for what I saw when I drove into Giacomo's yard on Sunday, January 23, 1977. I had been out of touch with the Rossi family for some time. I had sent a telegram from Rome saying that I would be down for the day, but it had not arrived. Maria was hanging out the wash. She was surprised to see me but not unduly so; life is full of the unpredictable. We embraced. Giulia Tassoni, her mother, appeared at the door, a frail figure in black, one hand holding the door frame for support; tears filled her eyes. Giovanni Battista Tassoni, her husband, had died since I had seen her last. After our sorrowful greeting I asked, "Where is Giacomo?" expecting to see his portly figure appear at the door. "He is working on the house with Luigi. Come, I will show you," Maria said. We started out the yard and down the dirt road that runs by the canal. "Giacomo has been working hard to finish it, for Luigi is getting married this summer to Silvia, a girl from Sessa," Maria explained as I, looking up, saw it, a house four times as large as their own, two stories high, surmounted by a handsome red-tiled pitched roof. It was impressive, the kind a successful California businessman might aspire to in midlife. My anthropological interest was strongly piqued by the fact that here was a modern family enjoying greater prosperity than it ever had before, planning a future centered on a variation of an extended family.

We met Giacomo coming toward us down the short piece of road that separated the houses, covered from head to foot with plaster. I could see that he was older, graying at the temples, his comfortable paunch protruding a bit more. We embraced and he asked after my children, Steve and Roxie. We returned to the house, where Giacomo cleaned up and Maria took her scissors to the hen run to dispatch one for the midday meal. The eldest son, Luigi, came in to greet me, now a full-grown man with a moustache; he told me that he would show me

1

the house after we had finished eating. I congratulated him on his impending marriage. Teresa, seventeen, and her younger sister Caterina, thirteen, drove up to the front door on the moped. They had been sent for fresh bread, cheese, and olives. Teresa had become a pretty, vivacious young lady. Caterina was more reserved with me. Bruno, their younger son, was in the military in northern Italy, Maria told me. She showed me a snapshot of him leaning against a tank, the military beret cocked at a jaunty angle on his head. Later Giacomo said he was going to add two floors onto his own house to make a home for Bruno.

Maria laid a place for me at the head of the table. I looked at the kitchen, which I remembered from a visit I had made six years ago with my son, Steve, for the celebration of the fiftieth wedding anniversary of Giovanni and Giulia. The table around which we sat was the same, as were the cupboard full of Maria's best cups, Giacomo's bottles of liquors, and Maria's purse, where the family money is kept. I remembered the refrigerator, the spotless gas stove, and the TV on the cupboard placed so that they could watch the evening news, but the freezer in the corner was new. Maria said that Luigi, who works in the frozen food depository plant, had given it to her last year. She opened it, Giulia's eyes following her every move, took out some frozen greens from the garden, and moved toward the stove. Giacomo slapped her behind playfully from where he sat at the side of the table. She cuffed him in return, as a large smile wreathed her face.

For a moment I had to pinch myself to realize where I was in time and space. I didn't feel that old but I understood, as if for the first time, that I had known these people for twenty-six years; more than a quarter of a century had passed since I first sat with my late wife, Emily, in Giulia's smoke-blackened kitchen in their old house in the village. It was June 1951. I remember Giulia leaning over the open fire stirring the pasta in the pot, while the sauce bubbled in the small earthenware bowl on a tripod snuggled up to the coals. Maria, then twenty-one, was grating cheese at the table. Giacomo, her dark, handsome young suitor, sat silently on a chair by the fire, stealing glances from time to time in her direction. Giovanni, a manual laborer, was recalling experiences from his great adventure, the two years spent working in Argentina, from 1926 to 1928. By the time the pasta was on the table we had been joined by Salvatore, then twenty-three, a manual laborer like his father; Pasquale, eighteen, a tailor's apprentice; Tonino, thirteen, and Michele, six. Michele we discovered was not Giulia's son but the illegitimate child of Concetta, their firstborn, who lived with her second husband, Felice, a night watchman in Piove di Sacco, near Padua. In the days to come the story of the betrayal of the family by Concetta's first husband was to be painfully and bitterly revealed. The shame that Giovanni and Giulia felt was still deeply palpable.

That evening we learned that Giovanni and Giulia Tassoni were both born around the turn of the century in Stilo, Calabria, and had brought their then family of four to Valmonte in 1933 to improve their lot. It was when the Fascist regime was embarked on a massive project to reclaim the Pontine Marshes for farming. It became clear, as they spoke, that although they would never have returned to the harsh land of Calabria, they were proud of their Calabrian heritage; they would never renounce it. For the Tassoni family life since 1933 in Valmonte had been a long struggle, and even now in 1951 times were hard everywhere.

From that day in June to the following July of 1952 we saw a good deal of the Tassoni family, especially Maria. She cooked lunch for us every day over the fire in our house, and often Giacomo would come to visit in the evening. We had settled in Valmonte for a year, a year that was to become eighteen months by the time we left in the late summer of 1952. A graduate student in anthropology at Harvard, I had come to study Valmonte as a community with a particular interest in the relationship between land tenure and family organization. I was struck by the fact that most households among the poor villagers, who were largely agricultural day laborers, seemed to be made up of nuclear families. But when some were granted new farms created by the reclamation of the marshes an interesting thing happened. In the course of time the head of the family would build an addition or even another house on the land for a married son to live in. The extension of households seemed like turning the clock back to an earlier agricultural time when land ownership both necessitated and permitted the co-residence of multiple families on the land. In a sense an important goal of the reclamation of the marshes for the Fascists was just that: a turning back of the clock to create a peasant population attached to the soil, politically conservative, and grateful and loyal to the regime. I wondered, as I later finished the analysis, what would happen to the impetus toward familial extension as the area became industrialized, as surely it was bound to. One plant, the French-controlled Accord factory, was already producing transistors. A common assumption, for which there seemed to be a good deal of evidence in the industrial West, was that industry had a corrosive effect on composite family organization. It was held that industrialism and nuclear families seemed to go together like fire and smoke.

After lunch I walked with Giacomo and Luigi to see the new house; Maria and the girls remained behind to clean up. There was still a lot of interior work to do, but Luigi showed me the finger-tip action on the sliding garage door on the ground level. Giacomo was proud of the exterior steps leading to a balcony on the second floor and to the front door. I was not prepared for the living room – it was immense – nor for the two bathrooms, one beside the other – one for Luigi and Silvia, the other for their children.

It was while we were slowly returning the few yards to Giacomo's house that it suddenly came upon me: I would have to return in my forthcoming sabbatical year to Valmonte, to the Rossi family, for there was a story worth telling – two stories, in effect. One, a domestic history of this family triggered by my esteem for them; the second, flowing from the first, would attempt to explain what I saw happening that day, a man building houses for his married sons so that they might live nearby rather than encouraging them to leave, to become "independent," as is the wont among most parents in Western industrialized societies. I did return and I did embark upon the writing of that story.

Introduction

An anthropologist's use of oral history constitutes one of those methodological and conceptual modes in which anthropology and history meet: an outcome of the more recent confrontation between the anthropologist and literate and hierarchical society. From its inception anthropology worked within the confines of an oral tradition: Rich in received wisdom but bereft of historical documents these cultures invited the anthropologist to focus on the present rather than the past. Questions of cultural derivation were undertaken by ethnohistory, involving painstaking reconstructions of distinct cultures and cultural patterns.

Before the Second World War the universe of anthropological investigation was almost exclusively that of preliterate peoples. After the war fieldwork began to include complex societies as well and the study of peasant populations within their midst. Then anthropologists, long accustomed to cultural homogeneity, had to begin to take into account social heterogeneity, dealing as they were with partial societies within larger nation-states. In time it became clear that what was being observed, both with respect to social organization as well as personal behavior, was as much a function of class specificity as cultural uniqueness. For the most part, working in that setting anthropologists undertook community studies of rural peoples, employing the traditional methods of fieldwork supplemented by other documentation: vital statistics, thematic apperception tests, film, and so on. But community studies organize the present without accounting for the past. This bias for the present resulted partly from the fact that anthropology had come into being through its engagement with "timeless societies." Not only were anthropologists ill-equipped methodologically and theoretically to undertake the burden of historical analysis of complex societies, but they appropriately felt that task better left to historians. And yet the very people that anthropologists have turned their attention to – people marginal to history – have been ignored by traditional history.[1]

History, as we have known it, has been a function of those privileged to have made a difference in the observable course of events. The lives and actions of ordinary people, lacking social visibility, have not been entered in the written record. For history is the possession of those who by casting light on themselves obscure others and thus justify their own existence. The sharp contrast between the few who stand in the light and the many in the shadows is to be found in Valmonte itself, home of a noble family, illustrious since the time of the medieval papacy. Their vast palace in Rome contains a magnificent library where scholars work on medieval family documents. The fact that the last remaining member died recently makes no difference at all upon the course of the research. What does matter is that they of titled blood were the only Valmontesi who made history, which was materialized in thousands of documents and personal memoirs.

It is another thing to reconstruct the story of a working-class family who did not make history but whose progenitors lived during the same historical period. Oral history, attending as it may to women, minority-group members, and workers, is not in and of itself a final corrective to the inequities of omission and commission made by traditional history, but it is a step in the direction of lifting a silence imposed upon them.

More than a decade has passed since Allan Nevins instituted the Oral History Research Office at Columbia University, and oral history has come of age, with a professional association and journal both in North America and Great Britain. Its practitioners are many and diverse, and its detractors remain skeptical if not adamant. Among historians it is seen as a way of more richly informing the written record – a valuable supplement. But where no such documentation exists it becomes the sole vehicle for reconstruction. In that instance historians find themselves in a situation long familiar to anthropologists bereft of the sense of authority that the written word can bestow. How does one know who and what to believe? Answers to those questions can only, at best, be partial, for they apply to the evaluation of written materials as well.

But the issue of the verification of oral data is not so important as the question of where history resides within that data. History is created not by the actions of historical actors themselves, nor by documents themselves, no matter how critical, but by the imposition of meaning upon them by historians. History begins when historians begin to think and write about the past. And so it is for oral historians too, except for one important difference: They are engaged with another living consciousness, the interviewee, in the act of historical reconstruction. What transpires between the historian and the interviewee is a conversational narrative, the telling of a tale.[2] The goal of this interchange is neither the establishment of fact nor causal explanation but elaboration, for in this context of mutuality the historian is pulled in the direction of Geertz's "thick description," where the aim of anthropology (history) becomes "the enlargement of the universe of human discourse."[3]

It was in this spirit that I asked questions of Giulia, Maria, Giacomo, and the others. Certainly I was interested in establishing a chronology of their lives, but my curiosity went beyond that to evoke their sentiments about what had befallen them. And what comes out of that critical dialogue is their form of historical consciousness, a consciousness that speaks to their own situation on the one hand and to that of the larger community on the other.[4] Shaped by their circumstances, it touches upon the outlook of other working-class people who find in their struggle more of a commonality than an individuation of purpose. It is not a tale of personal misfortune, for Giacomo's difficulties in finding work are perceived as belonging to matters beyond his control rather than an estimation of personal failure. (Indeed, where a consciousness of extreme individuation does not prevail, unemployment is less devastating than in the United States, where individuals assume responsibility for their own oppression.)[5] Above all else their story is seen by them as a continual act of sacrifice undertaken with patience and forbearance. *Sacrificare*, to sacrifice in the sense of sacrificing oneself for others, is an expression heard time and again in this household.

"To sacrifice for your children is a parent's lot," says Maria. Giulia nods her head vigorously in affirmation and hardly begins on her own litany of sacrificial acts when Maria interrupts her. "I always think," she says, "that one day Giacomo and I will go somewhere in the car just for the fun of it. We never drive anywhere together except to the cemetery to lay flowers on Papa's grave or to see Concetta when she is sick." Maria knows deep in her heart that they will never take that trip, for does not one responsibility follow another like day follows night?

When the traveling Neapolitan salesman stops with his truck invitingly full of toweling, sheeting, and bolts of bright cloth, Maria quickly hugs a piece of flowered cotton to her front but with a laugh and dismissive gesture lays it down, knowing that more towels and sheets for Teresa's and Caterina's trousseaux come first. What one does one does for others, or so it is perceived. Giacomo in his place at the table muses aloud about the next tasks he must undertake: reset the tiles over the kitchen sink in Luigi's house, or begin on Bruno's stairs. In both the myth and reality of otherness, there are seeds of an antihegemonic consciousness. The disposition of Giacomo and Maria's time and their affirmation of responsibility communicate a commitment to family without at the same time incurring allegiance to

authority. The Rossi family is not a template of that familism dear to
the heart of the nationalist state. Its adherence to otherness is also
incommensurate with the self-serving ideals of an advanced Western
society at the same time that its growth provides the space for resistance to domination. Oral history can reveal those exemplifications of
popular consciousness critical for our understanding of that universe
which hegemony attempts to subsume.

If oral history is a genre, a way of doing history, family history is a
subject of investigation. Although what I have done here assumes the
methodology of oral history, its content partakes of family history.
With very few exceptions (*Hanna's Daughters* by Dorothy Gallagher is
one), family history has made little use of personal recall.[6] Rather it has
employed "hard data" – census materials, church and civic records of
vital statistics, and so on – ever since such information was first systematically gathered. Its purpose has been the reconstitution of familial
forms in order to better understand the rhythms of change and constancy over time.

Much of the present argumentation about the alleged earlier existence
of large-scale extended families, most especially among rural peoples
and their eventual substitution by the small conjugal family, goes back
to the work of Frederic Le Play (1806-1882), French administrator and
social reformist.[7] In Le Play's eyes the weakening of the moral under-
pinnings of the nation resulted from the transformation of the stable
patriarchal household into the unstable nuclear family.

But the more recent heightening of interest in family history in the
1960s was derived, largely, from the work of another Frenchman, the
demographer Louis Henry. Although not a historian, Henry turned to
historical demography in order to obtain information on natural fertility (fertility unlimited by birth control). Henry applied the techniques
of reconstitution (the process of reconstructing the demographic history
of particular families) to estimate fertility and mortality rates.[8]

In the English-speaking world family reconstitution has found an
articulate spokesman in E. A. Wrigley at the Cambridge Group for the
History of Population and Social Structure. Although he has used the
technique of reconstitution in examining certain events in particular
groups through time, his fellow worker Peter Laslett often employed
an aggregate analysis focusing on the same events at one point in time,
providing a snapshot rather than a developmental perspective.[9] But if
the Cambridge Group has borrowed one of its methodologies from
Henry, their theoretical concerns stem more from a concern with Le
Play and what they perceive to be his ideological commitment to the
virtues of extended households. One of the main concerns of the Cambridge Group has been to dispel the myth of the historical primacy of

the extended family (the "Classical Family of Western Nostalgia," as William Goode has described it)[10] and this is done by dealing with actual family behavior rather than with idealizations made about it. Laslett's findings for one hundred communities in preindustrial England reveal that household size remained fairly constant from the sixteenth century until the beginning of the nineteenth. "There is no sign," Laslett contends, "of the large, extended coresidential family group of the traditional peasant world giving way to the small, nuclear, conjugal household of modern industrial society."[11] At the end of his introduction to *Household and Family in Past Time* (1972) Laslett asserts that a belief in the existence of extended families in earlier times resides alone "in the heads of the social scientists themselves."[12] The view that households of small size existed well before the industrial revolution has found support in Dupâquier and Jadin's study of Corsican households, in van der Woude's investigation of family structure in the Noorderk-wartier district of the province of Holland, and in Hélin's study of Liège.[13]

But since the publication of *Household and Family in Past Time* in 1972 a challenge to an exclusive emphasis on family composition and structure has come from a number of quarters. Most critical of Laslett has been the historian Lutz Berkner. What constitutes a meaningful household, Berkner argues, must reflect native perception and not the narrow definition of an outside observer.[14] Berkner shows that in the case of Austrian peasants, living under the same roof "is not the essential or even an adequate criterion for defining the household."[15] Of more general interest, though, is Berkner's contention that Laslett found the nuclear family to be ubiquitous because he disregarded the familial life cycle. Relying largely upon aggregate analysis, Laslett obscured the extent to which the nuclear family is often a phase in the developmental cycle of more complex family forms, Berkner argues.[16]

The year 1983 saw the publication of a new volume by the Cambridge Group entitled *Family Forms in Historic Europe.* Responding to the criticism of the ensuing years, it purports to be more attentive to the life cycle of the family than did the 1972 book and, equally important, recognizes the significance of regional variation in household organization in Europe. In 1972 Laslett stressed the contrast between nuclearity in the West and extension in the East. In 1983 he recognized the need for a fourfold division: West, West/central or middle, the Mediterranean, and the East; with the Mediterranean falling in the middle of a continuum stretching from the small Western household to the large multiple one of the East.[17] Laslett's representative date for the Mediterranean comes from central and northern Italy in the form of two studies undertaken in Emilia Romagna, and Friuli-Venezia Giulia, where extended families were found to be commonplace – one by Angeli and Belletini and one by Morassi.[18] Speaking of the data gathered by Morassi for late nineteenth-century Fagagna Laslett writes, "That the proportion of complex households (extended plus multiple) should rise in the village by one fifth between 1870 and 1890 . . . may still surprise us after all that has been recently published against earlier suppositions that kin complexity decreases over time, especially as industrialization sets in."[19] As it was Laslett who proclaimed the ubiquity of the preindustrial nuclear family, to now find "kin complexity" occurring with the advent of industrialism in central Italy is to call into question contentions of convergence between industrialism and specified familial forms. Indeed, the most intensive historical study of urban family forms is that undertaken by Michael Anderson for nineteenth-century Preston, a small Lancashire cotton mill city, and it reveals a significant increase in the co-residence of married couples and their parents on the part of its working-class population.[20]

It is obvious from the work of the last decade in family history that large-scale generalizations concerning industrialism are hardly useful in accounting for the forms that households may assume in any one place or time. And so it is encouraging to see the Cambridge Group calling (with some qualification) for the research of particular cases. The formation of households reflects the play of multiple forces and does not readily lend itself to linear or monocausal explanations. Furthermore, generalizations about the impact of industrialism upon kinship systems need to differentiate between the consequences for unilineal systems as opposed to bilateral ones for, as Rosenberg and Anspach have pointed out, the effect upon the former is always more significant than upon the latter.[21]

To arrive closer to Valmonte and to an understanding of the construction of the houses by Giacomo for his married sons, we need to move beyond the Cambridge Group's identification of a Mediterranean region manifesting a high degree of kin complexity and follow the way taken for the most part by anthropologists who have reported on family organization in Italy. It is commonplace among them to see a rather clear division between nuclearity in the south and extension in central and northern Italy. The thesis has been most succinctly put forth by Sydel Silverman, who has undertaken work in Tuscany. Essentially it has been argued that poverty of resources available to peasants in the south has selected against the formation of extended families, whereas in central and northeastern Italy, land tenure patterns allocated sufficient property to make possible the creation of large-scale multiple-family households.[22] Examining studies done from the south to the north, that generalization seems largely to hold true. Schneider and Schneider as well as Cronin in Sicily; Banfield, Davis, Cornelisen, and Tentori in Lucania; as well as Belmonte and Parsons in Naples – all note the prevalence of the nuclear family.[23] The only exception to this picture comes from research undertaken by William Douglass in Agnone, Molise. Douglass worked with censuses stretching from 1753 to 1970. Those figures revealed that in 1753, 63% of the households were nuclear and only 11% were fully developed joint families. By 1970 that ratio had climbed to 76% nuclear and 7% joint (leaving aside figures for stem households).[24] Despite the numerical preponderance of nuclear households, Douglass insists that the joint family was and still is regarded as socially desirable. In coming to this conclusion he refers to "certain pragmatic factors," which Silverman failed to consider, that encourage the formation of joint-family domestic groups. Chief among these were the economic benefits in sharing limited resources, which gave, at least in agricultural activities, an advantage to joint households over smaller ones. Furthermore, as the size of the household increases, so does its resource pool. Indeed, there is an increase in the per capita net worth of individual household members. The decline in the number of joint-family households in recent times is not because of a lessening of the "joint-family ethos," Douglass argues, but because of the emigration of young men who would otherwise constitute one of the married sons in such a household. Douglass concludes by saying that although he cannot claim that Agnone is typical of southern Italy, he does not feel it to be an aberration either.[25] Indeed, part of the apparent difference between Agnone and the other southern villages that have been investigated has to do with what has been counted. Douglass reminds us of the Laslett-Berkner debate and Berkner's contention that Laslett's use of aggregate analysis emphasizes the nuclear phase and obscures the possible expanded phase of the life cycle of a household.[26] But what are we to make of the disparity between the ideal of the extended family that Douglass reports and the statistical fact of nuclear preponderance? Is Laslett right in implying that the ideal exists, for whatever reason, more in Douglass's head than in the minds and hearts of the Agnonesi? I doubt it, for it is an ideal based upon the calculation of benefits that may accrue to those in a position to take advantage of household extension. The truth of this contention becomes clearer as we follow our way farther north in the peninsula.

Montecastello di Vibio in Tuscany, studied by Silverman, resides on a hilltop overlooking the valley of the Tiber. Silverman found that in 1960, 60% of the households consisted of a single nuclear family, and the remaining 40% were made up of stem- and multiple-family households – results similar to those of Douglass. Despite the predominance of the nuclear families, Silverman writes that "When people talk about the ideal family, they generally describe a three-generation family in which the sons all bring their brides into the paternal household."[27] The choice people actually make at marriage, as to whether to live apart or with parents, depends upon a number of considerations, most important of which are property, skills, and the need for labor. Silverman found that large peasant proprietors favored an extended household as did landowning families, whereas professionals, white-collar workers, artisans, and laborers did not. And yet the largest proportion of extended families was found among merchants, apparently because a business can often use the resources and talents of several adults.[28]

Evidence in the same direction is reported by David Kertzer for the countryside around Bologna. In a paper published in 1977, Kertzer writes of the households of Bertalia, a village a few kilometers from Bologna, as he was able to reconstruct them from census data for 1880. Kertzer found that 64% of the households were then conjugal and that the remainder were extended, about the same proportion Silverman reported for Tuscany and Douglass for Molise.[29] But even these ratios of nucleation to extension may be somewhat misleading, for they do not reveal the extent to which people spend time living in joint households. For if, as Kertzer suggests, one selects the individual as the unit of analysis rather than the household, as the historical demographers have done, then it becomes apparent that although at any one moment two thirds of a village population live in nuclear households, many more of them have participated in joint-household existence for significant parts of their lives.[30] Indeed, this experience may account, at least partially, for the idealization of familial extension even though the statistical reality of household composition may lead to another conclusion.

With Kertzer we come full circle to Laslett's Italian data, the sharecropping multiple households of central Italy. Writing in 1983, Laslett suggests the operation of a normative element in their formation, a cultural convention operating independently of the imperatives of work:

But important as their status as a work group was, it does not seem that it was the sole reason for the huge size of *mezzadri* households, some of the largest and most complicated in structure in Europe west of the Baltic and of Russia. It seems to have been a convention shared among landowner and share-cropper, the village community and local society, even Italian society at large, as well as the imperatives of work, which ensured that these share-cropping arrangements should give rise to such huge fraternal joint families of the Mediterranean type.[31]

If the data I have discussed so far are of recent historical origin, the possibility is left open that the movement of the Mediterranean toward non-Western familial forms may be a modern development having to do with the strengthening of, among other things, Italian share-cropping agriculture in the nineteenth century. But there is reason to believe that familial extension is a venerable practice in Italy. A recent study by historian Richard Ring, drawing upon records of the Monastery of Santa Maria di Farfa some forty-five kilometers north-northeast of Rome, reveals that the expectation that one would live in a joint family household is an old one. Ring reports that in the ninth century newly married couples took up residence with the husband's parents; brides would always marry out. Nor was it the custom as is the case in some extended families for the father to retire and turn over the management of the household to the eldest married son.[32] Ring's research would confirm, then, Laslett's conclusion in the 1983 volume, in which he refers to Italy as well as the East: "The evidence we have surveyed would seem to imply that neo-local tendencies were never part and parcel of the historical social structure of these societies as they have been for the west Europeans."[33]

Thus it would seem that what I found Giacomo doing the day I returned in 1977 was not at all out of keeping with an Italian convention for extended family formation. What was different from the practices I have been describing was the construction, commensurate with a more comfortable economic status, of an elaborate dwelling for his married sons near his own. What was traditional were the modes of sharing that this conjunction permitted.

That working-class people enter into patterns of sharing of limited resources with kin and neighbors has been testified to in a number of studies undertaken in recent years: Young and Willmott writing of a working-class London borough, Bethnal Green; Mirra Komarovsky's investigation of blue-collar marriage in a small American city, which she calls "Glenton;" and Carol Stack's study of a poor black community, the flats, in a midwestern American city.[34] Sylvia Yanagisako's description of kin networking among Japanese-Americans in Seattle makes it clear, however, that such strategies are not confined to the working and under classes.[35] Kin cooperation in Bethnal Green meant that many couples began their married life in the parental home. Later on with the mother's help they would find a place of their own, but always with the preference of living near their parents so that they might more readily visit each other. But in the flats, the option of establishing independent households was not available. There, writes Stack, "The life histories of adults show that the attempts by women to set up separate households with their children and husbands, or boyfriends, are short-lived."[36] The strategies for survival noted by Stack involve a complex pattern of kin alliances for the exchange of essential goods and services. Yanagisako, in her research of Nisei families in Seattle, stresses the extent to which facilitation of ties between kin-related households was almost totally woman-centered.[37] The centrality of Nisei women in the maintenance of kin ties involving the exchange of goods and services is also true for the women of Bethnal Green, the blue-collar wives of Glenton, and the black women of the flats. Kin cooperation in Italy may not be as exclusively woman-centered as among the Nisei, for working-class Italian women do not possess an independent basis for autonomy, and yet in both cases kin solidarity is undoubtedly embedded in a similar division between the man, who mediates family and community, and the woman, who solidifies kin relationships.[38] Whether the patterns of kin cooperation exist primarily in the mother–daughter, sister–sister tie as opposed to the father–son, brother–brother tie is not as important, however, as the recognition of the cruciality of kin affiliation as a survival strategy for the disadvantaged in different cultural settings.

A discussion of intra-kin patterns of exchange moves us away from a central concern of family history with household composition and size to the more complex and comprehensive issue of the relationship of family to society at large. Until quite recently this question was subsumed for the most part under the generous conceptual umbrella of modernization theory. The number of contributors to the cause of explaining the emergence of the modern family as a response to the process of modernization is legion; notable among them are Parsons, Aries, Goode, Shorter, Stone, and Wrigley.[39] Perhaps Goode has been the most eloquent spokesman for the point of view that not only sees modernization as inevitable, but the alleged worldwide evolution of the conjugal family as an absolute good.[40]

In recent years criticisms of modernization theory have come from various quarters, for example, Lasch, Appleby, and Hareven among others.[41] Even among those who still regard the explaining of the transition from traditional to modern society as the most crucial question for family history, there is disquietude about the effectiveness of that theory for the task. For instance, Stone points out that there is no consensus among those who use the model as to when or where the modern family first came into being. Was it among the Florentine bourgeoisie of the fifteenth century, the Amsterdam bourgeoisie of the early seventeenth century, or possibly the London bourgeoisie of the late seventeenth century? Then, too, there is even less agreement about which class gave birth to it. Aries and Stone favor the gentry and bourgeoisie, Degler and Norton the middle class, and Shorter the industrial proletariat.[42] And the variations in the explanation of the rise of the modern conjugal family are impressive. Indeed, modernization would seem to be one of those heuristic ideas that in explaining every-thing in general explains nothing in particular. The historical demogra-phers have efficiently demonstrated that aspects of family behavior gen-erally thought of as being modern actually preceded major urban and industrial growth, whereas Giacomo's familial housebuilding suggests that characteristics of household organization generally thought of as traditional can flourish in settings undergoing rapid industrialization.[43] One might, accordingly, be tempted to conclude that family operates as an independent variable and changes in ways unrelated to movement in the larger social and economic reality. But such a conclusion would be mistaken. In fact, it is the very need to understand that relationship more clearly that leads us beyond the tautologies of modernization to perspectives that seek out greater clarification about the connection of family to society, household to the marketplace.

Foremost among those who have opened up this perspective are feminist students of family and of work. Among the first steps they have taken in relating family to the larger society is to close the gap that modernizationists helped to widen between household and the market-place. And the arena in which they have helped us to understand the degree to which reproduction and housework are in themselves modes of production has been the working-class family. Such households depend upon participation in the production process, which exists outside the family itself. For the Rossis, survival means exchanging labor power, especially that of Luigi and Bruno, for necessary resources. But that exchange depends not only upon their labor as wage workers but upon the housework of Maria, Silvia, and Luisa (Bruno's wife) in feeding and caring for "their men," an undertaking that cuts the costs of reproduc-tion considerably. The domestic labor debate, however, has if anything erred on the side of overly externalizing woman's work by equating it with wage labor in the marketplace. A significant part of Maria's house-work has been devoted to not only caring for the household's wage earners but to more strictly "family" work, that is, preparations for the marriage of her children. Maria would, undoubtedly, not heed·her com-patriot Mariarosa Dalla Costa, who demands all women to "get out of the house" and "reject the home" – not just because her consciousness has not been raised to that degree, but because Dalla Costa's polemic that a woman's "slavery ensures the slavery of her man" is not relevant to the symbolic reality of her existence.[44] What Maria does, day in and day out, is drudgery. Pains in her feet and the small of her back testify to that. But her tasks bear not so much the stigma of exploitation and hierarchy as they do pride of place and validation as a person. Neither equivocation nor ambivalence mars the core of her central importance, grounded as it is in the family, an esteemed institution.

The close connection between the working-class family and the forces of production is in turn linked to changes in expectations for consumption. The story of the Rossi family is starkly revealed by the extent to which its exposure to market relations has created new demands among all its members. Almost year by year new items have been added to the inventory, a development that has its own dialectic. This development applies far less to Giulia, however, who still reflects the more economical appetites characteristic of the household that she and Giovanni created. For spending and installment-plan buying come into conflict with a traditional commitment to thrift and a desire to be free of financial obligation. Increased consumption demands ever higher levels of production in the form of wage returns and a never ending juggling act to make ends meet, an obligation that falls largely on the heads of the women. But in consumption as well as in production a calculation is made that the interests of all are best served by sharing their resources and aptitudes.

It is Maria who orchestrates everyone's contributions in the long-range strategy of buying year by year, towel by towel, sheet by sheet, plate by plate the trousseaux of Teresa and Caterina, preparing them for the transition from one household to another. At marriage, when they move into the house provided by their husbands, they will undertake those rituals of interchange with their new kin. On his own land Giacomo envisioned from the very beginning an arrangement of dwellings, one nested above his own with a third to the side, that would separate each household and yet facilitate interchange and sharing among them. In the last analysis the issue is not who lives with whom, under one roof or not. The family is not a thing to be understood in its composition so much as it is a system of relationships that change over time. Family is not stasis but process. Family history becomes most meaningful when it becomes truly developmental in subject matter. The emergence of the life course perspective, which encompasses individual development as well as the collective development of the family unit, is a desirable direction for family history to move in. The volume entitled *Transitions: The Family and the Life Course in Historical Perspective* edited by Tamara Hareven points the way.[45] For those authors the subject matter becomes family as a sequence of transitions rather than household as a unit of composition. The story of the Rossis is the story of a family in transition. Their history cannot be understood primarily in organizational terms, for its composition has varied over time. It has now become an extended family, even though not all under the same roof, because the quality and quantity of the relationships that bind the members of the separate households together makes of them a family.[46]

Now a final word of explanation. The major focus of my study is the

Rossi household founded on February 13, 1953, with the marriage of Giacomo Rossi to Maria Tassoni. In order to provide what I am convinced is an essential temporal perspective, I begin the story by introducing the lives of Giovanni Battista Tassoni and Giulia Mori, Maria's parents, and describing the events leading to their marriage and the founding of the household of Giovanni Tassoni in 1922 in Stilo, Calabria. The interests of symmetry and completeness ideally call for equal treatment to be given to Giacomo's family of orientation. I chose not to for two reasons: the addition of another family history would make this rendition unwieldy if not confusing, and my own long-term involvement with the household of Giovanni Tassoni in conjunction with the ongoing relationship of Maria Rossi with her mother Giulia convinced me of the importance of those relationships providing a significant link between past and present. A somewhat different bias could have easily led me to focus solely on the story of Giulia Tassoni.

My anthropological field technique was simple enough. Three or four mornings a week I took the local 8:04 A.M. train from Rome's central terminal and got off at Latina Scalo approximately an hour later. Almost always Giacomo or occasionally Luigi or Bruno would be there to meet me. I spent the day with them and returned to Rome in the late afternoon to greet my fourteen-year-old daughter on her arrival home from school. The day with the Rossis was passed talking, listening, observing, writing. For the first four months I confined myself to taking complete notes on what I saw and heard. In January I bought a tape recorder and began interviewing sessions, first with Giulia and then with all the other members of the household. Above all it was Maria to whom I turned time and time again for information stored in her intelligent and retentive mind. Also the hours spent with Giulia were particularly rewarding for the obvious pleasure she received from my persistent attention to her story. My only regret was that I was not able to pay similar respect to her husband Giovanni.

In the narration that follows the voices you "hear" while reading are those of Giacomo, Maria, and other members of the family. Sometimes what they say are direct statements taken from my notes and tapes and indicated by quotation marks. For the most part, though, I have attributed to them behaviors to which I have not been a direct witness and thoughts to which I could not be privy. The danger in doing that is that what I have written in their names is not an accurate representation. I can only hope that what follows, reflecting all that I have learned being in their presence for months and in some cases years of our lives, is consistent with the truth.

Valmonte from Mount Furchiavecchia, 1951

The road into Valmonte, 1951

Maria and Giacomo, 1951

Giulia, 1951

Giovanni working on the reforestation project, 1951.

Tonino in the street, Valmonte, 1951

Maria hemming her sheets, 1951

Maria, Bruno, Luigi, Giacomo. A Sunday afternoon in the village of Valmonte, 1959.

The Rossi family in their new house, 1966

Giulia preparing fennel, 1978

The house of Giacomo and Maria as it appeared in 1977 before the addition of the second and third floors for Bruno and his wife.

Giacomo and Maria at Luigi's wedding

Maria, Bruno, and Luigi leaving for the wedding of Luigi and Silvia, 1977

Teresa and Luigi at the wedding of their grandson

Tonino at the headtable presenting the pears to Luigi and Silvia

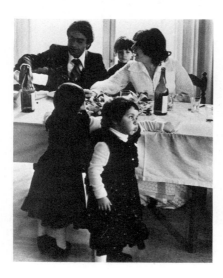

Tonino at the wedding of his nephew

Luigi and Silvia at their wedding

Bathroom fixture, house of Luigi,
1977

Maria and Giacomo on the road in front
of their house, 1977.

Giacomo and Bruno building
house for Bruno, 1978

Giacomo's house, with Bruno's in construction, 1978

Luigi's house (foreground), with Giacomo and Bruno's to the left and the village of Valmonte in the background to the right, 1978

Maria dousing slaughtered pig with boiling water prior to debristling, 1978.

Maria hanging out the wash, 1978

Maria making po-
lenta, 1978

Giacomo and Maria selecting intes-
tines for sausage casing, 1978

Giacomo and Maria in
their kitchen, 1978

1

Stilo, 1898–1933

I

Giulia Mori and Giovanni Tassoni were equally poor. They were born within three years of each other in the town of Stilo, Calabria, she in 1898 and he in 1901. Giulia's family had nothing. Giovanni's family had nothing either, although he did have a father, two brothers, and a sister. Giulia was illegitimate, her father being one of the wealthy land-owners of the region who had his way with Giulia's mother, Maria Luisa, a servant in his house. Giulia grew to womanhood in her grand-mother Chiara's one-room house with her and her mother.

Giovanni was brought up at the other end of the village in a one-room house belonging to his mother, Concetta, who died when Giovanni was six. Everything was made easier for Pasquale, Concetta's widower, their children, and the destiny of the house when Pasquale later married Concetta's younger sister Lucia. (Giovanni never called her "Mother" but rather "Aunt.")

Stilo hovers under Mount Consolino and faces the Ionian Sea, twenty-five kilometers away. On clear evenings the moon etches a luminous path to the edge of the fluid darkness, but in those days the sea and Stilo might as well have been a thousand miles away. The people of Stilo were, for better or for worse, wedded to the land, and a poor land it was. In the summer the sun scorched the vegetation to a brittle gold and molded the clay-rich soil to crust or intractable clump. Torrential winter rains pressed deep cuts in field and pasture. The best land, such as it was, was owned by the great families of Stilo: Count Crea, Count Contestabile, Baron Grillo, Baron Musco, and the Mar-chese Sersale. The remainder was divided into tiny plots and clusters of olive trees coveted by a few fortunate peasant families. Of the three thousand people living in Stilo at the turn of the century, most had little or nothing and had to work for others. Even the better-to-do peasants had to do the same to survive.

Giulia's grandmother, Chiara, owned five olive trees left to her by her father, until she gave them to the doctor who attended the fatal illness of her first child. The doctor willingly accepted the trees in temporary payment for the money that neither Chiara nor her husband, Alberto, possessed. They were never able to recover the trees, and with their loss Chiara and Alberto sank even deeper into the abyss of Stilo poverty. Then came two sons in rapid succession followed by Maria Luisa. A small, quick, and pretty child, she was her father's favorite. But she was not destined to know him long, for, an inveterate gambler, he was fatally stabbed in the back in a heedless moment by a young man whom he had insulted just an hour before over a game of cards. Chiara lived on in the one-room house given her by her father and with which she had caught Alberto for a husband, for in Stilo it is the custom for the woman to bring the house to the marriage. Giulia remembers her grandmother bent over the loom in the corner of the room, where she transformed flax into linen. But when she was young, Giulia spent most of her time with her mother helping her to do other people's wash at the river. Every day Maria Luisa would carry on her head a large tub of dirty clothes assigned to her by a *Signora* of one of the great families, but on the way someone would thrust a shirt at her saying, "Here, take this and wash it," and another would thrust a pair of pants at her saying, "Here, take these and wash them." The next day the shirt and the pants would be returned washed and ironed, but rarely did Maria Luisa receive anything for her trouble.

Pasquale Tassoni's household was more typical of the poor peasant of Stilo than was that of Chiara Mori, although his family was smaller than some. For Pasquale had neither a parcel of land nor a cluster of olive trees, only the house that Concetta had brought. Early in the morning, just as the sun was rising over the low mountains to the east and beginning to cast its shadow over the statue of Tommaso Campanella, the great sixteenth-century philosopher and most famous son of Stilo, Pasquale Tassoni would enter the piazza from the upper right-hand corner and, resting his back against the wall, wait for the call of a day's work by a steward of Count Crea or Baron Musco. He had nothing to leave his sons except the advice to marry a woman with a house; he would leave Concetta's to his daughter. When Giovanni was six his father enrolled him in school, but it was of no use. The world of words and numbers was as remote as the sea. Pasquale, resigned, withdrew his son before literacy made a mark upon him, and from then on his course was set. Survival was to be wrung by the muscle of back, arm, and leg.

Below Stilo stretched the fields, the farthest requiring two hours to reach by donkey, and above lay the mountains and the woods. Giovanni followed whichever road assured work. Although short in build, he could do the work of a giant, and by the time he was fourteen he already had a reputation as a skilled axman.

No matter how long Chiara worked at her loom or Maria Luisa scrubbed at the river's edge, there was scarcely enough money for bare essentials. By the age of seven, Giulia began to earn her first *centesimi* by looking after the children of neighboring peasants who left for the fields at four thirty in the morning and returned by six in the evening. If she was asked to watch more children than she could handle, she would instead accept a commission to sell a basket of eggs or beans or onions in the piazza. For every 100 *centesimi* that she received, she was allowed to keep one for her troubles. Later on when she was twelve and stronger, she carried stones on her head for the masons constructing the new town hall. In the beginning she was paid half a lira a day, but later, when she was able to manage stones "as large as a table," she was paid like the older girls. There never was time for Giulia to go to school.

II

In a town the size of Stilo, everyone knew everyone else, and so it was with Giulia and Giovanni. Giulia knew Giovanni by his nickname, La Caicala, just as he knew hers, La Pecerula, even before they knew each other's full Christian names. By the time Giovanni was seventeen, he found even more excuses to visit an aunt who lived near the house of Chiara, in hopes of catching a glimpse of Giulia. If Giovanni was seen coming, word was passed along that he was on his way, ensuring Giulia time to find a haven so that they would not meet face to face in the street unexpectedly and alone. But necessity brought them together more than propriety permitted, for the road that Giovanni took to the mountains and the woods was the same that Giulia had to follow, and it was not to Giulia's displeasure that this was so. More often than not, Giulia would go with her cousin to collect firewood in the part of the forest where Giovanni was working with a cutting crew. Giulia could not help but feel excited to see the way that Giovanni would go after the biggest trees and bring them down in what seemed like no time at all. But when Giulia and her cousin asked him if they could have the branches, he refused saying that he had done all that hard work to bring them back to his own house at the end of the day. Whenever Giulia's cousin's collecting took her out of earshot, she and Giovanni would talk about less practical things. One day Giovanni took such an opportunity to tell Giulia of a plan that he had worked out, by which he would signal to her with his handkerchief when he started for home with the other men on the main trail, so that if she walked slowly with her cousin down the shortcut, their paths would converge and they could meet again, even though momentarily.

Giulia used to wonder what it was about her that attracted Giovanni. There were other young women who had houses – and some with olive trees as well – whom Giovanni could have had if he had set his course in the right way. Giulia knew what it was that she liked about Giovanni: It was that he was as poor as she was and that he was a hard worker. Giulia, too, had a reputation for seriousness and hard work, and those virtues had attracted some attention. There was, for instance, the man who came to Maria Luisa and told her that her daughter should marry his son, for he knew what kind of person she was and one day his son would have a parcel of land. But his argument fell on deaf ears. Giulia knew that she did not want to marry someone who was better off than she, for then everyone would say that she had married only for interest. The thing that Giulia hated above all else was gossip. She wanted to stay clear of it at all costs.

One day when they were within speaking distance of each other in the woods and Giulia's cousin was out of earshot, Giovanni took the opportunity to propose marriage to her. Giulia accepted on the condition that they not have a long engagement. She was already twenty-one and did not need much time to collect her trousseau. Chiara had sold the house some years before when one of her brothers claimed that he had a legal right to some part of it. He told Chiara that he had made the papers say that the house would go to him if she died rather than to Maria Luisa and Giulia. Chiara, frightened, promptly sold the house for four hundred lire, giving a hundred to her brother for his share and then putting the remaining three hundred away in a postal account to buy Giulia's trousseau when the time came. Shortly after that she died, leaving Maria Luisa and Giulia living together in a one-room rented house.

Neither Pasquale nor Maria Luisa were pleased at the idea of the marriage, or at least that is what they said. Maria Luisa told Giulia over and over that it was a mistake to marry a man who had not yet done his military service, for no sooner would they marry than he would leave her pregnant while he went off to soldier. Pasquale was, for his part, exasperated that Giovanni would choose to marry a woman without a house. Were there not those in Stilo with a house? Why marry La Pecerula, who had nothing? the father demanded of his son. But Giovanni closed his ears. He knew why he wanted to marry her: because she was a hard worker and as poor as he was. Let other men marry for interest, he told his father, he would not. Parental resistance wavered, then crumbled, and it was agreed that the wedding would take place after the harvest, in the fall of 1921.

Now Giovanni could visit Giulia every evening. They would sit opposite each other with Maria Luisa, knitting to while away the time, between them. But after a while Giovanni did not visit anymore, for he came down with typhus. For several months he was in bed, hardly able to move. He was nursed night and day by his stepmother, Lucia, and his sister, Annunziata. Despite their ministrations he lay close to death. The priest was called and the last rites were administered, finally the crisis was surpassed – although not before every hair on his head had fallen out. Even so he wanted Giulia to come to him, but she could not let herself go for fear of the gossip that would follow her. It would not be decent for an unmarried woman to visit a man neither her husband nor her relative. One time she found herself halfway to his house before she came to her senses and returned home. Instead, it was Maria Luisa who made the visit every day, always bringing something to eat and sometimes small amounts of money.

Almost half a year passed before Giovanni was well enough to marry Giulia. A new date was set for the wedding, February 5, making it midwinter of 1922. Giulia took the three hundred lire that Chiara had deposited for her in the postal account and bought what they would need to start their life together. By stretching the three hundred lire to make every one count, she was able to buy six sheets, six towels, the ticking with which to make a cornhusk mattress, two blankets, a bed spring and two sawhorses and boards to support it, plates, glasses, knives and spoons, a new set of copper pots, and pans. Maria Luisa would let her have the table and chairs, cupboard, and chest.

III

The wedding was held on a Saturday morning in the Chiesa Matrice of Stilo. Only Maria Luisa, Pasquale, and Lucia were in attendance, for there was not enough money to have invited guests as well. Pasquale bought a kilo of almond cookies and a bottle of liqueur. Giulia and Maria Luisa provided a demijohn of wine. The service and refreshment completed, Giovanni and Giulia bid good-bye to Pasquale and Lucia and retired to their new bed which was separated by a curtain from Maria Luisa. They remained at home Sunday, Monday, and Tuesday, the last day of *Carnevale*. On Wednesday they both went to the neighboring town of Pezzano to work, he to hoe in a vineyard and she to gather wood. That evening she returned with a large bundle of wood on her head, which she sold in the piazza for five lire, more than enough to buy oil, pasta, cheese, and a bit of sausage with which to make her first meal as a married woman. Even when she was a girl, Giulia would buy whatever was needed at the store. Maria Luisa was deaf and was ashamed to go into public places. Giulia was quick and enjoyed bargaining and the feel of the *centesimi* rubbing together in the pocket of her shirt. "I would have felt dead if I did not have one piece of money on me," she said later. And so it happened that for all the years that they were married, Giovanni turned over to Giulia the money that he brought home when he was paid – but in that they were not different from other Southern households.

Giulia fondly recollects that early time at the beginning of their life together. In those days there always seemed to be enough work for both of them. Maria Luisa would go for wood for cooking while Giulia earned a day's wage hoeing or carrying stones and Giovanni found work in the vineyards of Count Crea or Baron Musco. On the days that Giovanni went to the mountains to cut wood, Giulia would go with him. "We would eat and talk and we were happy," as Giulia put it.

IV

In August of 1922 Giovanni was called to perform his military service. An earlier call had come when he was still convalescing from typhus and now Giovanni prayed that the doctors would find something else, but to his regret he was deemed fit, although short, and sent off to the barracks in San Remo for fourteen months. Giulia was in the sixth month of pregnancy, and it seemed as if Maria Luisa never lost an opportunity to remind her that she should have waited until he had finished his military service before they married. A husband, she said, should never see his wife in labor, but he should not be halfway around the world either when the time came.

Giovanni detested soldiering and returned to Stilo on his first leave. Blackened with soot from the long train ride, he immediately went in search of work to earn whatever he could against the expenses of the baby. The little that Giulia earned was just enough to buy the bare necessities for herself and her mother. She continued to work until two days before the baby arrived. The birth went easily enough; it was attended by her mother, who did nothing but pray, and the midwife, who held the baby boy in the air so Giulia could see it and cut the cord. Giulia named the baby Vincenzo, after Giovanni's grandfather. Giulia had someone who could write send a telegram to Giovanni. The baby was strong and healthy, the delight of his mother and grandmother. Maria Luisa confided to Giulia that the shame of Giulia's own birth had now finally been removed by the birth of this legitimate boy.

When he was three months old, Baby Vincenzo contracted meningitis and died after a few days of high fever. Giulia had another telegram sent to Giovanni, who was himself too ill to leave the barracks until after Giulia and her mother had buried the baby.

Giulia soon became pregnant again, but this time Giovanni would be finished with his military duty when the baby arrived. It was a difficult birth. The cord wrapped itself around the baby's neck. Maria Luisa became hysterical. The midwife worked frantically, but it was no use. The baby was born dead. Giulia felt that she was cursed and turned angrily on her mother. Giovanni buried this unnamed one next to the first. In a few days Giulia's breasts began to swell with milk. It was a bittersweet relief to suckle the baby girl next door. Soon word spread that La Pecerula had milk, and shortly a baby boy was brought to Giulia by a servant of one of the great families. The master, she was told, had had his way with one of the servant girls. He did not wish to keep the baby, but the girl was too sick to look after the boy. The story suffocated Giulia but when she looked at the pale, emaciated creature fed on goat's milk, she was overcome with compassion and pressed him to her breast.

The servant said that the master was willing to pay her ten kilo of wheat and fifty lire a month if she would keep the baby, christened Giulio, at least until it became strong again. Giulia assented, but when Giovanni came home he was furious. "With us babies only die. I do not want to have another one in the house," he shouted. But Giulia reminded him of the fifty lire a month, and before the day was over Giovanni relented. Giulia suckled Giulio for eighteen months, and he grew so large that Giulia could not carry him easily under her arm. On every eighth day she would take him to see his father, and he would give Giulia additional wheat and dried figs to take home. When her milk finally dried up, Giulia sent word that she could no longer feed him. When the servant came to take Giulio away, he cried bitterly at being separated from his "mother." Giulia wept also.

With the death of their second child, Giovanni became convinced that the house where they lived brought them only bad luck. He wanted to have one of their own so that he could nail a shelf here or a hook there without fear of the landlord. He wrestled with the problem for weeks and months until he came to the conclusion that he would have to emigrate, like other men did, in order to make enough money to buy a house. He knew several who had gone to Argentina and spoke favorably of it. There were even Italians there who could help you to make your wants known. He told his dream to Giulia, and she agreed that he must go or they would never have a house of their own, for surely they had no money. "Many are going to America now, but how are you going without money?" she asked, and he replied, "I do not know. The ticket costs twenty-five hundred to go and to come back, and who is going to give that money to me who has nothing?" The more Giulia thought about it, the more certain she became that she could find it for him, and she set to work. She went to each of those persons of property for whom she had worked. She had always given them more than she had received. It was as if she were collecting her debt from them. She would say to each in turn, "Would you give me money to send Giovanni Battista to America? There is no work here, and he must go there to find work. In that way he can buy a house here and make a family. You know me. You can trust me." Before long she had borrowed fifteen hundred lire on her good name; more she could not find. The remainder eventually came from Pasquale, who put up what property he had against a loan on the condition that another son, Salvatore, would go with Giovanni. Salvatore had married a war widow with a house on his father's recommendation, and he had enough money in the postal account to pay his way. But it was Giovanni's fortune to be a good sailor during the two weeks crossing in the old vessel. Salvatore had to be carried ashore when they landed in Argentina in March of 1926.

Giulia was already three months with child when Giovanni left Stilo. She continued to work as usual at whatever she could find, but it was difficult being with people without Giovanni as her condition began to show. Malicious gossip was cast in her direction, and she would have liked to have remained closed in her house until Giovanni returned, but she had no choice. It was Pasquale, her father-in-law, who consoled her the most in the absence of her husband, and she him in the absence of his sons. Once every eight days he would pay her a visit, and on those occasions she would accord him proper respect. She would give him a few *soldi* for cigars and then clean him, first shaving him, then trimming his hair, cutting his fingernails, and last removing his shoes and socks to cut his toenails and wash his feet.

V

The eighteen months that Giovanni spent in Argentina constituted the great adventure of his life. Hard work earned him more money than he had ever seen. Within six months he had sent enough to Giulia to repay the amount borrowed for the ticket. After that, Giulia deposited in the postal account all that was sent to her toward the purchase of the house. In the evenings after work, even though tired, Giovanni set himself to learning a few words in Spanish so that he could make his wants known when he went to the city. When a letter arrived dictated by Giulia, he copied the words over and over until he had learned how to make them and then began to write letters to his wife himself. In November, the cablegram that he had been waiting for arrived. Giulia had given birth to a baby girl and named her Concetta in honor of Giovanni's mother. Giovanni got drunk that night and had to be carried back to the boarding house by his compatriots from Stilo. His friends commiserated that his wife had produced a girl rather than a boy, but Giovanni paid them no heed and sent a tiny silk dress so that his daughter could be baptized as if she were the child of *Signori*. At first Giovanni paid no attention to the suggestion, and then the warning, that he should be more generous with his earnings toward his compatriots rather than sending them all to his wife. He told them that what he did with his money was his business, but when he was told of a plot to kill him after the next payday, he knew that the time had come to return to Italy. He and Salvatore set sail for Naples in August of 1928.

VI

Giulia first knew of his return when one day in September someone came running to the door to say that La Caicala had been seen walking up the hill toward Stilo. Giulia caught her breath and then quickly carried Concetta to a neighbor's so that she and Giovanni Battista could be alone. Then she went home to wait, to avoid meeting him in the street where people might see him embracing her.

"It seemed as if the whole world was in our hands" is the way Giulia described how she felt in those months after Giovanni's return from Argentina. They bought a one-room house for four thousand lire, an eighteen-year-old donkey, a pig, and a goat, and rented a small piece of land – large enough to sow a quintal of wheat and room enough to grow some eggplant, tomatoes, beans, and corn. Giovanni made a partition in the house, so that Maria Luisa could sleep apart in the back, and a loft for children, as there had been in his mother's house.

In the summer, and in good weather, Giulia did the cooking outside and baked bread in the oven that Giovanni rebuilt for her. The aroma of Giulia's bread intoxicated the neighborhood. It was said that no one in Stilo baked better than La Pecerula. And so it happened that the *Signora* who had written Giulia's letters to Giovanni persuaded her to start baking bread for a nearby *collegio*. In the beginning all went well and Giulia had a hard time keeping up with the orders, but the payments from the *collegio* came later and later, with one excuse or another from the priests. When there was no more money to buy flour, Giulia suspended baking.

VII

Giovanni returned to hoeing in the vineyards of Count Crea and Baron Musco, and when they had no need of him, he worked wherever there was a job to do. But it seemed in those years as if it rained all the time and as if days on end would pass waiting in the piazza to be called. Finally a call did echo through the piazza, but for a different kind of work: laying track for the new railroad line being built to Cutro. Giovanni agreed to go even though it meant seeing his family only for a short time every eight days. Giulia was pregnant and gave birth to a baby boy on the eighth day of July 1928, when Giovanni was in Cutro. They named him Salvatore in honor of Giovanni's brother. Giovanni brought Giulia his earnings when he returned to Stilo, but they were never enough to tide the growing family over from week to week. With Maria Luisa at home to watch after Concetta and Salvatore, Giulia looked for work wherever she could find it, hoeing tomatoes, corn, or beans in the fields, collecting wood, or carrying stones. On the fifth of October 1930 a baby girl was born, and this time Giovanni was in Stilo. They named her Maria in honor of Maria Luisa. Eight months after the birth of Maria, Giulia was startled one night by a loud knock on the door. When she opened it she saw at her feet Giovanni covered with a blanket on a makeshift stretcher. He was shaking with malarial fever. His companions told Giulia that he had had the fever for some time, as did many working on the line, that he had tried to hide it, but now it was so bad that he could no longer stand, and so they had brought him back home in a cart. They helped Giulia put him in bed, and he remained there for months – wracked first with fever and then with chills.

VIII

The need for money was now greater than ever, and Giulia knew the time had come to do something she had not tried before but had watched other women do. She had seen them load their donkeys for the long trek to the mountain village of Serra San Bruno to sell fruit. Now she joined them, getting up at four in the morning and walking her donkey into the country below, collecting or buying whatever fruit was in season. At about noon, they would return to Stilo and unload their animals to store the fruit in the shade. Giulia would eat some bread and cheese, take a short rest, and then reload the donkey, nurse Maria, and at about three join the caravan. She learned after her first trip that it was best to carry a basket of fruit under her arm so that when they passed the charcoal makers along the way they would let her pass; if she gave

them some fruit they would refrain from going through the large baskets strapped to the side of the donkey, taking whatever they pleased.
In time Giulia learned how to sleep while walking, hanging on to the
donkey's tail. After six hours of climbing, the little caravan would stop
on the outskirts of Serra San Bruno, where the animals were unloaded.
Giulia would then lie down for a fitful sleep, pressing the baskets close
to her side, for she had learned that she could not trust even her fellow
paesani. At daybreak they would arise to feed themselves and their
animals, then load up to arrive in the main piazza by seven, in time to
arrange their produce for the first customers. Giulia prided herself on
the rapidity with which she managed to sell her entire load, so that by
eleven she would be on her way back down the trail to Stilo. On the
trail she would stop and collect wood wherever she found it, which she
was able to sell in the piazza for five lire a bundle.

And so Giulia continued her trips back and forth to Serra San Bruno
until Giovanni could return to work. He decided not to return to the
railway at Cutro again, where malaria was endemic, but to try instead to
wrest a living from the small piece of rented land. It was now Giovanni's
turn to take the donkey, carrying hoe and mattock, to the field far below
Stilo, while Giulia became a transporter of wine. In those days trucks
were still few and far between, and a woman like Giulia could earn fifty
lire a trip as well as a liter of wine by carrying a load of fifty liters on her
head to a neighboring town. Giulia was the sort of person ready to help
others with a load of wood or wash, and she was given a liter of oil here
and a chilo of flour there for her troubles.

In this way and with the help of Maria Luisa, Giulia and Giovanni
held their small household together. On Sundays Giulia would turn
everyone out in clean clothes so that they might attend the sung mass at
eleven at Chiesa Matrice. Maria Luisa went to an earlier mass so that
she could come home and prepare the noonday meal, which might
include a bit of pig or sheep or goat along with a big bowl of pasta.

For Salvatore's baptism they invited guests to partake with them at
their house. For the godfather they chose a man of good family for
whom Giulia had worked. He accepted expecting that the ceremony
would take place in the Chiesa Matrice, but Giulia had to explain to
him, with some embarrassment, that if they had it there people would
come from the church to their house for refreshments, and she would
be ashamed, for she would not have enough to feed them. The baptism
was held in the house. Giulia and Maria Luisa had prepared sweets, and
there was a guest who brought some coffee, one who brought sugar,
and another who brought liqueur. The godfather gave Salvatore a small
gold medallion on a chain.

The children grew straight and strong and suffered no serious illness.

Giulia prayed unremittingly to San Antonio, Santa Rita, and Santa Anna for the health and well-being of her children, Concetta, Salvatore, and Maria; her husband, Giovanni Battista; her mother, Maria Luisa; and herself.

Unlike Giovanni, Giulia was a strong believer in the wonder of miracles and the power of saints. She revered the pious Madonna, Her suffering son, and God's shepherd on earth the pope, but for priests she held little respect. They spoke with forked tongues, although they too were part of the inevitable scheme of things, in which everyone had a place.

As for politics, Giulia knew it belonged to the world of men. At the top were the *Signori*, who commanded, and at the bottom was everyone else. That is the way it had always been. There were political parties in Stilo: at first the Liberals and the Socialists, then only the Fascists. But in truth, each *Signore* had his followers. In the days when there were elections, before Mussolini commanded everything, one master would say at election time, vote for me, and his friends would vote for him; another master would say, vote for me, and his friends would vote for him. But Giulia paid politics no heed; what mattered was work. Giovanni, for his part, distrusted the politicians as much as he did the priests. He wanted to be free and independent, so he aligned himself with one faction or another as little as he could.

IX

Giovanni, though, became ever more restless and unhappy with their lot. The eighteen months that he spent in Argentina had opened his eyes, and since then he had wanted to free himself from the soil of Stilo, which demanded so much and gave so little in return. But most of the rumors that he heard in the piazza led to discouragement. It appeared that the government of Mussolini did not want its men to migrate to other countries in search of work now that there was so much talk of the glory of the fatherland. Then in 1932 and 1933 it seemed that everything that he planned failed. The pig and goat failed to produce. Giulia was pregnant again and Maria Luisa died, making it more difficult for Giulia to leave the children for a day's work. In 1933 Concetta was seven. Giulia put her in charge of Salvatore and Maria and locked them in the house when she left early in the morning for field or forest.

The baby was born on the fifth of June 1933, and they named him Pasquale in honor of Giovanni's father. Giulia had no choice but to take all four children with her when she went to work. Like all her children before him, Pasquale was swaddled. It was the only way that Giulia knew to make sure babies' legs grew straight and strong. She had seen too many little children with crooked legs running the streets of Stilo, their mothers never having properly swaddled them. Then, too, for a peasant woman like Giulia, swaddling kept a baby quiet and out of harm's way when work took a mother to the fields.

In July of 1933 the quintals of wheat that Giovanni had planted in the winter rendered only fifteen kilos of wheat to bring home after the master had taken his share. Giovanni was now determined to leave Stilo at all costs. Later Giulia swore that it was an act of God, but Giovanni knew that it was a turn of fortune that presented him the opportunity he had been praying for. A *signora* for whom Giulia had done several favors told Giovanni one day while he was waiting in the piazza for work that there was an opening for him in Rome as a street cleaner. She herself had been given the opportunity to move to Rome to educate her children by one of the great families of Stilo for whom she had done favors. She was well established there by now and returned to Stilo to visit her crippled husband from time to time, for there was no room for him there. That day in the piazza she told Giovanni that it was now his turn to leave Stilo behind and establish himself and his family in the great city. She went on to say that there was work there for everyone, for Mussolini was building new buildings and new streets everywhere; her son was already a street cleaner and would be able to find work for Giovanni. That evening Giovanni and Giulia talked at length about her proposal. Giulia pointed out that there were many things about travel and life in the city that they did not know, and that they could easily be taken advantage of, for she herself had never been farther from Stilo than Serra San Bruno. Giovanni reassured her that he knew how to travel about and how to live in cities, for he had lived near Buenos Aires, a great city like Rome and Naples. Giovanni was eager to get started as soon as possible, and seeing him Giulia knew that their going was inevitable. Then she said, "What about the things that we have planted and the donkey and the house? We cannot just go off and leave them." And so it was decided that Giovanni would go first and Giulia would remain behind with the children and harvest the crops. Giulia felt afraid at the thought of leaving Stilo, whose every nook and cranny she knew better than the back of her hand, and at going to live in a great city full of the terrors of the unknown, where people had no shame. Where did you go to the bathroom, where did you find water, where did you wash clothes?

As soon as word spread that the La Caicala and La Pecerula were going to leave Stilo and go to Rome to find work, others said that they wanted to throw their lot in with them. So when Giovanni left in the middle of July 1933, he was accompanied by two nephews and two *paesani*. It was their intention, as it was Giovanni's, to call their families and friends to Rome, if they found work. It was a sad but joyful morning on the day that Giulia bid farewell to Giovanni at the door of their house. She did not want to go to the piazza for all to see, but the children ran after him for a long way as he walked away bearing the same suitcases, carefully bound with rope, that he had carried to Argentina.

As soon as Giovanni left, Giulia set about, with a heavy heart, to get everything in order for her departure with the children from Stilo. Early every morning she would load the donkey, putting Salvatore and Concetta in baskets on either side of the donkey and wedging Maria in between them on the donkey's back. With Pasquale swaddled and held in her arms, she would start on the long trek down to the land. They would arrive when the morning, still cool from the evening before, did not yet stifle. At the edge of the land she would make a cradle out of a sack and hand it between two trees, leaving a cord long enough for Concetta to pull the baby slowly back and forth. It was Salvatore's task to help his mother as best he could and keep a steady eye on his lively younger sister, who seemed to have a passion for throwing herself into every ditch she could find. When the harvest of wheat was completed, Giulia sold their share for what little she could get. For the donkey she received two hundred lire and it almost broke her heart to part with the faithful animal. As for the house, she found someone to live there when they left who would pay her father-in-law five kilos of wheat, or its equivalent, per month. It made her feel somewhat better at the thought of leaving to know that they would still have a place in Stilo. Then she waited for Giovanni to come and take them to Rome, but he did not come. One day the *signora* knocked on her door and exclaimed that she was returning there and that it would be best for Giulia and the children to accompany her, for she could show them the way. As for Giovanni, he was probably having difficulty finding work – for in the city you could trust no one – and by now he would need to have his family with him. Giulia knew that her worst fears had been realized but felt that she had no choice, for how could she manage the long trip along with four small children? Anxiously Giulia packed a chest and two large sacks with their clothes, bedding, and mattress cover, and then filled a basket with dried figs and broad beans. She was ready to leave. She bid farewell to her neighbors and to her father-in-law. He held Giulia for a long time; tears welled in his eyes. "Who will clean me now that you have gone, Giulia? Tell me, who will clean me?" he cried.

The train ride, which took the better part of the day and all night, seemed endless to Giulia who held Pasquale in her arms. For Concetta and Salvatore all was new and fascinating. Maria remembers only the lullaby that the wheels sang as they sped along the tracks.

2

Valmonte, 1933–1943

When they arrived at the Rome station in the morning, terror struck Giulia's heart. She had never seen so many people as were crowding the platform beside the train. And everywhere there were soldiers. She had heard in Stilo about Mussolini's war in Africa, wherever Africa might be, but she had not expected to see so many soldiers so far away from the fighting. When they had descended to the platform, the *signora* told them to follow her. Giulia lifted the chest on her head and thrust a bundle apiece into Concetta's and Salvatore's waiting arms. Then she picked up Pasquale with one hand and the basket with the other, and they started off. Maria, holding on to her mother's skirt, ran as fast as her legs could carry her. Fortunately the place where the *signora* lived was not too far away from the station; it was a single room up five flights of stairs, with a kitchen and a bathroom off to one side. The *signora* assured Giulia that Giovanni would be there to meet her and then take them all to the room that he must have located for them by then. She herself had been away for two weeks, she explained, so she did not know where the place was that Giovanni had found. Giulia was crushed when they opened the door to find no one there. She sat down in the middle of the room with the chest, the two bundles, the basket, and her four children and quietly wept.

That evening the oldest son of the *signora* returned and told them what had happened. He said that the day after Giovanni arrived, he had taken him to the city employment office on his way to work and told the clerk there that his friend from Stilo, Calabria, was looking for a street cleaner job like the one he had. He needed work, he explained, so that his wife and four young children could come to join him in Rome. The clerk nodded and handed him a form, which the *signora*'s son

helped Giovanni fill out. When he returned it to the clerk, he asked
Giovanni to show him his party card. Giovanni felt pleased that he was
prepared for that request, for his card was neatly wrapped in paper and
tucked away in his pocket. He had been told in Stilo, before he left, and
on good authority, that he could find no work in Rome unless he
belonged to the party, so he had joined. His blood chilled, though,
when the clerk shook his head and handed the card back to him. "But
what is wrong?" asked Giovanni. "It is signed by the party secretary
himself of Stilo. I saw him do it." The clerk responded, "It does not
make any difference who signed it. It has not been stamped for 1922,
the year of Mussolini's march on Rome, and without that you are no
good. Without it you can do nothing, you are out."

That same evening, as they were wondering what to do next, the
other brother came to the room. When he heard the story and looked at
Giovanni's crushed figure bent over the kitchen table, he told him not
to worry, the next day he should come with him by train to a place
called Valmonte, where there was a big project going on to drain the
marshes. He worked there himself in a reforestation project. The foreman was sympathetic and did not worry about party cards, and besides,
there were other *paesani* there. So the next day the two of them left.
That had been about a week ago. The *signora*'s son said that there was
nothing to do but to wait until Giovanni either returned or sent word.

When she heard this story, Giulia was somewhat heartened to know
that Giovanni Battista was well and would be coming for them soon.
That night she prayed that he had found work so that they could all go
to this Valmonte and leave Rome forever, with all its noises and people
who walked about with no shame.

For two weeks Giulia waited for Giovanni to arrive. The room was
small for seven people to live in at the same time. At night Giulia slept
on the floor with her children on the bedding she had brought. During
the day she would do her best to keep the children quiet, but it became
more and more difficult once the food they had brought was finally
eaten. When that happened, the *signora* told her that if she did the
cooking and the housework she would give her some food. Giulia
accepted the proposal. She put Concetta in charge of the children, and
after nursing Pasquale, went to the kitchen. She was amazed to find
such a room, with a gas stove in it and water that ran into a basin when
you turned the knobs. To her dismay, though, Giulia found that the
signora's offer of food did not extend to the children, whom she did not
want crowding into her kitchen; nor did she want the responsibility of
providing food for them all. So Giulia would wait until the *signora* had
gone out and would then bring her children the food that had been set
aside for her.

It seemed shameful to Giulia that the place to go to the toilet was a little room next to the kitchen. At first she did not know how to use it and was too embarrassed to ask the *signora*. But then she discovered that it was proper for the water to run as if there was to be a flood.

By the middle of the second week, the nerves of the *signora* were stretched to the breaking point. When Salvatore woke up one night crying from a nightmare, or from hunger, she grabbed him and put him out on the balcony. Giulia wept in bitterness and indignation.

On Sunday morning of the second week Giovanni arrived. He had finally received the news from the letter sent by the *signora* to her son saying that Giovanni's wife and children were waiting for him in Rome. Later he discovered that the letter had been intercepted by a man on his work squad who was angry at the arrival of those Calabrians coming to take their jobs away.

It was a joyful reunion for everyone. Giulia's spirits recovered immediately, and she began to pack their belongings. Concetta and Salvatore crowded around their father as he held both Maria and Pasquale in his arms and asked him where Valmonte was. He explained that they would have to take another train but that this would be a little train, not like the big one they had taken from Calabria, and it would take them only two hours. There was work there. The *signora* was delighted to see them go, but all was reconciliation. She gave Giulia her bedspring to take with them, saying that her son was doing so well that she was going right out tomorrow to buy one in the market at Piazza Vittorio. Giulia was so relieved to leave that she did not even mind the figure she cut as she balanced the bedspring on her head and followed Giovanni, bowed under from the chest on his back, through the streets of Rome toward the station.

II

When they stepped off the Rome–Terracina train at the little station at Valmonte, Giulia's heart lifted at the sight of the mountains looming up behind the village that Giovanni said was Valmonte. It all reminded her of Stilo, and what was even better were the familiar faces at the station – Giovanni's nephews and the two *paesani*. The four young men divided the spring, chest, two bundles, and basket among them, and they started off on the dirt road. Concetta and Salvatore clung to Giovanni's hands while Giulia carried Pasquale in her arms, and Maria followed as usual, holding on to her mother's skirt.

Giovanni led the way to Titalo, a little settlement belonging to the forestry at the base of the hill on which Valmonte was perched. The foreman turned out to be as *simpatico* as the *signora*'s son said he was.

Right on the spot he told Giovanni that his wife could work on the project, too, as he needed someone to plant seedlings while the men cut and trimmed the young trees. Giulia's heart filled with joy. It seemed as if they were going back to those early days when they were first married and worked together in the forest behind Stilo.

Giovanni, Giulia, the children, the two nephews, and the two *paesani* remained for three days with the foreman at Titalo and then moved to a house in the village, which a friend in the forestry squad had found for a rent of five lire a month. There was already some furniture, a table, chairs, and a cupboard, and Giovanni set to work immediately to divide the room in two, so that the nephews and *paesani* could be by themselves to play cards and tell stories. They agreed to pay Giulia ten lire apiece a month for food, lodging, and washing their clothes.

Early in the morning Giovanni and Giulia would leave the house and children in care of Concetta and head down the mountain toward Titalo, taking Pasquale with them. The work was not as hard as some that Giulia had known in Stilo, and it was regular, so that Giovanni did not have to go to the piazza in the morning and wait to be called. The walk back up the mountain at the end of the day seemed long, though, and the children were waiting to be fed. After the evening meal, Giulia still had several hours of washing and ironing to do. There were times when she was so tired that she found herself going to sleep with the iron in her hand and would have to catch herself before the coals burned a shirt.

Having so many in the house made for a good deal of extra work, but it was good to have people close by who spoke the same language. For in Valmonte they felt like foreigners. They had only to go outside on the street to feel the disapproving stare and hear the angry whisper. If they went into a shop in the piazza to ask for wine or cheese, the owner would say, rudely, "What kind of language is that? Don't you know how to speak Italian?" Giulia knew that there were different ways of speaking even in the same village, for the *Signori* of Stilo spoke Italian among themselves even though they talked to her in dialect. But in Stilo they did not insult her for the way she spoke. To Giula and Giovanni, the nephews, and the two *paesani,* the Valmontesi seemed cold and distant even among themselves. They had only been there a month when a prominent member of the community died. Giulia went to the fountain with the excuse of getting more water, but in fact she wanted to see the procession pass. She had expected that a great many people would be following the body, but in fact there were very few, and the bells tolled for only a short time. How very different these people are from us, she thought to herself, remembering how it was in Stilo when somebody died. There the whole town would join in the procession and the bells would toll and toll. The family of the bereaved would be fed by relatives and neighbors for eight days.

Even at work there were those who harassed them because they were Calabrian. There was one older man who blamed them for everything that went wrong. If one of the seedlings died or a tool was missing, he would run to the foreman and say that it was the fault of one of the Calabrians. At first this old man tried to influence the foreman by bringing him presents of fruit from the orchard of the house where he was boarding. When that failed, he went about saying that Giovanni was a cuckold, for he had discovered that Giulia did not know who her father was. It was then that Giovanni had to be restrained from trying to strike him, and Giulia herself remembers the rage she felt: "I could easily have killed him, and I felt like driving the knife that I always carried deep into his black heart."

After the wheat had been harvested in July of 1934, Giulia followed other women to the fields to collect the gleanings. In Stilo the wheat had never grown so abundantly as it did in Valmonte, and Giulia was surprised at how much she could glean in the large fields that were being reclaimed from the rich soil of the drained marshes. When she had collected as much as she could carry, she would take the sheaves to the mill at Ronticchio to be ground. At the end of the day she would carry the flour home to make into loaves. She would then place them on a board and carry them on her head to Titalo, to bake in the oven there the following morning while she worked at the forestry. Giulia was careful that these chores did not interfere with her work of planting and thinning, but even so there were those who complained that she had no right to use the forestry oven, even though Giulia knew that no one baked in it except her. It seemed at times that there were no bounds to the rancor of these jealous and malignant people. The saying that they had first heard shortly after they arrived, "In Valmonte first they feed you and then they tear you apart," seemed now to be the truth.

In February of 1935 Giovanni found a new house to rent, one in the upper end of town in the *contrada* known as Torrevecchio, for which they paid nine lire a month. Indeed, they had little choice but to move, for the Ministry of Education had decided that Valmonte was to be graced with a new school – one that would do justice in its size and equipment to the regime. The site chosen was that on which their rented room was located. As he had before, Giovanni made another division in the single room so that the children slept on one side and he, Giulia, and the baby Pasquale in the large bed on the other. By then the two *paesani* had found quarters of their own and Giovanni's nephews had returned to Stilo to find themselves wives, for they regarded the women of Valmonte as too frivolous.

III

In November of 1935 Giulia gave birth to a baby girl, their seventh child. They named her Annunziata in honor of Giovanni's sister and made plans to baptize her as soon as they could afford to have a feast. Giulia did not like to wait too long in case the baby sickened and died a creature, not a Christian. She asked a neighbor with whom she had made friends, Margherita, to be the godmother. Margherita accepted but insisted that the baby's name be changed to her own. Neither Giovanni nor Giulia liked the name Margherita, but did not want to offend the godmother, and so the baby was baptized Margherita. She was a lovely baby who delighted Giovanni by the way her face crinkled in a smile upon hearing his voice when he returned from work. Within a month and a half of Margherita's birth Giulia returned to work, carrying the baby with her, wrapped in swaddling. Concetta was left in charge of the house and the other children. Suddenly one day the baby began to run a high fever. Giulia took her to the pharmacy to buy some medicine. She sent Salvatore to tell his father to come home from work immediately. When Giovanni arrived, the baby opened her eyes and smiled when she heard her father's voice. Giovanni exclaimed later, "I was as happy when I saw her smile as if I had won a lottery." The following day the fever went higher, and Giovanni stayed home and walked about the house with the baby in his arms so that Giulia could go to work in the forestry. The next day the doctor was called. He hurried into the house late in the afternoon, saying that he could spare only a minute. He looked at the baby and exclaimed cheerfully, "Look, look how your baby is looking at me! Oh yes, you can see there is nothing to fear, she is getting better." And so it seemed for a while; but then she became very agitated. Giulia took her in her arms and as she did so Margherita turned her head and died. Giulia screamed and all the neighbors came running to see. Concetta sent Salvatore to fetch his father, and when Giovanni returned and saw the baby laid out in a white dress on the kitchen table, he fainted. Margherita was buried the next day in a coffin that Giovanni and Salvatore made for her, in a plot set aside for small children in the cemetery of Valmonte. Giulia and Giovanni had now laid to rest three of their children.

IV

One of the first things that Giulia did after Margherita died was to enter Concetta in school. She was then eleven and had never gone to school, because there were always so many things that Giulia needed her to do at home – look after the younger children and help Giulia when she was expecting another baby. But when Margherita died there was no longer a pressing reason to keep her out of school. When Giulia went to see Maestra Renata, the teacher told her that it was too late in the year for a student to enroll, and besides, the girl was so old, why bother to send her? "It is my experience that girls like that just waste their time in school," she said. Giulia knew as she stood with Maestra Renata, who was talking to her so loudly, that she wanted to get rid of them because she thought they were ignorant Calabrians, but Giulia was determined for Concetta to go to school. As soon as they left the building, she told Concetta to go to the store and buy two notebooks and two pencils. That night she quickly sewed together a white smock; the *grembiuli* were too expensive to buy. The next morning she sent Concetta to school with a ribbon in her hair. Concetta was terrified but Giulia was right, Maestra Renata allowed her to stay. At the end of the year Concetta was promoted to second grade. She enjoyed school and would have liked it more if the children, as well as the teachers, had not taunted her so much about her dialect. But by the middle of Concetta's third year Giulia was pregnant again and Concetta was needed at home. She left school at the end of that year and never returned. For Giulia it was a source of satisfaction to have a daughter who could read and write.

With Salvatore it was different. Being a boy he did not have to stay at home and look after his younger sister and brother, and being two years younger than Concetta, he could start first grade when he was six. From the beginning he had made some friends in the street, and by the time he was ready to go to school, he had learned how to speak the Valmonte dialect. When he came home he would often tell the rest of them how to say this or that according to the Valmonte way. For Salvatore, going to school presented no difficulties. He never missed a day and would always start early enough in the morning so that he would not be late. He especially enjoyed reading, and whenever he could find a book about heroes and their adventures he would read it at home until it was finished – no matter how bad the light. When he was eleven he read *The Three Musketeers*. It became his favorite. He and his friends fashioned swords from sticks and cans and performed breathless duels that carried them to the highest ramparts of the castle that dominated the village of Valmonte.

By the time Maria began first grade in 1936, a new teacher had been hired for the beginning students. It seemed to Maria that she took a liking to her almost from the beginning, for she would entrust her with little errands, like carrying messages that she wrote to other teachers, or even going to buy cigarettes. Maria was gratified that the teacher trusted her so much and was pleased when the teacher asked if she would like to do her shopping for her and take the purchases home and put them away. Maria was thrilled, for it made her feel like a young housewife to ask for this and for that "for the *maestra*" in the piazza on market day. By the time Maria had done the shopping and put the teacher's house in order, there was little time left to spend in the classroom. At the end of the year she was easily promoted to the second grade where she continued to win the teacher's praise, and Giulia too was happy to know that Maria was doing so much to please the teacher, and so little to anger her. Maria's fortunes changed, though, in the third grade, for the teacher was Maestra Renata, who believed that children went to school to learn. Maria, unaccustomed to passing the school day in the classroom, would bring a pair of scissors with her so she could cut out designs in her notebook, and she therefore failed to respond correctly to Maestra Renata's questions. When this occurred, Maestra Renata would sweep down the aisle to where Maria sat, grab her hair, and bang her head down on the desk until Maria cried for mercy. After several encounters of this sort, Maestra Renata commanded Maria to tell her mother to present herself at the school the following day. When Giulia arrived, Maestra Renata spoke to her very loudly, telling her that Maria, even though she was nine, would have to return to the first grade, for she knew nothing. Giulia replied that she intended to do no such thing, but rather would take her daughter home and keep her there, where she was needed to help her mother. And so Maria's schooling came to an end at the beginning of her third year.

V

Giovanni and Giulia waited until the spring of 1936 to have Concetta, then ten, and Salvatore, then eight, confirmed. By having them confirmed on the same day they were able to save by having a single feast. For Concetta they chose Nina Monte and her husband, both Calabrians from near Catanzaro, to be the godparents; for Salvatore, Giovanni had his mind set on Arnaldo Laino and his wife, also Calabrians. Just before he spoke to them, a fellow worker at the forestry by the name of Gustavo Corvino asked Giovanni if he could have the honor of being his son Salvatore's godfather. Giovanni was greatly flattered, for Gustavo was not even a *paesano* but was one who came from the neighboring town of Sora to live in Valmonte, where there was more work. Giovanni did not like Gustavo very much but, in order not to offend him, accepted the offer. The ceremony was held on Palm Sunday with the bishop of Terracina in attendance. Giulia had dressed both children in sparkling white, including white gloves. Both she and Giovanni kept saying that they did not know where the money was going to come

from to pay for such an extravagance, but they were determined to
make a *bella figura* and show the Valmontesi how serious people did
things, even when they had nothing. Giulia made a fine *ciambella* to be
served with liqueur following a meal that included two kinds of meat—
rabbit and goat. The feast pleased everyone, including the priest, Don
Antonio. Nina Monte and her husband gave Concetta a ten-lire piece,
which delighted her, but Gustavo gave Salvatore nothing. Giovanni
then knew that it had been a mistake to have accepted his request.
Salvatore was crestfallen to have received nothing, not even a lira.
Giulia tried to console him, saying that she herself would find something to give him, but he insisted that that would not be the same as
receiving something from your own godfather. In time Giovanni settled the matter by dividing Concetta's ten lire between them. When it
was all over, Giulia felt that she had acquitted herself well; perhaps now
the Valmontesi would hold their tongues a bit.

VI

In the summer of 1936 Giovanni moved his family once more, now to a
rented house in that part of Valmonte called Il Martello, not far from
where they lived when they had first arrived three years ago. For the
first time in their lives they found a place where the roof did not leak,
and there was a little space in the back where Giulia could keep chickens. She had kept no chickens for three years, and she missed them
terribly. By then Giovanni was no longer working in Titalo, for almost
all of the replanting had been completed. For the next two years he
worked in the area of Sabaudia, some forty kilometers from Valmonte,
where the plan was to reforest that part of the Agro Pontino from
Valmonte to Monte Circeo. While there, he lived in a barracks and
came home every eight days, as he had done when working on the
railway line at Cutro, almost ten years before. He often dwelt on how
differently things had turned out from the way he had thought they
would when he left Stilo. Here they were living in the country again, in
a village even smaller than Stilo, and being offended by people who
lacked a proper sense of respect. But for all of that, he was glad that
they had come. The children were not sick, and he and Giulia always
had work, and that was the most important thing of all.

It came as a shock when the government terminated the reforestation
project in 1936. Giovanni did not know where to turn. The great
reclamation program of the Pontine Marshes, hailed as the monumental
victory of Facism where Caesar and the popes had failed, was now
completed. The land had been divided into farms, almost all allotted to
Venetians, who had had experience cultivating land as peasants, rather

than to the Valmontesi, who were for the most part agricultural day laborers. Now that the reclamation work was over, no plan existed to occupy the labor of all those who had come from the South to dig canals and clear the land. The war in Africa had come and gone, and now there was talk of building a great empire for Italians in that continent. From time to time, Mussolini came from Rome to speak from the balcony of the town hall in the new provincial capital of Littoria. Giovanni would be rounded up with many others by the Fascist Party of Valmonte and taken in trucks to Littoria to cheer the great leader, who promised that plowshares would be changed to swords to fight the battles that it would be their great fortune and honor to engage in. Giovanni found out that he was not alone in wondering why it was that notables collected the peasants' gold rings on those occasions to buy more guns when there was so much need of work right there in Valmonte. But he had always known that politics was not the concern of a person of his position in life. It was the work of the *Signori*, just as laboring with his hands was his assigned lot.

In the morning he would walk down the mountain to the abandoned house at the base, where everyone deposited their bicycles, and then would peddle off toward Littoria and the employment office. Day after day he would wait in line to register for work but to no avail. Finally he was given work as a manual laborer with a construction firm and was assigned to the building of a new church in Littoria. As the work drew to completion after several months, he noticed that all the men on the crew gave presents – one a ham, another sausage – to the foreman in hopes of being kept on. Giovanni discussed with Giulia what he should give, for they had no pig to provide them with a fine ham or sausage. They decided that Giovanni should try artichokes. He bought twelve of them and presented them to the foreman. Two days later he was let go.

Giovanni began to feel the way he had in Stilo years ago, hating to live in someone else's house, always being beholden to others. Back then he had only to find the price of the ticket to Argentina to earn enough money to buy a house, but now with the dictatorship more fully entrenched there were rules as to what you could and could not do. More than anything else he wanted to get out of the village and away from the harsh looks and gossip. He was tired of trying to convince Valmontesi that his hard work was not earning him money that he sent back to Calabria. The truth was that they were barely able to make ends meet. Giovanni knew the house that he wanted to have. It was a one-room wooden shack at the base of the mountain near the sulfur spring and just a short distance away ʿrom the railroad track. There they could be by themselves, raise some crops, and keep chickens and a pig. Their neighbors would be *paesani*. He had heard that the shack was for sale and that the owner wanted two thousand lire for it. Giovanni thought that he could probably purchase it for fifteen hundred, but even so, where would that amount of money come from? It was Giulia who found the answer, as she had once before in Stilo. She had been gleaning wheat in the fields of Valmonte for three years, and as the production of wheat increased with every harvest, so did the amount that she was able to collect. She was convinced that with one good season of gleaning they would make enough money to allow them to purchase the *baracca*. Giovanni recalled that he knew the guardian of the Vivaldi estates, and he thought it a good idea to work those fields, for other gleaners would not dare to do so, as Vivaldi peasants were particularly hostile to gleaners. Giovanni bicycled to have a word with him and found him well predisposed. He told Giovanni that he had his permission, for he knew him to be a serious and honest man, and if anyone stopped them, he should say that they had his leave to glean. Giovanni thanked him profusely. The following day he set out early by bicycle with Giulia on the handlebars and Salvatore on the back. Giovanni felt some trepidation, for he knew the Vivaldi peasants to burn their fields after the harvest or let the poultry root in the stubble rather than allow the likes of them glean. Leaving the bicycle in a ditch, they moved out onto a field farthest removed from the first farmhouse they came to. Barely fifteen minutes had passed before they heard them – five peasants with raised pitchforks bearing down on them. The three of them fled toward the bicycle and sped off as fast as Giovanni could pedal. They returned to the village with heavy hearts, but by evening Giovanni was convinced that they should not be stopped by those malevolent peasants. He returned to talk again to the caretaker and related all that had happened; the caretaker shook his head. He counseled them to lay low for a few days and then return to another farm farther down the road where the peasant family did not mind gleaners, even if they were Calabrians. He was right; when they returned they worked those fields for three days with good results. Giovanni and Giulia walked the rows, dropping the piles of wheat they had collected every twenty meters. Salvatore, who was only ten but skillful with his hands, tied the gleanings into sheaves. From that farm they moved to another, and then another, and by the end of the harvest of 1937, they had collected six quintals of wheat. At the mill, Giovanni received a good price, and with what they had earned, plus the two hundred lire that Giulia had hidden under the mattress, they had enough – fifteen hundred lire – to buy the *baracca*.

VII

When Giovanni paid the owner he felt happy and relieved to have a place of his own again. But there was work to do before they could move in. The wooden hut measured eight meters in length and four in width, and Giovanni set to work making a partition out of the long stalks of the hemp plant. When they were all in place he plastered the wall on both sides and papered it. Now the children could sleep in one room and he and Giulia in the other. Giovanni built Giulia an outdoor oven for baking bread. In the summer Giulia cooked outside to keep the house free of smoke and the yard free of mosquitoes. In the winter she cooked in the room where the children slept. It was lit by two oil lamps; the other room remained dark. The toilet was the area behind the Indian fig trees on the lower corner of the land away from the railway track. The small piece of land was in lamentable condition, full of rocks, underbrush, and vipers. Giulia set to work with a sharpened pole slaughtering the vipers with a vengeance, and when the land was cleared of snakes and scrub, Giovanni turned it over with a mattock. Then they set to planting beans and tomatoes and lettuce for the first time since they had left Stilo five years before. It was hard work to make that soil render, but it made them both want to sing to see the young plants slowly grow to fruition.

The hut was a quarter of a kilometer away from the gravel pit where Giovanni found employment – making lime in the lime kiln. The work was heavy and dirty but regular, and it was a source of considerable satisfaction to Giovanni to have only a short walk home at the end of the day and to be able to work in the garden until dusk. Giulia too enjoyed hoeing and weeding, and caring for the chickens and the pig, but she was restless without paid work, without the feel of some money in her pocket that she had earned herself. Not far down the track in the opposite direction from the gravel pit was a small barracks where the forest wardens lived. It was their duty to see that the citizenry did not chop down trees for firewood; only roots and broom were allowed for that purpose. Giulia set her sight on the sergeant in charge and every week paid a visit to the barracks to tell him that she needed work, for she had four children at home and her husband was paid barely enough to feed them. The sergeant would tell her that he had no work for her but if he did he would send a message. Giulia was not to be deterred and kept up her visits for two months. The sergeant finally relented and told her that she could wash their clothes. It was agreed that for every ten items washed and ironed Giulia would receive ten lire – but she would get nothing for socks. Giulia was overjoyed to be working again, and every week she watched the money grow in the leather bag that she kept under the mattress. The time was coming when she would have to start collecting a trousseau for Concetta and every lira would count.

VIII

A few months after Giulia started washing she became pregnant. She was then forty years of age and was carrying her eighth child. As soon as her condition began to be evident, she set to work making herself a special skirt that fit her in a way to allay suspicion. She wore it every day to work, for she was convinced that if the sergeant discovered her condition he would use that as an excuse to let her go. On payday she would turn quickly away from him when he handed her her money so that his eyes would not linger on her waist. Her ruse was successful, for she was able to work until a week before the birth. It was a difficult pregnancy, and Giulia felt very tired during the last months. To add to that hardship was another. Giovanni was recalled by the army in April of 1938 to serve in the Italian imperial forces in Tripoli. Giovanni was stunned. His detestation of the army made him feel faint at the prospect of going to an unknown place in Africa. Privately he cursed the day that Mussolini had become the commander of all of Italy, but he felt helpless, for he knew of no one in a high place who could put in a good word for him. Within four days of when the *carabinieri* had knocked on his door he was gone. Giulia was distraught. Left alone with the four children, it became all the more important that she keep her job as laundress. The day after Giovanni had tearfully departed on the bus she went to the mayor. That day she did not wear her special skirt and to him she admitted her pregnancy, begging him to have her husband recalled, for her time was coming. Words flowed from her mouth. She told the mayor that when she was young and Giovanni Battista was serving in the army at the time her first boy came it was not so bad, or even for the third when he was in Argentina, but now with the eighth she was forty and afraid that if something went wrong there would be no one to help. Her own mother was long since dead and her daughter Concetta was still young and, besides, it would be brutal for Concetta to have to see her mother in pain. The mayor, a wealthy landowner not known for his compassion, was moved. He said that he had not been aware that Giulia was in an interesting condition. He agreed to send a telegram to the military commander of the Tripoli district saying that Giovanni Battista Tassoni of Valmonte should be sent home for reasons of domestic hardship, for his wife who lived in a hut in the country with four small children was about to give birth to a baby. Tears came to Giulia's eyes for the pity that the mayor showed for her. The following days passed slowly, but three weeks later, in early May, Giovanni walked into the house. He quickly changed out of his uniform. He had been granted a leave of eight days, but he requested an extension, for by the seventh day the birth still had not occurred. Then he requested another extension. After the second extension, the *carabinieri* did not bother to come to the house anymore.

The baby was born on the eleventh of June 1938. The midwife arrived in time and let Giovanni come in as soon as the baby's cord had been cut, and the baby had been washed, swaddled, and placed in Giulia's arms. It was a boy, but there was no time to name him now. Giovanni was shocked by the way Giulia looked, drawn, pale, old – not as he remembered her looking after the births of their other children. The midwife said that the baby was all right but that the mother had a high fever and he had better call the doctor. Giovanni ran all the way up the mountain and, finding the doctor in, implored him to come and see his wife. The doctor muttered that it was not his responsibility to look after peasant women who, if they had had any education, would not have babies at that age. "You Calabrians are like Africans, like beasts," he roared, but Giovanni paid no heed to what he said. He only wanted him to come and save Giulia. The doctor told Giovanni that he would come as soon as he could get a proper ride. Later that afternoon he arrived and announced that Giulia was a very sick woman and must go to the hospital at Littoria at once. Then he left. Giovanni pedaled as fast as he could the twenty kilometers to Littoria to find an ambulance. He had a hard time persuading the authorities at the hospital to send the ambulance to the hut. It was already dark when it came. Giovanni rode back to Littoria with Giulia and the baby clutched in her arms in the back of the ambulance. He left Concetta in charge at the *baracca*. At the hospital Giovanni was stunned when they told him that they could not admit his wife, for the baby had not been born in the hospital. He would have to go to the hospital at Velletri, some thirty kilometers away. Furthermore, the ambulance would not be able to take them there because Velletri was in another medical district. The only thing left to do was to travel by bus; the last one left in an hour and a half. The ambulance driver, now commiserating with their plight, left them at the bus stop. Giulia collapsed on a bench, and Giovanni made her and the baby as comfortable as he could. When they finally arrived at the hospital the authorities began to tell them that they could not possibly take a sick mother with a newborn baby who had been born at home rather than in the hospital. Giovanni pleaded with them, saying that he was at his wit's end. It was already eleven thirty at night. They could not just throw a woman and a baby out on the street. The admitting officer emitted a heavy sigh. He said that it was indeed fortunate that they should have come there, for he would make an exception in this particular case. Giovanni was ushered out of the hospital and Giulia was wheeled with the baby into a large room filled with women in beds; some were moaning, some were screaming, some just lay on their backs or sides staring. Giulia had never been in a hospital before, but she knew that it was a place in which to die. Her fear was exceeded only by her shame when the doctor examined her the next morning. No man, other than Giovanni Battista, had ever looked at her. She raised her hands to hide her face while the nurse taunted her, saying that she should not think that she was the first woman to have been seen by a doctor.

The next day they placed her and the baby in another room with three empty beds, for they said it was not right for other women to have to suffer the sound of a screaming baby. The empty beds made her fearful, for she could think only of the women who had died in them. She wished the baby could be baptized before it could sicken and die, too, she thought, for her milk had not come in. The doctor said it was because she had an infection, and her husband would have to take the baby away the next time he came and find a wet nurse for him, for she would be in the hospital at least a month. On hearing the doctor's words, Giulia could only turn her head toward the wall and moan. Giovanni came with food prepared by Concetta, but Giulia had lost all desire to eat. She handed the baby to Giovanni and told him to find a woman who had good milk so that the baby would not sicken and die. Giovanni did not come to the hospital for another three days, because it was not an easy thing to do to find the proper wet nurse for their baby. His search finally took him to the neighboring town of Priperno, for he had heard that there was a woman there whose baby had just died. When the woman agreed to take theirs he was greatly relieved.

For the next six weeks Giovanni came twice a week by train to visit Giulia. She had developed large abcesses in her left leg that had to be drained. After the doctor had completed that procedure, a nurse gave her an injection in a way that left her leg paralyzed. Convinced that she would never be able to walk again, she prayed day and night to San Antonio, Santa Anna, and Santa Rita to intervene on her behalf.

One Sunday Giovanni brought Salvatore to see his mother. He told her about school and how he was helping his father at the gravel pit by carrying water for the kiln. With all her strength she hugged her son and told him how proud he made her feel because he was such a good worker. Once Salvatore had made the trip, Maria said that she wanted to go, too, but her father said that she was too small and, besides, he was too busy to take her. She pleaded and pleaded but he would not listen. So one day she set out along the railroad track to find her mother. She got as far as the first crossing when the wife of the guard recognized her as the daughter of Giulia Tassoni. "And where are you going?" she called out. Maria answered that she was going to find her mother in the hospital in Velletri, because she missed her and had not seen her for such a long time. The woman, moved by the girl's story, asked her to come inside. "You will need to eat, for the way is long," she said. She kept Maria there all day. When the train carrying Giovanni back to Valmonte from Velletri passed by, the woman flagged it and told Giovanni where his daughter was. When he descended from the train he said nothing to Maria. She was terrified, for she had never seen such anger in his eyes. He ordered Maria to start walking down the road toward their house. As soon as they had rounded the first bend, he caught up with her, grabbed her, fastened her to a tree with his belt and then with a sapling switch started beating her as hard as he could. Maria remembers the pain and the humiliation of that beating as the most severe she ever suffered at her father's hands. She knew him best as a gentle man.

By the time five weeks had passed Giulia was pleading with Giovanni to take her home. He said that she was not cured yet and would have to stay longer. By the next visit she was even more upset and said that the nurses hadn't given her water when she was thirsty or a bedpan when she had a need. When they finally did come they made insulting remarks under their breath, saying that she was an ignorant Calabrian. The more Giulia talked, the more agitated she became. Reaching for the bed railing behind her head, she pulled herself up to a full sitting position and shouted "I want to go home! I want to see my baby!" Giovanni felt very troubled to find his wife so upset and went looking for the doctor. It was difficult to make the doctor listen to his story, but at last the doctor agreed to release Giovanni's wife if he would sign a document in which he would assume full responsibility for her. Giulia was overjoyed. She did not mind that she had to be carried by Giovanni and a male attendant to the bus.

When she returned home she was exhausted and had to remain in bed for a month. She was still weak from the infection, and her left leg remained partially paralyzed, because she had also developed sciatica in it. Giovanni fetched the baby from Priperno and gave him to a woman nearby, called Nina, who had lost her baby just two weeks before. When Giulia saw her baby for the first time in five weeks, she cried for joy but also gasped with pain, for he had become very thin. He had weighed 3 kilos, 500 grams, when he was born and in the meantime had lost 600 grams. Every day Nina brought the baby for Giulia to see, and she watched him gain day by day, for he seemed to thrive on Nina's milk. When she saw this, she made a vow to San Antonio that if her baby son continued to grow well and strong, she would honor the good saint by naming her son Antonio. Then she thought of another vow: "If you let your namesake grow well and strong, I will bake as much bread for you as Antonio weighs in a year and a half." When she had finished saying that aloud she felt better.

After a month Giulia began to get out of bed and move about. She was regaining the use of her left leg. It was then that Nina came to her and said that a *Signora* from Littoria was willing to pay her more money for her milk. Giulia knew that they could not afford that much and asked for Antonio to be given back to her. She then sent Maria quickly to the pharmacy to buy a bottle and a nipple, and sent Concetta outside to kill a hen for broth. She knew that if the baby was to continue to grow as he should, he would have to have her milk. The broth would bring back her strength and make her milk flow again.

She gave the broth two days to take effect. While she waited, she fed Antonio formula from a bottle. On the morning of the third day she called Maria and Pasquale, who was then five, to her bed where she lay. She bared her breasts and then pointing to the left one said to Maria, "Here, suck that breast." Little by little the milk began to flow. Then she said to Pasquale, wide-eyed with astonishment, "Here, suck that breast," and little by little the milk began to flow. Giulia told them to spit out the first milk on the floor because it was not good. She then told Maria to bring Antonio to her and, setting him to her breast, she lay back on her pillow with a great feeling of joy in her heart. She thanked San Antonio for all he had done and then sent Maria and Pasquale to the store with a *soldo* apiece to buy caramels for themselves.

When she was fully up and about, she made a tiny habit out of brown sackcloth resembling that of a Franciscan friar. Before dressing Antonio in it, she brought it to the church and had it blessed by the priest. Then, properly clothed, she carried the baby to old Doctor Maolelli. He was amazed, saying that he had never seen such a change in a baby in his entire career. He said to Giulia, "Well you see, the old proverb is right, 'It is the eye of the owner that makes the horse grow.' "

Whenever the habit became too dirty she would carry Antonio to the public laundry, strip him, wash the frock, dry it on a bush, and put it back on him again. So she continued until it wore out. When he was a year and a half, she had Salvatore glean several kilos of wheat, from which she made six loaves of bread. She took them to the church to be blessed before the statue of San Antonio, and then she asked Don Antonio to distribute them to the poor. Antonio was growing to be a fine little boy. For Giulia, this was proof that if you ask a saint for his help in time of need with a full and sincere heart, it will be granted to you. She was as certain of this as she was that the hospital in Velletri had ruined her. Her experience there was one that she would never forget. She would never forgive them for the pain and shame that she suffered there. She passed that way once more on a pilgrimage to Rome in 1950, and when the bus drove by the hospital, she averted her eyes so as not to be offended by the sight.

IX

After the birth of Tonino, Giulia never worked again for a wage. Her leg bothered her, and she had five children at home to care for. She turned over more and more of the housework to Concetta, so that she could spend more time in the garden. By the time she was nine, Concetta had already learned how to make bread and then how to balance the loaves of dough on a board and take them to the oven to be baked. Concetta liked to help her mother in the house, whether it was cleaning or cooking, but more than anything else she enjoyed sewing. Giulia taught her what little she knew by example, for that was the way Giulia instructed her daughters. Before long Concetta was cutting out patterns on the kitchen table. She taught herself how to make a man's shirt by stretching out her father's as a model and cutting the cloth to measure. By the time she was thirteen, she was so clever at making shirts and skirts that Giovanni decided to try and find his daughter a secondhand Singer sewing machine. But it was not until 1941, when she was fifteen, that he found one through a *paesano*. With the machine Concetta was able to make some money, sewing a shirt for this person and a skirt for that one, and with her earnings she bought sheeting and toweling for her trousseau. The cleverer she became as a tailor, the less sadness she felt that she had not been able to finish school. She could read and write, but she envied the ease with which Salvatore could read a page of a book without faltering or write sentences in proper Italian.

Salvatore completed the fifth grade, at the head of his class, when he was twelve. His teachers urged him to go to the middle school in Littoria. The thought of doing such a thing stunned Salvatore; he knew that it was not his destiny to be a student. He had already gone further in school than anyone in his family ever had before, but now it was only just that his father, who had worked so hard, should have him at his side. Salvatore had a dream that maybe someday he would have a son who would be a student like those fine young men he saw standing in front of the *liceo* in Littoria, but it was his lot to be a worker and make his way through life by dint of the muscle of his arms, back, and legs. As soon as he graduated from elementary school, he started working with his father in the gravel pit hauling water. The boss was glad to have him, because he worked so hard and never missed a day, but because of his youth, he was paid very little. It angered Giovanni that the boss did not pay Salvatore like the others, for he worked just as long a day as they and harder than many. But he did not dare speak up on his son's behalf, for fear that he would be fired. With Giulia not working for money anymore, the burden of supporting the household fell almost entirely on his shoulders.

On one glorious Fascist holiday, the party secretary himself came to Valmonte to award prizes. All the student groups, the militia, and the town hierarchy were aligned in the piazza in full regalia. Salvatore, as a member of the *Balilla*, looked resplendent in his black uniform that Concetta had sewed for him. It was a proud moment when Salvatore stepped forth from rank to have a medal honoring him for his excellence in school pinned to his chest. Tears welled in Giovanni's eyes as he saw the Valmontesi around him applaud this son of an ignorant Calabrian.

Maria, standing with her family in the piazza that day, had a pang of remorse that she had not stayed in school, for if she had, she could have been one of the *Piccole Italiane* standing out there, proudly, in a black and white uniform receiving applause like the rest. She knew that she was different from her older sister and brother, Concetta and Salvatore; she was easygoing, whereas they were more serious. She loved to talk, to joke and laugh, and in that way she was more like her younger brother Pasquale. From the time Tonino was born in 1938 until Maria was eleven in 1941, she was Tonino's constant companion. She felt like a little mother carrying him here and there, changing his swaddling, feeding him. She loved him as if he were her own creation, and he loved his sister, which he showed by running after her when he was two and three.

When she was twelve in 1942, Maria began to search for outdoor work. She was more like her mother that way than Concetta, for she liked to work outdoors more than in the house. She began to work a day here and a day there, picking beans, hoeing tomatoes, carrying stones on her head, and then in the winter harvesting olives – as her mother had done in Stilo. Maria had reached the age where she had to begin thinking about collecting her trousseau.

For Pasquale it was different. He was a boy, and nothing should interfere with his completing elementary school, even though he was not the good student that Salvatore was. In 1942 he was eleven and the next year he was planning to follow in his brother's footsteps and become a member of the *Balilla*, even though Salvatore's uniform would not fit him, because he was so short. But in 1943 the war overtook life in Valmonte, and nothing was to be the same again.

3
The war

I

In the beginning the war had little effect on Valmonte in general or on the Tassoni family in particular. As 1941 gave way to 1942, more and more young Valmontesi men were called to arms; the town became increasingly a community of women, children, and the elderly. By 1943 food rationing was the law of the land, and for Giulia, as for everyone, it was a source of great frustration; it seemed that she never had enough coupons to feed a family of seven.

The only news that they had about the course of the war was rumors, for no one in the area had a radio or a newspaper. What everyone did know for certain was that German soldiers appeared suddenly in August of 1943. The Germans told those who dared to ask that they were there to help their Fascist comrades-in-arms achieve a final victory over the Allies, but from the way they gave orders it was clear that it was they who commanded. With the Germans in charge food became even scarcer. From time to time soldiers would come by the hut, knock at the door with the butt of a rifle, and ask Giulia for some eggs or a loaf of bread. It took all her resourcefulness to find enough to send them on their way and keep something in reserve for her family. At the sight of the German soldiers, all the children, terrified, would run and hide – all, that is, except Tonino, who would remain at his mother's side, holding on to his mother's skirt and looking up at the strangers with a large smile lighting his face. It seemed that he always reminded them of a son or grandson at home somewhere in Germany.

By November of 1943 voices were heard to say that in the South there was more food to be had, for there were few or no Germans south of Naples, and life was going on there much as if there were no war. Giovanni and Giulia talked about this news and what it might

51

mean for them. It was finally decided that someone must return to Stilo
to procure whatever they could, and it would have to be Giulia, for it
would not be safe for Giovanni to travel without special papers. Already the Germans were beginning to round up able-bodied men to
work for them. It was thought best for Giulia to take Tonino, as it
always aroused less suspicion for a woman to travel with a child. Besides, Tonino seemed to have a way of charming all who noticed him.
Giulia packed three large sacks in the suitcase, took money from the
bag under the mattress, and started her journey to Calabria with
Tonino.

Giulia found that Stilo looked much the way she remembered it
when she left, except that so many people she had known were now in
the cemetery. Her father-in-law, Pasquale, was much moved to see her
and his youngest grandson. He had never expected to see Giulia again,
and to show her respect for him, she cleaned him as she had in the past.
When she was through she asked him about food and how difficult it
was to procure wheat and oil and beans. He replied that the people of
Stilo refused to accept the black flour available with the rationing cards,
for plenty of white flour could still be found. As soon as Giulia heard
this, she started to call upon persons she had known to ask them if they
would buy the black flour for her, for which she would repay them. In
that way she collected twelve kilos of flour, as well as ten liters of olive
oil, beans, and the dried figs she loved so well. Before long she had
filled the three sacks and the suitcase and was ready to start her journey
to Valmonte. She knew that she would be severely punished if appre-
hended with so much food, and she was anxious to get the journey
over with. She cleaned Pasquale for the last time and departed with his
fervent best wishes. At the station it was most fortunate that some
soldiers took pity upon her and helped her lift the sacks on the train, for
she could not have managed by herself. During the trip, which seemed
as if it would never end, one of the soldiers held Tonino in his arms,
sang to him, played with him, and laughed at the bright things he said.
Giulia felt as warmly toward the soldier as if he had been her own son,
and when he told her of the long way he had to go and of the dangers
that faced him, Giulia's heart filled with pity; she shared some of her
dried figs with him. At the station at Littoria he helped her down with
the sacks and the suitcase. Giulia was at last off the train. She made a
small pile of her possessions and sat down on them with Tonino to wait
for Giovanni to arrive for her at the time agreed upon. Barely had she
sat down when she saw a man of stature dressed in sober civilian
clothes approach her. She could tell by the way he looked that he was
an official and she knew what he was going to ask. He stopped directly
in front of her and demanded to know what she was doing there, and

what were the contents of her bags? Didn't she know, he went on to say, that it was illegal to transport food during wartime and that penalties were very severe if one was discovered doing so? Giulia looked at the man directly and said, "I am waiting for my husband Giovanni Battista, for I have just returned from Calabria where I went to get some food for my family. Now take these figs, be quiet, and go away." The man looked both ways up and down the platform, nodded his head, slipped the figs under his jacket and strode quickly away. When Giovanni arrived, she gave one of the sacks to him to carry on his back, and she balanced the other two on the suitcase on her head. So they began the long walk home, Tonino running by his father and recounting to him the adventures of the long journey.

II

By 1943 Concetta had turned seventeen, and if the times had been normal, she would have been engaged to be married by then. But many of the young men had left Valmonte and, too, it was difficult to meet prospective suitors when living in the country. Concetta was not allowed to join the work gangs of unmarried women who picked olives in the winter. Those who beat branches with long poles to make the olives fall to the ground were young men, and the mutual effort in the grove was an occasion for courtship to ripen. So, too, was the nocturnal hour of the promenade, which was made along the road that led to the main gate of the village. On rare occasions Concetta would be allowed to participate, chaperoned by Salvatore or Maria, for Giovanni and Giulia were of the opinion that one could not be too careful in these matters. They disapproved of what they regarded as the loose morals of the Valmontesi, and they liked the Venetians even less, for they seemed not to have any morals at all.

One evening a Calabrian by the name of Marone, who lived nearby and dropped in to drink a glass of wine and play a hand of cards with Giovanni, came to the door with a young soldier whom he introduced as Domenico Collobiano. Domenico was stationed in some barracks to the east of the Via Appia near Littoria, and it seemed that he had a considerable amount of free time from his military duties. Domenico enjoyed himself that evening, and Concetta also admitted later that she found him an easy person to sit and talk to. He then began to come more often and finally every other evening. He would sit at one end of the table, and Giovanni or Giulia, or both together, would place themselves between him and their daughter, and so passed many pleasant evenings in conversation.

Seeing that the situation was becoming serious, Giovanni set about to discover as much as he could about Collobiano. He found out that his mother was dead and that his father was a road worker in the province of Reggio Calabria. Domenico told Giovanni that before the war he had been a mason and that he was looking forward to returning to his village after the war to pick up his life there again. What Giovanni heard was reassuring, but he felt uneasy that he could not meet Domenico's family. One day when he met Marone on the way to work, he stopped and asked him if he would swear to the good name of Domenico Collobiano. Marone replied that Giovanni should rest assured, for he knew his family by reputation and they were serious and respectable people. By that time Domenico had deserted the army, as had so many others after the fall of Mussolini in July of 1943.

In November of 1943 Domenico asked Giovanni and Giulia for Concetta's hand in marriage. They both knew that the inevitable had happened, but they could not help but feel some resentment toward this stranger who had come into their midst and was now proposing marriage to their daughter. Giovanni warned Domenico that if he intended to take advantage of their daughter, or to make light of her in any way, then he should leave immediately. Giulia added that if Domenico, distant from the women of his family, wanted to marry Concetta in order to have someone wash and iron his clothes, then it was not necessary – for she herself could do that for him. Domenico answered that he had no intention of taking advantage of the innocence of their daughter and that he was not looking for a maid but a wife. He finished by saying that they should allow Concetta to speak for herself so that they could see whether she wanted to marry him of her own free will. Concetta then spoke and said that in these months she had had the chance to become acquainted with the character of Domenico. She trusted him and knew that he came from a poor but respectable family like their own. She consented to marry him.

There remained one more barrier to cross, however, before Domenico could claim the hand of Concetta in marriage. He would be required to go before the bishop and swear upon the cross that he had not already taken a wife. The dislocation of the war had been so severe that the Church, by Article 13, absolved soldiers like Domenico of proving through documents that they were unmarried. Now a simple oath would suffice. By all rights Domenico should have gone to the archbishop's site in Terracina. But by December of 1944, the war had made travel that far impossible. Instead, Domenico, Concetta, Giovanni, and Giulia took the bus to nearby Sessa and there, in the presence of the bishop, Domenico, clutching a crucifix in his hand, swore that he had never been married before. With the ceremony completed, Giulia, now reassured, began immediately to make plans for the wedding. The service itself would take place in the church of Santa Anna in the village and the reception in the hut. There was no question but that a bus would have to be chartered to bring the guests down to the country. Giulia had to use all of her ingenuity to find the ingredients for a wedding feast. She was consoled, though, that at least they did not have to provide for the relatives of Domenico, for conditions prohibited travel of such a distance. That would save some expense.

From Giustino Cervino, a storekeeper in the village, she bought two bottles of contraband vermouth and the ingredients to make several different kinds of liqueurs, as well as four kilos of flour. She was able to find a little more here and a little more there until she finally had enough to make the pasta and the sweets. Over the sauce, though, Giulia despaired, for she had little more than tomato paste, some oil, and herbs. She was elated when just two days before the wedding Giovanni was able to locate a kilo of meat. Now she felt she could be proud to have guests sit at her table. There was even a solution to the total unavailability of coffee and sugar. It lay in the five kilos of sugar and one kilo of coffee that a Calabrian had left in their house for safekeeping. Giulia borrowed just enough for her needs.

The wedding took place on the twenty-second of January 1944. The day broke fair and clear, and before long the hut was full of guests who were taking great pleasure in Giulia's coffee and sweets. As Giovanni looked about he took pride in the thought that when he first came there in 1933 he knew no one and now there were all these people, not a relative among them, who had come to the wedding of his daughter. His pride was even greater when the old bus pulled up and they all boarded it for the ride to the village. The boss at the gravel pit had made the expenditure possible by making an advance on Giovanni's pay in honor of the wedding. When the guests returned from the church, Giulia had the first course all ready. The times made it impossible to prepare all the dishes that a wedding feast called for, but nonetheless the guests remained at the table drinking wine and singing *stornelli* until late in the afternoon. From time to time a voice would call out, "Viva gli sposi," and Concetta and Domenico would rise to their feet to the sound of applause and cheers. The party became livelier when the accordianist and guitarist struck up a tarantella. Domenico and Concetta were the first to dance and then other couples joined in. Darkness descended but it was clear that no one wanted to leave – all were having such a good time.

At first the distant rumbling and flashes that lit the sky to the northeast seemed like a thunderstorm, but it was January; it must be cannonading instead. But where and why? Rumors began to ebb and flow. Some said the Germans were blowing up Rome; others claimed that a giant munitions dump near Littoria had been hit. But soon it became clear that the Americans and the English were landing at Anzio, some twenty-five kilometers away, and already men were dying. There were those who wanted to know why, if they were to be liberated, the Allies were landing so far to the north, and there were others who were saying that an operation like that would endanger them all, for it would bring the war right down on their heads. Surely the Germans would respond with great force and they, the defenseless, would be caught in the middle. All of a sudden, in the midst of the confusion, two German soldiers appeared. Terror struck at everyone's heart; had they come to round up the men as they had begun to do a short time before? The Germans grinned. Giulia advanced with two bowls of pasta and glasses of wine, which the Germans accepted eagerly and began eating with relish. The fear lessened. The Germans thanked their hosts and moved on. The cannonading increased in intensity, and it seemed now as if it were coming from all around them. The guests began to leave, not knowing what fate might be in store for them before the evening was out.

After all the guests had departed, Giovanni and Giulia blessed their daughter and new husband, and then Concetta and Domenico walked nearby to the hut of Allesandro, a Calabrian who was Concetta's honorary godfather. Out of respect for Giovanni and Giulia, he allowed the newlyweds to sleep there for three nights without being disturbed. On the morning of the third day they moved to a rented room nearby but continued to take their meals with Giulia; for in times of rationing, what little food there was went further if it was shared. Concetta had little to furnish their room with, since conditions had made it difficult for Giulia to accumulate a proper trousseau for Concetta. Domenico said that he understood and that he would not expect her family to provide for her as they ordinarily would have done. Giulia and Concetta carried over the bed, mattress, cupboard, table, and chairs. In the way of linens Concetta was better off, for she had managed to put by a good number of sheets and towels herself, buying the materials with the money she had made by sewing. Giulia had wanted to buy a whole set of copper pots and pans for Concetta, but copper was out of the question. As for plates, Giulia had acquired them earlier from a Neapolitan itinerant salesman. She had bought twelve of them after the gleaning in July of 1942, paying for each with wheat equal to a brimming plateful.

Now that the wedding was over, Domenico reassumed the trading in oil and wine that he had begun when he had walked away from the army. At first it had bothered Giovanni that Domenico was a deserter, but now it seemed that almost every young man was. What had become more troubling was his dealing in the black market, for Domenico insisted on hiding the demijohns of wine and bottles of oil in the hut. It was bad enough to have the Germans banging on the door, but the thought of the Italian police descending upon them was even more terrifying. Domenico would reassure Giovanni that they had nothing to fear, and besides, his business was making money. The sight of the lire notes that Domenico would then pull from his pocket sufficed to silence Giovanni. At home Concetta sewed on her Singer and awaited the arrival of her first baby. It was born in their room on January 8, 1945, with Giulia and the midwife in attendance, and was named Michele Collobiano in honor of Domenico's father.

III

From the day of the wedding life became increasingly precarious for the Tassoni family. The area where they lived became a military encampment from which Germans hoped to throw the Allies back into the sea at Anzio. Everything in sight was commandeered by the Germans. Indeed, they once ordered the family from the hut, claiming they needed it. But as they shouted "Raus, raus!" Giovanni pointed to all the mattresses on the floor, and they relented. By then godmother Rosina and her husband, godfather Alessandro, had moved in as well as another Calabrian couple and their two children. At night the floor was covered with bodies, and it was all but impossible to move across it without stepping on man, woman, or child. One evening Giovanni counted twenty-two persons seeking refuge with them, and food became ever more scarce. The ration card allowed one hectogram of bread per person per day, but a growing boy like Salvatore was constantly hungry and could have easily eaten the whole seven that were allotted to them as a family. Like every other apparatus, the flour mill at Ronticchio had been requisitioned by the Germans, so Giovanni reconstructed an old coffee mill for the milling of flour. When properly fastened to the table, it was possible to produce four to five kilos of flour if one worked all night. At first the only wheat that was available was black, and when that ran out *fave* and *ceci* beans were ground to make the flour for bread. The garden was turned over almost entirely to the production of potatoes, and Giulia coaxed her hens to make more eggs so that she could trade some for bread, which the Germans baked in their giant ovens nearby.

For a while it was Salvatore who was the best-fed member of the family, for every morning two German soldiers would come by to accompany him to a nearby stable where he milked cows and fed animals. For his efforts the Germans would give him a big bowl of minestrone at noontime, but even so, he would come home hungry at night, and there was hardly any bread to eat.

Almost equal to the preoccupation with hunger was the fear that the Germans would one day take Giovanni away to build fortifications at the front line – and then he might never come back. During the day Giovanni would hide himself in a small cave not far from the hut, and at other times when he was home he would flatten himself between the spring and the mattress if he heard their voices or banging at the door. He grew a beard, slumped his shoulders, and walked with a slow shuffle to make them think he was too old to be useful to them. But one day, when he was alone with Pasquale, two soldiers caught him before he was able to run for the bed. When Giovanni resisted they threatened him with their rifles. Pasquale threw his arms around the legs of one and pleaded with him to leave his father, but his anguish was to no avail. Instead they dragged off Pasquale with his father, although after they had forced them to walk as far as Due Ponte, they released Pasquale, concluding that he was too young for their purposes, even though eleven. Pasquale ran home as fast as he could, convinced that he would never see his father again. But to his overwhelming joy, Giovanni appeared at the door two hours later. Breathless from his running, he told his son that he had managed to escape but did not have time to tell him how he had done it; the important thing was to go into hiding, which he did for two weeks in a more distant cave.

While in seclusion he came to the belief that his best chance to survive and to help his family was to collaborate with the Germans. When he thought the immediate danger had passed, he went to the gravel pit where he used to work before the Germans had requisitioned it for a kitchen area. He told the sergeant in charge that he would work for them in exchange for food. He told them he was strong, despite being short, and straightened his shoulders, grabbed a pail full of water nearby, and swung it at arm's length. The sergeant nodded his head and told him that he could haul water from the spring to the kitchen. From the large bowl of minestrone they gave him at noontime, he would take a couple of spoons full for himself and carry the remainder home to his waiting family. If he was attentive he was able to procure, from time to time, some salt and some sugar. Almost every morning Tonino, who was then six, would come along with him to play in the kitchen area. The Germans became very fond of him, nominating him their mascot; Tonino was not at all afraid of them. Grinning from ear to ear he would say, "Comrade, marmalade, marmalade," and they would give him a big piece of bread smeared with it. Tonino would take a couple of bites and then store it safely in his hiding place, to be brought home later to his mother, brothers, and sister.

In the late winter of 1944, the bombing by Allied warplanes trying to destroy German gun emplacements became intense. Reports came back about the screaming of the wounded and the dying in the German hospital set up in the renowned medieval Benedictine monastery of Valvisciolo; it was in that monastery, too, that slain American and British troops were buried. More than once shrapnel pierced the roof of the Tassoni hut. Terrified, Giovanni and Giulia withdrew with the children to a large cave behind the sulfur water spring. There they crowded in with seven other families, so that there was barely enough room to stretch out on the cave floor at night. In the cave they were safe enough, but when the bombs or shells began to land nearby, the children cried with fear and buried their heads under whatever cover they could find. It was during one such bombardment, which killed seven persons nearby, that Giulia yelled out that Tonino was not with them. Giovanni, convinced that his son had been killed with the rest, or at least wounded, dashed from the cave even before all the planes had passed. He saw him cowering behind a large boulder. He rushed to him and took him in his arms, and yelled Tonino's name over and over again for the joy of finding him alive.

By the end of May, people were saying that American soldiers had been seen near Sessa and were pushing toward Valmonte. Every day more and more Germans could be seen retreating northward. Some who came by the hut stripped themselves of their uniforms and begged Giulia for civilian clothes. But she was afraid, for she did not know what the new American masters would do if they found her helping the enemy escape. On one of those days two wounded Germans appeared at the door. Giovanni immediately hid under the mattress, but Giulia could see that they were more to be pitied than feared and called Giovanni out. They had already walked thirty kilometers that day and were clearly exhausted. Giulia gave them two eggs and invited them to sit down at the table. They pulled out photos of their relatives. "*Kaput, kaput*, all *kaput* from the bombings," they said. For the first time Giulia found herself genuinely sorry for these men, who now seemed to have lost their great power. When they left they said that they would return the next day with some bread to repay them for the eggs, but Giovanni and Giulia never saw them again.

The last fighting occurred around the ruins of the old convent above Ronticchio, where thirteen Germans held out until the last man was killed. Then the American jeeps began to appear, a tank or two went by, and the men leaning from the turrets scattered caramels. Maria, Pasquale, and Tonino ran down the road after them, picking up as many of the candies as they could. It was on the way back that Maria saw a black hand protruding from a grave. It was all that remained to be seen of six Italians executed by the retreating Germans. She had heard the shots earlier in the day. Numbed with terror, she went running home. It was then that the sickness, the fevers, and the boils began that were to plague Maria for so long. Even today Maria attributes some of her ailments to the terrors of the war.

Once the Americans had cleared out all the Germans, they bivouacked down the road at San Giuseppe, so no one saw as much of them as they had of the Germans. But when it came to the Americans, it was not so important that they were kind or cruel but that they left so many good and valuable things behind. Word spread quickly that the fields near Cisterna and Anzio, where the Americans had been dug in, were full of such treasures, and so people from all over bicycled, ran, and walked in that direction to bring home whatever they might find. The scavenging was always dangerous because of the possibility of touching off a land mine. The food was as welcome as it was unfamiliar. Everything was in cans – even the spaghetti – and tasted of sugar. But there was an abundance of things, especially cigarettes, caramels, and gasoline. One day Maria walked as far as Nettuno, some thirty kilometers away, and returned exhausted with a sack full of chocolate bars.

IV

Little by little life began to return to normal. As soon as the Germans left, the owner of the gravel pit took repossession and in a short while started operations there again. After so much uncertainty and fear, Giovanni found it good to be working once more, backbreaking though it was. In the beginning it seemed as if the war had taught a lesson to the *padrone*, for he was punctual about giving the men their money. That enabled Giulia to pay off the debt that had piled up at the store. For her, it was important to be scrupulous. She knew of a number of families who had not paid their debts and went right on eating anyway, and they were the ones who maligned the Calabrians. In a few months, though, the *padrone* went back to his old ways and began giving only a fraction of the pay that was due, saying that if he paid in full he would have to close the plant down and then there would be work for no one.

The war had changed nothing. It was a bitter pill to swallow, following on the hope that things would be different after so many years of sacrifice. Before Giovanni had worked in the lime kiln, but now he had to break, with a pick, the giant rocks that had been loosened by dynamite. Within two months of his return, Giovanni had lost twelve kilos.

Salvatore, who had turned seventeen in 1945, also came back to work in the pit, pushing the railed carts loaded with stone from the place where his father labored to the crusher. Salvatore worked even longer hours than his father, for he wanted to assume more of the responsibility for helping the family get back on its feet. The *padrone*, though, refused to recognize the extra hours that he was devoting to the job. Salvatore, angered, threatened to lodge a complaint with the representative of the CGIL, the General Confederation of Italian Labor. Giovanni counseled him not to, saying that if he did so the *padrone* would accuse him of being a spy and fire him – fire them both, perhaps. Where else could they find work? Salvatore responded that things were different now; the Fascists were no longer in charge and workers were free to bargain and to strike. The workers had to learn to stand up for their rights. No one had ever talked back to the *padrone*, and he was going to be the first, he added. Giovanni was proud of his son's courage and impressed when his strategy worked, for when Salvatore went to the CGIL representative and lodged a complaint, the *padrone* was forced to give him nine hundred lire in overtime pay. Giovanni had the uneasy feeling, however, that sooner or later the *padrone* would get his revenge, for he knew that once a *padrone* always a *padrone*, and it did not make much difference whether the Fascists or the Communists were in command.

4

The travail of Concetta

When the war ended Domenico seemed to change. He gave up the buying and selling of wine and oil, for with the termination of rationing there was little to be gained. Instead he took up being a mason again and rode the train every day to Frascati to work. But he seemed to be always on edge and distracted. Before he had been kindly disposed toward Concetta and his baby son, Michele, but now he rarely was. At first Concetta tried to pay no heed, but as time went on she became more and more upset, and then Giulia too began to notice that Domenico was mistreating her. Furthermore, he began to make strange comments to his mother-in-law, such as "You do not really know who I am" or "You do not know the family that I come from." Giulia's answer was, "Well, we are a poor but honest family. What kind of a family is it that you come from?" Such talk aroused Giulia's suspicions about Domenico all over again, and she went to a Calabrian neighbor who knew how to write and confessed to her her fears. The friend agreed that her doubts were justified and advised that Giulia should have a letter written to the parish priest of the village from which Domenico came. Later Giulia confided to Giovanni what she had done. He was angered that she had not asked his permission first but admitted that they owed it to themselves as well as to Concetta to find out about Domenico. They waited day after day, and the longer they waited the more agitated they became. Finally a letter arrived from the priest at San Lucca. When Salvatore read it their worst fears were realized, for the priest said that Domenico Collobiano of San Lucca was married to a woman of the village and had two children by her. Giulia screamed and Giovanni banged his fists on the table so hard that Salvatore had to restrain him for fear that he would hurt himself. The shame was like a hot rod that seared their insides. Both had a hard time catching their breath. It had become the worst day of their lives. It was made more bitter by the realization that daughters of other families had married under Article 13 and yet this terrible thing had not happened to them. Giulia and Giovanni had tried so hard to find out everything there was to know about Domenico. How cruel fate could be, they thought, for now they would become the laughing stock of the town. What to do? Giovanni reached for godfather Alessandro's shotgun, which he had left in the hut for safekeeping, and hurried out of the door in search of Domenico. He was going to blow his brains out — even if he had to do it in front of Concetta and Michele. But Domenico had left home, for he knew Giulia was becoming suspicious and had written a letter. It was true all along that he had married Concetta in order to have someone take care of him while so far away from home. But now the war was over, and he was ready to return to San Lucca and rejoin his first wife and children.

Giovanni was prepared to travel to San Lucca by train, gun in hand, but Salvatore finally persuaded him not to. He said that the family, especially Concetta, needed him during this terrible time. It was finally decided that the wise course of action was to send for Giovanni's brother, Salvatore of Stilo, so that he could help them decide what to do. It took considerable time to locate Salvatore, but when he finally arrived, he found Giovanni and Giulia in a state of considerable agitation. "Why," they kept asking, "did this terrible disgrace befall us who have always been so careful to do the right thing?" After several days in Valmonte, it was clear to Salvatore that it would have to be he who would go to San Lucca and confront Domenico Collobiano.

When at last he located Domenico in the house of his first wife and confronted him face to face, he felt an overwhelming urge to attack him in the name of the honor of the Tassoni family. But he restrained himself and told him, without referring to him by name, that he must go to the parish priest immediately and tell him all that happened so the marriage could be annulled at once. In time Salvatore returned to Valmonte with a letter from the priest of San Lucca setting forth the whole case. But even armed with the document, it was not clear what should be done. It took several weeks of being directed first here and later there for Giovanni to arrive at the proper ecclesiastical authorities in Rome. They replied that, yes, the marriage of his daughter could be dissolved, for a mortal sin was at issue. It would cost Giovanni Battista Tassoni no money, but it would be necessary that his daughter Concetta appear in person before them. The following week she made the trip to Rome with her father. Fortunately Concetta's memory was good, enabling her to answer all the questions that the ecclesiastical authorities put to her in a most convincing way.

A year passed before the entire procedure was completed. For Giovanni, Giulia, and Concetta it seemed like a lifetime, and even when Concetta was finally a single woman again, the bitterness in their hearts did not pass. As Giovanni said, "In life one has to suffer every kind of displeasure, but that was the greatest unhappiness that can befall a man."

II

After the humiliation of Concetta, Giovanni thought more and more of leaving the hut, for it bore all the fearful memories of the war and the bitterness of the marriage. And Giulia, thinking of all the troubles that had befallen her in that terrible hospital in Velletri, decided she wanted to be in the village so that she could get help more readily if she needed it. Giovanni began to make inquiries about a house to rent and in time found one not far from where they had lived years before, near Il Martello. The rent was five hundred lire a month. When it came time to sell the hut, Giovanni found the transaction far easier than he had thought it would be. It seemed that owing to the destruction of the war, habitations of any kind were in great demand. He was stunned to find that he could sell it for as much as 39,000 lire – he had paid only 1,500 for it in 1937. He had never seen so much money in his life, and he quickly deposited it in the post office for safekeeping, advising Giulia that her leather bag under the mattress was no longer a secure place in this day and age. The day the house was sold, Giulia, Concetta, and Maria began transporting pieces of furniture – the three beds, table, chairs, cupboard, and bread chest – on their heads to the house in the village. By nightfall, after several trips, all had been moved, and for the first time since 1937 the family passed a night together in the village. Everyone was pleased with their relocation. Not far away was the piazza, with its two stores, butcher shop, bar, barbershop, and pharmacy. Now it would be easy for Concetta to do the shopping. Salvatore joined the village band. Pasquale escaped as soon as he could from any task at hand to the *loggia*, which provided a vantage point for viewing the girls of the village as they passed. Tonino loved roaming the streets, performing tasks for anyone who gave him a command. Maria joined the Daughters of Maria, a Catholic Action group, and participated in all the religious processions as they wove their way through the village.

Pleased as he was to be back in the village, it was Giovanni's ambition to own a house of his own. He had never liked being beholden to a landlord and feeling restrained from pounding a nail here and putting in a hook there. Furthermore, he reasoned that if he bought a house now, it would probably increase in value just as the hut had done in the years that he had owned it. Once again he began to make inquiries, but it wasn't for some time that he was told of a house for sale just down the street that he had been by countless times, hardly noticing it. When he took Giulia to see it, she liked it immediately: It had a window that looked to the southwest over the Agro Pontino that let in light, and there was a storage room where she could have an oven and space enough to dry beans and fennel. Giovanni liked it because the kitchen was large and there were two other rooms as well – a bedroom and a living room. Now Concetta and Maria would be able to sleep separately in the living room, and the three boys could sleep with Giulia and Giovanni in the big bed in their room. For the first time Giovanni would not have to make a two-room house out of one room. Even so there was much to do; the house was in serious need of repair. The flooring was torn up, the walls had large cracks, and the roof leaked in several places. The price was forty thousand lire, which meant that Salvatore had to put in overtime before the purchase could be made final.

A whole year passed before the house was ready to move into. Every evening and on Sundays each member of the family would collect gravel along the side of the road. It would be scraped into piles, loaded into pails and buckets, and carried back to the house to be mixed with cement to make mortar. Crushed stone was also sought as a filling for the floor. Concetta, Salvatore, Maria, and Pasquale would carry twenty-five kilo sacks of the stone from the far part of town, where a soccer field was being made, up the long flight of stairs from the west gate, to where Giovanni was working, all the while feeling that their arms would fall off. The last thing they built was the oven where Giulia's bread was to be baked. Now for the first time they had a real house of stone and mortar, and a kitchen with its own fireplace for cooking!

It was in June 1947 that the family moved into their new house. Never before had they felt so well sheltered, so proud of a dwelling. They had their first meal in the living room so that they could enjoy the view from the window overlooking the Agro Pontino, and on a day like that one, the eye could stretch as far as the sea beyond Latina. Not long after they moved in, Giovanni applied for electric light; they had always lit with oil or gas lamps before. After considerable delay, a single fifteen-watt bulb was suspended over the kitchen table. Everyone assembled the first time Giovanni turned the switch on late one July evening. Giulia gasped. Pasquale began to dance an abandoned tango with Maria. "This must be the way it is to live in the city," exclaimed Tonino, his hands clasped over his eyes. The current went on at dusk and went off at dawn, enabling them to pay the lowest rate. Later on they changed the fifteen watts in the kitchen to ten and suspended a five-watt bulb from the ceiling in the living room.

Maria and Concetta's bed in the living room could be made into a couch with the bedspread and the pillows for which Concetta had sewn covers. Next to the bed was a table on which rested the secondhand phonograph and six popular records that Pasquale had bought from a friend leaving for military service. Above all else Pasquale loved to dance, and for hours in the evening and on Sundays he would glide and pivot with an unseen partner in his outstretched arms. Such comportments drove Giulia to her wit's end, and when Pasquale could tolerate her interjections and occasional blows no longer, he would escape to the *loggia* in the piazza to observe the girls passing.

In the new house the toilet was a chamber pot. Giulia or Concetta or Maria would empty it every morning in the corner of an old foundation behind the house, but eventually the chamber pot went the way of the oil lamp. After they had been in the new house for two years, Giovanni and Salvatore set to work building a privy that was attached to the front of the house, just to the right of the door. The design was simplicity itself, being a hole in the middle of the floor down which water was sluiced. But the job took a long time, because the floor had to be reinforced by two iron girders. It was Maria who was most relieved by the new addition, for she hated more than anyone else the task of emptying the pots in the morning. Giulia knew of a few families, the more well-to-do, who had running water in their houses, and some were even cooking over gas ranges rather than an open fire. But for her, the advent of the light and the toilet was so monumental as to make her wonder if she was not already living in the America that she had heard about.

III

It was in the autumn of 1947 that Felice Centallo moved to Valmonte. He was the second of three sons in a family of eight children who lived in Piove di Sacco near Padua. Finding no work there after the war, he had traveled to Valmonte to visit his uncle with the hope of finding employment. Being resourceful, he was soon able to find work as an ironsmith. When he first met godfather Alessandro, he told him that he wanted and needed a wife – someone poor but honest like himself. Immediately Alessandro thought of Concetta, and after a moment's hesitation began to tell the story of her great misfortune. When he finished he expected Felice to say that he would have nothing to do with such a woman, but instead he said right out that it would make no difference to him if she had been married before, as long as she was a serious person. Alessandro did nothing for a while, to give himself a little more time to think over what had been said. He finally decided to go and speak with Giulia about what he had on his mind. He knew that it would do no good to speak to Giovanni, for he was still so embittered that he didn't want to even hear of the possibility of Concetta marrying again. But when Alessandro raised the subject with Giulia after mass one Sunday, she dismissed him immediately. Alessandro returned to Felice that very day and told him that he would have to be very patient, and maybe in time Giulia would change her mind. In fact, after her meeting with Alessandro, that is exactly what she started to do, for she knew that it was not right for a young woman, a mother, to live without the protection of a man; already people were talking, and in a place like Valmonte there were always men who would try and take advantage of a single woman like Concetta. Even Calvino, the mayor and owner of one of the shops, had told Concetta that if she came shopping alone, without Michele, he would give her a hectogram more here and there for the same money. Concetta, knowing what he had in mind, left in a fury and told Giulia about it. Giulia, hurt and angered by the humiliation that her daughter had suffered, commanded her to never go shopping alone again. From then on Concetta busied herself at home with her sewing and rarely went outside.

When Giulia first began to broach the subject of Concetta marrying, Giovanni shouted at her and banged the table for silence. The wound was still too deep to even contemplate such a thing, he cried. But little by little he began to see the wisdom of what she was saying. He finally agreed that she should talk to Concetta. After the annulment had been passed down by the ecclesiastical authorities in Rome, Giulia never thought she would ever, as long as she lived, speak to Concetta about another man entering her life. She did, however, find the courage to tell her of Felice and all the things Alessandro had said about him – how he was poor but honest like themselves and not the kind of person to try and take advantage of them. She went on to say that she and Giovanni were already old, and Concetta would need someone to help her and care for her, for there were always men, as Concetta herself knew very well, who would take advantage of a single woman. Concetta listened to her mother and saw that what she said made sense. She agreed to meet Felice. When Alessandro brought him to the house, she could see that he was indeed poor but honest and had not come to take advantage of her. At the end of the visit, it was agreed that Felice would call upon Concetta every other evening. Concetta found that he was an easy person to talk to and that he had a way of making her laugh in spite of herself. Sometimes he would sing, for he had a good voice and knew all the *stornelli* that Concetta liked. After three months of courting, Felice asked Giovanni and Giulia for the hand of their daughter in marriage. Giovanni, ever cautious and protective of his daughter, answered that considering the great evil that had befallen them they would be willing for Felice to marry their unfortunate daughter, only, if she herself was of a mind to do so.

Concetta replied that it was God's will that had brought Felice to Valmonte, and now it was her destiny to marry him. Felice concluded by saying that he was a poor man from a poor family and had very little to bring to the marriage. Giulia replied that she knew he was of the same condition of life as themselves, but they would do right by Concetta as best they could.

At first Giulia did not know what to do, for they had absorbed Concetta's furniture into the new house – her table and chairs as well as the cupboard were in the living room. The bed had been sold, so strong had been her repulsion at the thought of sleeping in it again. As there was no extra money in the leather bag under the mattress after all the expenses of repairing the house, it was clear that there was only one thing left to do, and that was to sell the house in Stilo. It was decided that Giovanni and Salvatore should make the trip, for Giovanni knew that his father could not live much longer. When they arrived, Pasquale was very moved to see his oldest son and grandson. He wanted to keep them there as long as he could, but Giovanni said that they had to sell the house in order to have Concetta marry, and so could not stay as long as they would have liked. Pasquale said that he understood and held them both close to him for a long time before their parting. That was the last time they saw him. Two months later Giovanni received a telegram from Lucia – which arrived three weeks after it had been sent – saying that Pasquale had died and had been buried in the cemetery in Stilo.

With the money from the sale of the house, Giulia bought the furniture for a bedroom and a kitchen for Concetta, as well as some extra sheets and towels. Felice and Concetta were married in May of 1948 in the church of Santa Anna. Concetta wore a white dress, since her first marriage had been anulled. Giulia and Concetta, with Maria helping, had cooked and cooked in preparation for the wedding feast. On the day before the wedding they made the egg noodles and the sweets; the rabbits that they had been raising for some months were slaughtered; Giovanni made several different kinds of liqueurs. Almost all the guests were Calabrians, except for the close neighbors. Giulia was thankful that she did not have to prepare for any members of Felice's family, for there was hardly room as it was. Even so, there was so much more space than there had been in the hut for that first wedding that she said she felt like a *Signora* with the guests in the *salotto*. There was no dancing this time, although Felice sang some *stornelli*, and early in the evening he and Concetta took the train to Padua and then on to Piove di Sacco, where they stayed for two weeks with his family. With Concetta married, Giovanni began to feel for the first time that some of the terrible wrong had been righted, and he could begin to hold his head straight in public again.

When the newly married couple returned, they took a room in the upper part of the town near the castle. Felice returned to his metal-smithing and Concetta to her sewing. He had made it clear from the beginning that he did not want Michele for his son, nor did he want him to call him father. It fell upon Giulia to avert a serious falling out by offering to raise Michele as her own. Giovanni had become very attached to his first grandson, and he understood why Felice would not want to raise the child of another man. It made Concetta heavyhearted to give up the small son who had been the center of her life for three years, but she knew that Felice's feelings in this matter must come first. Felice had said that he wanted to have several children, for they would be his hostages to the future; this being the case, she must give over Michele in order to make room for his. In fact, shortly after they were married, Concetta became pregnant. When the baby was born in April of 1949, they named her Costanza in honor of Felice's mother. By then Felice was finding it more and more difficult to pursue the trade of ironsmithing in Valmonte; it seemed as if the hard times were getting worse year by year. So it was decided that Felice would go on ahead to Piove di Sacco, where he knew more people and felt he had a better chance of locating work, and find them a rented room. After a month Felice sent word to Concetta to come and join him. It was a tearful occasion when she parted with the baby in her arms, leaving Michele behind. Giulia was disconsolate, lamenting that no one understood what it was like for a woman to lose her first daughter. Concetta comforted her the best she could, saying that she had Maria to take her place.

When Concetta finally arrived in Piove di Sacco, she was sorely disappointed to find that Felice had not been able to find a rented room. Instead, they had to lodge with his mother, father, and five brothers and sisters. In time they found a place of their own and in the next fifteen years, Concetta gave birth to six more children, five of whom survived. On each occasion Giulia made the trip alone to be with her daughter and remain with her for a month after the birth to help her get settled.

IV

It was not long after his first trouble at the gravel pit that Salvatore was again at loggerheads with the *padrone*. Even though he had turned nineteen in 1947, the *padrone* did not contribute to his social security tax and treated him as if he were still a minor. No amount of discussion and persuasion would make the *padrone* see the error of his ways. Finally, it was Giovanni who became so incensed that he announced that he was going to the employment office in Latina to find out what indeed Salvatore's rights were. He left work early one day on the pretense of not feeling well and bicycled as fast as he could to Latina. There he was surprised to find the clerk very helpful; indeed, he seemed gratified that Giovanni should take so much interest in the welfare of his son and assured him that he would get in touch with the company and set things right the very next day. He was as good as his word, for everyone knew in the pit that a call had come to the office the following day. Sometime after that the *padrone* called in Salvatore and said that he had decided that the law was the law and that from then on he was going to begin to contribute his share of the new social security tax. Giovanni was delighted and basked in the pride that his son expressed toward him for being a man of courage, willing to take a risk to help his son.

A week later *padrone* called in Giovanni and told him that he was fired for incompetence. He said that there were many others waiting to take his job who would not make trouble. Giovanni, of course, did not know that when the office in Latina had called the company, the *padrone* had demanded to know who among his workers had been the informer. His name was given; and so goes the law among those who command. Giulia chided Giovanni for having been so innocent.

For days Giovanni stood in line at the employment office until he was given a job with a construction company in Latina. There he worked through 1949 and then was let go. Business was getting worse, the *padrone* told him, and there were many others with more seniority. After that Giovanni worked a day here and a day there. He went to the piazza early in the morning, as he had done in Stilo, to wait to be called to hoe tomatoes for this owner or harvest wheat for that one.

V

Giovanni was now forty-eight and though he knew that he still had the strength of a younger man, it was the younger man who was called before him for a day's work. His thoughts began to turn again to the land, toward his desire to work a small piece of it. He began to make inquiries and was told that Doctor Maolelli was looking for a tenant to sharecrop a parcel of land near the village. It was just what Giovanni was looking for – he would not have to walk too far, and Giulia could get to it without bothering her leg too much. He was glad that it was old Doctor Maolelli, for he liked him more than all the rest of the *Signori* and was grateful to him for his treatment of Tonino when he was so small and sickly. When Giovanni went to call on Doctor Maolelli, the doctor walked with him to the parcel of land just below the west wall of the village. It had not been worked for three or four years, and the olive and fig trees had been neglected. Doctor Maolelli said that he wanted to bring it back so that he and his wife could have a nice supply of fresh vegetables on their table all the time. Doctor Maolelli stipulated the terms: Two thirds of the vegetables would go to Giovanni, and Doctor Maolelli would take two thirds of the tree crops – the olives, figs, nuts, and oranges. Giovanni accepted the bargain with a shake of Doctor Maolelli's hand.

Giovanni set to work with his mattock immediately, and when it was ready to plant he and Giulia stooped over the furrows, dropping in seeds. From then on, they were there every afternoon after the heat of the day had passed and worked until dusk. Giulia liked nothing better than pulling up every weed or blade of grass that she saw while Giovanni worked over the fruit trees with a knowing and loving care. As soon as one crop matured and was gathered they would seed the next, so that something was always ready to be harvested. Not only did Giovanni rebuild the retaining wall, but he planted Indian fig trees to provide both a boundary and, in time, an additional crop as well. At the end of the first year, Doctor Maolelli was pleased with the way his land had been brought back and with the quality of the produce.

From then on the contract was renewed orally each year. Every Saturday Giulia would carry a large basket of produce on her head to Signora Maolelli, as well as a little something as a gift. Then, too, on Easter and Christmas she would present the doctor and his wife with a chicken. It was always more pleasant to deal with the doctor than with the *Signora*; she had a reputation for being very strict with peasants, for she had been brought up to know that they were never to be trusted. She would check everything that Giulia brought with great care, and whatever was extra she would divide like the rest. In that way she was different from other great ladies, who would allow the peasant to carry away the extra as well as a bottle of wine or oil for their troubles. But both of the Maolellis must have known what dedicated caretakers of their garden they had in Giovanni and Giulia, for the contract continued for eight years, until Giulia's asthma became so bad that she could barely make it back and forth. Both she and Giovanni regretted having to give Doctor Maolelli notice that he would have to find another tenant. All during that time Giulia had not had to throw away good money buying food in the piazza, except for staples. She liked to live that way. Most especially, she enjoyed sitting with Giovanni under an olive tree at the end of their work, looking out over the Agro Pontino as the swallows winged their way above them in the twilight.

During the olive harvest in December, Maria and Tonino would help collect the olives under the trees as Giovanni or Salvatore beat the branches to make them fall. Then Maria would carry the heavy sacks on her head to their house, where Doctor Maolelli would come to oversee the division. Maria, like her mother, preferred working outdoors to being inside cleaning and ironing. The one member of the family who did not work in the garden was Pasquale. He did not seem to have the stamina for field work. Many times Giulia would take him with her to collect wood, only to find that he could not carry even one bundle for long without getting tired and having to rest. Giulia was exasperated, for when it came to dancing, it was as if his legs never tired. Like Salvatore, he had graduated from the fifth grade when he was twelve, and then for a while he apprenticed himself to a cobbler. He liked cobbling better than any sort of manual labor, and he became determined to become an artisan. At first Giovanni did not think that his son was serious in his intentions, for he never seemed to be serious about anything. Pasquale persisted, however, and Giovanni began to go about saying that his second son was going to be an artisan. But the more Pasquale cobbled, the more he thought that he wanted to be a tailor and work with fine cloths rather than tough leather.

He had watched Concetta sew and had even helped her when she was making a pair of pants for him. One day he went to Enrico Pizzorno, the tailor, and asked him if he would take him as an apprentice. Pizzorno dismissed him with a wave of the hand, saying that he had four sons to teach. But Pasquale was not to be deterred, and when a tailor from Carpineto came to settle in Valmonte at the other end of the village, he approached him. This time the answer was yes. The new tailor agreed to teach Pasquale everything he knew of the art of tailoring in exchange for meals prepared by Giulia, for he was a single man and did not have a woman to cook for him. Giulia agreed and even felt relieved, for now it seemed that at long last a place in the order of things had been found for Pasquale. For two years he remained at the tailor's side from eight in the morning until eight in the evening. There was little time to dance other than Saturday evening, and occasionally on Sunday. In 1950 Pasquale moved to Latina Scalo to work for a new tailoring establishment. In exchange for his efforts, he was given a cot to sleep on in the back hall and a small wage. He opened the shop in the morning and swept it out in the evening, and during the day he became skilled in cutting cloth for suits. Pasquale remained in Latino Scalo for three years, returning the fifteen miles to Valmonte on Sunday to be with his mother and father, Salvatore, Maria, and Tonino. Then in

November of 1953 he left for Piove di Sacco to stay with Concetta in hopes of establishing himself as a tailor there.

The family that Giovanni and Giulia had established through their union in 1922 was dissolving year by year; and so the wheel turned. Maria was to be the next to leave.

5

The engagement and marriage of Maria Tassoni and Giacomo Rossi, 1948–1953

I

During the winter of 1947-8, Maria picked olives as she had for the past several years for Nestore Matera and received one hundred fifty lire a day. She would rise at five in the morning, make two or three trips to the fountain for water, leave the house at quarter of six and walk directly to the Portella gates, where she would meet the ten or fifteen other girls who made up the Matera work crew. They would walk as much as an hour or an hour and a half before reaching the grove, depending on where it was located. It was uncomfortable kneeling on the cold ground for hours on end, but it was pleasurable to be together with her friends for the whole day, with time to talk and laugh. Then, too, at the noon-time break the young men who beat the branches with long sticks would show off and generally get things in an uproar, although this sometimes led to quarreling and bad feelings among the girls.

One evening when they were walking home, Maria became aware of a young man whom she had not seen very often. When she asked him what his name was, he answered that it was Giacomo Rossi. He seemed edgy, determined to say something to make the girls come to blows. Maria, angered by his interventions, told him to mind his own business. He quickly turned on his heel and walked off. The next day he appeared again, but now in the company of his friend Gerardo. And so he returned the following day, and the next, always with the excuse that he was looking for his girlfriend, Olivetta. One day he confided to Maria that he was in love with Olivetta but she refused to recognize him. Maria felt sorry for Giacomo and began putting in a good word for him with Olivetta, in the meantime telling Giacomo that Olivetta was a serious girl and should not be taken lightly. But whenever Maria talked that way to Giacomo he would laugh at her and she would ask,

"Why do you make fun of me?" It went along that way for a month, with Giacomo appearing almost every day in order to approach Olivetta, but in fact talking with Maria.

One night on the way home he asked Maria if she ever went to the movies and Maria answered him, "Why do you ask me if I go to the movies? What does it matter to you?" Giacomo said that he did not care at all, but from that moment on Maria knew that, in fact, Giacomo had been interested in her all along. She continued to walk with her friends as if nothing had changed, but she knew that something was going to happen. One night as they approached her house, she could see that Giacomo had something particular to say to her. She was tempted to lead him on, because she was curious to know what he wanted to say. At the same time she was not prepared to be asked by him to the movies, so she feigned disinterest and Giacomo didn't speak. During the rest of the week, however, Maria could think of little else.

On the following Thursday, as Maria was approaching her house, she noticed Giacomo following her. Maria gasped. She knew that if her father should leave the house now and see her in the street with Giacomo, he would beat her. Giacomo came up to her and asked her then and there if she would become engaged to him. She did not know what to say; it was as if her mind was a blank and she had closed the door on all her feelings. All that she knew was that she was trembling all over. She finally found herself saying, "I do not know anything. You will have to talk to my parents and see what they have to say." Giacomo replied, "I do not care what their answer is. Right now I want to know if you are happy about what I said, and then I will think about your parents." But Maria couldn't speak except to say, "I do not know anything," and she turned away and walked into the house. She did, however, know one thing: She liked him.

Maria was ashamed to bring up the subject with her parents, and days went by before an opportune time arrived one morning when she was alone with her mother. She took a deep breath and then said all in a rush, "If I should find someone, would you let me become engaged?" Giulia's instant reply was a firm no, and then after a slight pause she said, "Why, is there someone who wants you?" Maria could not deny it and began to tell her mother who it was. Giulia had not heard of him, but it would have made no difference, for she was adamant. "But why don't you let me, mama," Maria asked. "Others become engaged for so many years, so why don't you let me? Why?" But no answer was forthcoming from her mother, nor her father, nor her brother Salvatore. Maria felt that there was no hope, and when she later saw Giacomo toward the end of the week she had to say to him, "Listen, my mother told me that I am too young to become engaged, and she will

not let me. When I asked my father, he did not even answer me."
Giacomo shook his head and muttered something about "those Calabrians." He then turned to Maria and said, without the slightest hesitation,
"Saturday I am coming to your house." Maria thought that he could
not be serious, but when Saturday evening came and he arrived at the
front door, she knew that he was. Her heart stood still when she saw
him, for fear of the impression he might make on her parents. She
knew how vivid their memory was of the shame of Concetta and how
difficult it would be for them to see anything but evil in Giacomo's
intentions. Maria could see that Giacomo was nervous, but even so, he
spoke right up and said that he wanted their permission to become
engaged to their daughter. Maria was surprised by her father's reply.
He began by telling Giacomo that they had no desire to see their
daughter engaged, because she was still young, and that it would be
better to wait until she was older, for there was still time. But then he
said, "If she is happy with this proposal, I cannot force her to abandon
the idea. You should know that your parents must also be happy with
the idea, otherwise I cannot permit it. Furthermore, if my daughter is
to be engaged, the courtship must take place in the house." Giacomo,
now relieved and emboldened, jumped at the opening and said, "Do
not worry about my parents, for I am ready to bring them the Sunday
after next. But for right now, it is enough that you are happy." The
Sunday proposed by Giacomo was the week before Easter, which
caused Giovanni to prick up his ears and tell Giacomo that if he was
coming to take advantage of them, he had better look elsewhere, for
they were poor. And if he was coming to amuse himself, he had better
think again, because his daughter was serious and had never been engaged to anyone before. Giovanni never finished his polemic, for Giacomo raised his hand to stay the older man and then said that he had
come neither for money nor to do his daughter a disservice, for if he
wanted to amuse himself there were lots of women he could go to.
Then he added, "I have come because I love your daughter. I know
what she is like, and I do not have these strange ideas of which you
speak." And so passed the first evening.

   Giacomo brought his parents as he said he would. It was Palm Sunday and Giulia offered them coffee, cordial and biscuits. It was a pleasant enough occasion, to the relief of everyone. And though it was too
early to talk of definite plans, Giulia and Teresa Rossi did discuss expectations, just to clear the air. Giulia told Teresa of the state of Maria's
trousseau, pointing out that because of the dislocations of the war and
the marriage of her oldest daughter, she had not been able to do very
much yet; but, God willing, she would have all in hand by the time of
the wedding. She was planning on eight sheets and towels, she said.

Teresa nodded understandingly and said that they, too, were poor and would not be able to do very much for Giacomo, but they did have one room in their house where the couple could live until they found something better. She pointed out that Giacomo still had his military service to perform. By the end of the visit it was decided that, everything considered, it would be another four if not five years before they were ready to be married. As Giulia pointed out, they were still young, so there was no rush; and besides, they needed time to get to know each other's character. As Giacomo was leaving with his parents, Giovanni said that it would not be necessary for him to come to visit with them every evening. Four nights a week would suffice – Tuesday, Thursday, Saturday, and Sunday. So indeed it began, but after a while Giacomo came every evening and continued to do so for seven months.

If Giacomo hoped that his persistence would lead to their having some time alone, he was mistaken, for they were never left in the same room by themselves. Indeed, Giovanni would not allow Maria to sit next to his future son-in-law. In fact it was not until three months after they had become engaged that Giacomo first kissed her. Maria knew that his attempt would come sooner or later, but she was afraid. She felt that if she granted Giacomo a kiss, he would become bored with her and leave her because she was not a serious girl any more. It happened the day that Doctor Forlari died, and the Tassonis went to church for the funeral. But Maria remained at home, and Giacomo seized upon the opportunity to come to her. Maria felt weak when she saw him, thinking of what her father would do if he found them alone. Giacomo immediately began to say that all engaged couples kissed, she would not be the first girl to have done it, and there was nothing evil about it anyway. But Maria was persistent in her resistance, and Giacomo finally said, "Either yes, or by force," and without waiting for an answer grabbed her from behind and kissed her on the mouth. Maria never dreamed that it would be so. She knew how men and women kissed each other on the cheek, but was aware of the other only because of a movie she had seen. She knew it to be a scandalous thing. All that Maria could do after Giacomo released her was to cry. She was so embarrassed that she could not look at him when he left, and that night she hardly slept for the shame of what she had done. Yet even so, she felt that she loved him more than ever.

II

The first two months of their engagement were the happiest of their lives, but by the summer of 1948 things began to change between them. On the twenty-seventh of July, Maria was operated on for appendicitis at the hospital in Latina. Every day Giacomo would come on his bicycle to visit, after he had finished harvesting wheat for Nestore Matera. He would arrive hot and sweaty, and Maria would feel sorry for him, but she also found that he got on her nerves – even though he did not scold her and was nothing but attentive. He noticed her coolness and asked, "What is the matter with you, why do you act like this to me?" She told him that staying in the hospital made her nervous. But the truth of the matter was that Maria had begun to hear stories about Giacomo, that he always fought with his mother and had known lots of women. When she returned from the hospital, Giacomo continued to visit every night, and it was then that she began to tell him what she had heard about him. Giacomo, angered, wanted to know who had spoken to her of these things, but Maria would not say, and Giacomo as he left said that she would be sorry. She did not know what he meant by that except that he did not come to visit for three days, and when he did come on the fourth, they quarreled. After that, they found that they could not make up. Maria wondered why she had become so disapproving when she had been so much in love with him before. Giacomo felt himself going mad with unhappiness at the turn that their love had taken, and he never missed a Saturday to have Maria serenaded in order to rekindle her affection for him. The music worked its effect upon her. "If I could only describe how passionate the music was," she said later. "I felt as though someone was behind me saying 'tell him yes,' 'tell him yes.' " And so she decided to make up seven months after their engagement had begun, but she was immediately disappointed to find that happiness did not return as she had hoped. She found that she could not feel the affection for him that she had experienced before, although she did not know why. Whenever she knew that he was coming to visit her, she would absent herself at some function or other at the church, and when they were around each other, she would be as mean as she could so that he would tire of her and leave. Finally one evening Giacomo said, "Can it be possible that every time I come here you are brooding and sulking?" Maria found the courage to reply, "But you have not understood by now that I do not want to see you again. Look, it is obvious that we are not destined to be together, because I do not feel love for you anymore. I tell you sincerely that when I see you, you get on my nerves, and so we cannot keep on like this anymore." When Maria had finished speaking, Giacomo said, "You still had all that poison in you when we made up, but in fact you did not love me anymore." Maria replied that she had hoped she could love him again but found she could not, and then added, "But do not think that I am the only one – there are many more beautiful and better than I." When she said this, he did not answer for a long time and remained with his head bowed. Then he drew himself up and said, "I can say goodbye and not good night. I wish you every good fortune and hope that you may find the man who will make you truly happy, for it seems that we are not fated for each other. I would not want you to suffer as you do now once we were married, so it is well that you spoke as you did." While he was saying those words, Maria experienced a sharp pain of grief but told herself that she didn't care anymore, and said, "I, too, wish you fortune and happiness." With that Giacomo turned and left, and they made a point of not speaking to each other even when they passed in the street or the piazza.

III

During the day Maria picked tomatoes and after work on Sundays she attended church functions, becoming ever more involved in Catholic Action. Day by day she found herself loving the Church more and more and began to think about becoming a nun. At first she thought it was a passing fancy, but as the days passed, she felt herself being pulled increasingly toward the convent. The more she prayed for direction, the more she heard a voice that said, "Come." One day she told her mother that she had decided to become a nun because she no longer wanted to get married. Giulia replied with feeling, "No, my daughter, stay with me as long as I live and then you will have your brothers to support you, but do not take the vows." Maria reflected upon what her mother said but knew that her words could not stop her, for she had to do what she had to do. When she told her mother her decision, Giulia immediately began to cry, saying that if she became a nun, she would be dead to the family. Between sobs, she asked how it was that even with two daughters, she could not keep either one near her, not even if she became ill. If she was young again, she continued, she would not get married, for children were nothing but grief. When they grow up they forget about their mother, who has sacrificed her whole life for them. Giulia cried so much whenever Maria mentioned the nunnery that she finally resigned herself to never becoming one, and in time the desire passed.

IV

Whenever Maria and Giacomo passed each other on the street, she on her side and he on his, they never looked at each other or spoke. But one day Giacomo asked a friend to speak with Maria to see if she would not mind at least greeting him – for as he said, "What evil has happened that we cannot look, even look, at each other when we pass." Maria agreed as long as it was in the spirit of friendship only, and so little by little, their regard for each other began to develop again. One evening Giacomo asked Maria, after they had stopped to exchange a greeting, whether she was still happy with his proposal of marriage, because he, for one, had never changed his mind. Maria found herself confused and did not know what to think. But the next time they met, she had decided what to say and told him that if they were destined to be married, so be it. First he had to do his military service, and in the meantime, she was not going to become engaged to anyone. With that, Maria turned and walked away. Giacomo resigned himself to leaving for his military service without really having made up. In fact, they did not even say goodbye.

V

Giacomo departed for the military in October of 1950 and was immediately sent to the outskirts of the far northern city of Gorizia. Giacomo had never been farther from Sessa and Valmonte than Rome, on two different occasions, and everywhere there was much to see that was new and different. In the beginning soldiering was exciting – the uniform, the parades, the camaraderie, and the passes that took Giacomo to Gorizia, Udine, and even once to Venice. But then monotony set in – hurrying up and waiting, policing the parade ground, just lying in the bunk. Even more distasteful were the long marches every Friday that resulted in painful blisters on his feet. The maneuvers of March and April of 1951 were even worse; the second one, which lasted forty days, was spent on a mountaintop in a tent that leaked the never-ending rain. Only the thought of his release and his reunion with Maria sustained and comforted him during those days. One day he wrote a postcard to Salvatore Tassoni and included greetings for Maria. He was overwhelmed with joy when, a short while later, a postcard from Maria came back. Immediately Giacomo set about writing Maria a long letter, saying that he still felt badly that he had not bid her goodbye the day he left Valmonte; at the time he felt angry, because she did not seem to take seriously what he was saying. Maria replied by letter saying that by now it was clear that fate had destined them to come together again, and as their love was like a chain that had never broken, she now consented to become engaged once more. Giacomo wasted no time in replying, saying that he had never been happier in his entire life, and all he asked of her was her photograph; he included his. It was November of 1951, and Giacomo lived only for the time when he would be granted a leave. Whenever cessation of his loathsome duties gave him the opportunity, he thought only of her, stared at her photo, and read and reread her letters.

A leave was granted for Easter. Giacomo thought of the hours it would take the train to cover the distance from Gorizia to Rome, the hour ride from Rome to Latina Scalo, the half-hour bus trip to the piazza. Maria found that she loved Giacomo more every day, and if she felt like that when he was faraway, she wondered what it would be like when he was beside her again. The thought of it made Maria's heart beat faster. Maria remembered how it was when the six o'clock bus arrived in the piazza two days before Easter. "He came all of a sudden, and when he saw me, he embraced me and kissed me in front of mama. I thought that later she will scold me, but she didn't say anything. He stayed for five days and it was like a dream. I was happier than I had ever been in my life, and I loved him more than ever; from that time on, I began to understand what love meant, how you suffer. He left, and when I said goodbye to him he was almost crying, but he did not want me to see. I was so sad that I would have gone with him if they had let me."

From then until he was discharged, Giacomo wrote Maria every day. They never quarreled, and if there was some misunderstanding, another letter would be sent off to explain and to forgive.

VI

Giacomo was discharged in January of 1952 and immediately went to work in the gravel pit. He felt that fate was smiling upon him when the *padrone* agreed to take him on, for he had always hated field work and had not been looking forward to hoeing and picking. He was at first assigned to the second shift, 4 A.M. until 2 P.M., and like Salvatore, his job was to push the carts full of stone from the blasting area to the crusher. For this he was paid one thousand lire a day, more than he had ever received before. At first he was paid regularly, every fifteen days, but after two months the *padrone* announced that he could not pay his men any longer on the day due, or else he would be forced to close the plant. It was a bitter blow to Giacomo, who had wanted to prove to his mother that he could be a good worker and provider, for she had many times cried and accused her son of being shiftless, and interested only in chasing after women. Then, too, he wanted to put money aside to buy a good dark blue suit to marry in.

Giacomo found that being reunited with Maria was far more difficult than he had ever thought it would be as he lay on his barracks cot in far away Gorizia. It seemed as if everything went badly, and he found himself treating her poorly despite himself. Not being paid made him nervous and irritable. Then, too, he was jealous, and everything Maria did was cause for it. What bothered him the most was the way she talked easily and openly with everyone. He could feel it coming as they walked in the street arm in arm; Maria would pull away slightly as they approached someone she knew – and she seemed to know everyone. Giacomo was certain that Maria provoked him on purpose, for she knew how much he loved her. But when she asked him what it was she was doing that made him so upset, he did not know what to say.

The possessiveness of Maria's parents also offended Giacomo; it was as if they never trusted him, even after all this time. It seemed as if they were making him suffer for the pain they had suffered over Concetta. Indeed, they kept such a tight rein on Maria that it made him want to take advantage of her, to hurt her. "I had always thought of taking advantage of her, and I do not know why I had all those scruples, because I did not with other women. When I saw how jealous her parents were, how they did not trust me, I always thought I would, but I could not touch her. I was always moved because she said that she wanted to go to the church dressed in white."

Maria pointed out to Giacomo time and again that it was not that her parents did not trust him; they would not trust anybody who was courting their daughter, for they were Calabrian, "and there was nothing you could do about that." The reason that they were so strict, she added, was to keep people from talking. It was the gossip that had gone on about Concetta that had all but killed Giovanni and Giulia. They were determined to do everything in their power not to give people any reason to gossip.

VII

The situation at the gravel pit went from bad to worse, and by the end of April Giacomo had not been paid for a month. Furthermore, he and others had been ordered to work on Sundays without credit for overtime and threatened with dismissal if they did not comply. When Giacomo went to the office on the next payday, the clerk gave him a fraction of what was owed him. Giacomo held the money in his hand for a few seconds, counted it, threw it on the floor and then spat on it. He demanded that the clerk give him all his back pay, plus what was owed him for overtime. When the clerk refused, the *padrone* came out of his office as if by signal, and fired Giacomo on the spot. Giacomo had to be pulled out of the office by his friends to prevent him from hitting the *padrone*.

After being dismissed, there was nothing to do but to take on odd jobs, play cards in the bar, call on Maria, and in the evening go in search of the widow with three daughters who did not care what they did.

VIII

During the winter of 1952 Maria again picked olives for Nestore Matera and put the money she earned toward the purchase of the final linens for her trousseau. As winter turned to spring, she worked in the fields of Bruno Sardo, who was a share tenant of one of the largest landowners, Matteo Alva. In March the wheat was cultivated, followed by the sugar beets and the tomatoes. From Maria's house it was a walk of ten kilometers to the field, so she had to get started very early in the morning. Maria was exhausted at the end of every day but gratified that she was able to bring money to her mother nearly every week during the spring and summer of 1952. Yet as September approached, she was still not ready to marry in the fall as they had planned. So the date for the wedding was postponed. She said of her feelings at that time, "We were always quarreling, and we couldn't make anything go right. If he tried to touch me in front of mother, I didn't want him to, and tried to get away and that made him angry. Then I began to blush because I was timid with my parents about him. I didn't think that they were ever going to trust him, because it had been five years now and if they did not know what sort of a person he was now, they never would. On one side he was right, because since we had been engaged they had not left us alone for more than half an hour. Still, if I had wanted to, I could have done plenty of things in that time, but I did not because, after all, if anything happens it is the girl who has to pay – not the parents. My mother is certain that he has never kissed me, except for the time he got off the bus. But I would like to have as many lire as the kisses that we sneaked; I would be the richest woman in Valmonte. My mother always tells me that my father finally kissed her the day they were married, and she thought at the time that if anything had happened to make them separate, he could always have boasted that he had kissed. So it is clear that my mother continues to be the same old jealous Calabrian."

Fortunately, Giacomo found work at the beginning of October 1952 with a government-subsidized reforestation program created to give jobs to the unemployed during the fall and winter. The purpose of the program was to terrace and plant olive trees on the great expanse of bare rocky hill that stretched up behind Valmonte. The land, once common in medieval times, was being held in trust for the people of Valmonte by the Universita Agraria for eventual division among the citizenry. The pay was only six hundred lire a day, but the work was not arduous. Giacomo felt a weight lifted from his shoulders. He quarreled less with his mother and also with Maria. One sunny day in November Giacomo and his parents came to call upon Giovanni and Giulia. It was agreed that now that five years had passed, Maria and Giacomo had had enough time to get to know each other's character, and no purpose would be served by waiting any longer. It was decided that the wedding would take place on February 15, immediately following the olive harvest, so that Maria would have the opportunity to work until the end.

Giacomo was greatly relieved to know that what had been his dream for so long was finally going to come true. Maria too was pleased: "In spite of our differences we loved each other very much then – more than ever before. When we made peace, he couldn't bear to not see me and neither could I. Our love had always been so sad but happy."

IX

As soon as the date for the wedding had been set, Giulia and Maria began to make their plans. Giulia knew that it would take several months to get ready for the wedding feast and that she would have to start laying things aside almost immediately – oil, flour, and sugar especially. Originally Maria had thought of having rabbit as the main course, but one of the mating pair died, and her plan to breed them was abandoned; she turned to chickens instead. She knew that her best source was the peasant she had been working for all summer, Bruno Sardo. When she mentioned to him that she was getting married in February and was planning to serve chicken to their guests, he agreed to sell her thirty eggs, which he was willing to set under his brooding hens. Maria was delighted, and when the chicks hatched, she carried them to Valmonte and set them out in a neighbor's cellar hole in return for some favors. With the chickens in hand, Giulia and Maria felt much relieved. With the *galline* they would make broth, the *polli* would be roasted, and the eggs would be set aside in an old well that was always cool, for making the noodles and the sweets. The chicks grew well. Although three died, Maria figured that twenty-seven would be enough, as long as there was another meat of some kind. She hoped that Giacomo would do something, but he did not seem to take the hint when she brought the subject up. Just a month before the wedding, he said that his family would contribute two sheep that they would procure from a shepherd from Carpineto who owed them a favor. Then, as if all good things happened at once, Giovanni said that he was willing to kill one of their two pigs to make pork chops, just in case. It would mean that half of their meat supply would be eaten up in one

day, but Giovanni knew as well as anyone else how important it would
be to make a good impression.

Maria had begun to make lists several times in her head of the guests
that they should invite, but every time she started, the list got longer. It
seemed that either her father or her mother would think of another
paesano who should be included, or she would suddenly remember
another friend. By November the total had already reached seventy-
five, a figure that was both alarming and gratifying. Where would they
put them all? Giacomo himself did not understand why they had to
invite so many, but that was just the way it was with Maria; she
seemed to know everyone. Evenings were spent discussing how the
table would be made up and where it would go. It was clear that some
people would have to sit in the bedroom, others in the hall, and the
most privileged in the living room. Chairs, plates, glasses, and cutlery
were a problem, and Maria went from friend to friend asking whether
she could borrow a chair here and a plate there when the time came.
Everything was complicated by the fact that there was going to have to
be a reception as well as the feast itself. At first it was an idea, a wish on
the part of Maria to make the best possible *figura*. "Rinfresco, rinfresco," shouted Giacomo. "Where did you get that crazy idea?" Maria
patiently pointed out that serving a refreshment before the meal was the
proper thing to do and that all right-minded people had them. But it
was only when she went to speak to Don Antonio about the hour of
the ceremony that she found out that it was a necessity. He told her that
February 15 fell during Lent, so they would have to marry at eight-
thirty in the morning. Maria was stunned; she had never heard of such
a regulation. At first she thought of changing the date, but she knew
that it was too late to do that – so many plans had already been made. It
would mean that the guests would have to be at the house by 7:30 or
7:45 at the latest; they would have coffee and then make the procession
to the church. At the close of the ceremony everybody would flock
back to the house and be there, underfoot, until the feast was served at
about one. Now Maria and Giulia had to figure out how to keep the
company happy with food and drink for almost four hours before the
first course was to be served. This required making cordials – five different kinds, two bottles apiece. Giovanni would tend to that, buying
the essence at the store and then adding sugar and water and laying
bottles by in a safe place. Four days before the wedding Giulia and
Maria would set to making three different kinds of sweets to go with
the coffee, liqueur, and hot chocolate. As for the hot chocolate, Maria
decided not to mention that to Giacomo, for he regarded it as effete and
would not understand that it was the proper thing to do, and there was
no point in having another argument.

As the day drew near, Maria found herself getting more and more tired. By the middle of December the last pieces of the trousseau had been assembled in the lower two drawers of the bureau. Six sheets and pillowcases neatly folded were at the bottom of the pile. Maria had paid for them herself. Giulia had bought the sheeting, six meters at a time, for six thousand lire, from the traveling Neapolitan. There was enough to make two sheets. The hand-embroidered sheets that the Neapolitan always produced first from his battered suitcase were lovely but beyond Giulia's means, so Maria would sit down with the plain ones and add a little design on the border of each one. On top of the sheets were folded twelve towels, three tablecloths, two bedspreads, and one wool blanket. Next to them lay Maria's personal trousseau: twelve slips and eight nightgowns.

At the same time that these soft goods were being accumulated week by week, month by month, the pile of hard goods for the kitchen had been slowly growing as well. Giulia had acquired a set of six knives, forks, and spoons, and six glasses and plates; but it was the copper cooking pots and pans and the two-handled water amphora that took the longest to save for and were bought piece by piece.

Now they had only to get the furniture and Maria's wedding and going-away dresses. Maria had had a thousand fantasies about the furniture – whether it would be antique or modern, light or dark. She had a secret dream about what she wanted but kept it to herself, for she knew that with Salvatore being the only member of the family bringing in money on a regular basis, she could expect nothing more than the basic bedroom and kitchen furniture. She knew, of course, of girls who married with less, as well as others who married with more – the living room, for instance – but she had never seriously expected more than what was finally decided upon. After Christmas Maria and Giulia took the bus to Latina to see for one more time what there was, how much it would cost, and what could be ready by February. When Concetta had married her furniture had been made locally, but now it was easier to go to a store and buy on layaway. Pitoni's store had everything except the armoire for the bedroom, but he promised to have that by the first of February. When Giulia asked the price, Pitoni quoted 160,000 lire. Giulia angrily retorted that it was an outrage, if not indeed criminal. She reminded Signor Pitoni that they were poor, but honest folk from Valmonte, not *Signori*. Besides, she said, he could count on her making the payments on time. She would not pay one lira more than 120,000, and she began to make her way toward the door, pulling Maria with her. After half an hour of heated discussion, a final price of 130,000 was decided upon.

On the first Tuesday in January Maria went with her future mother-in-law, Teresa, to the market in Valmonte to buy material for her wedding and going- away dresses. They had agreed to follow Valmonte custom, which holds that it is the family of the groom that honors the bride with her wedding dress and, more recently, the honeymoon dress as well. Teresa paid for the material that they agreed upon; later her sister came from Sessa to tailor it and sew it as her present to Maria and her nephew Giacomo. Maria had hoped that Teresa would offer to buy her shoes and coat as well, and was too embarrassed to ask her when she did not offer to. Later Giulia, not surprised to hear of Teresa's oversight, shrugged her shoulders and said that the cost of a coat and a pair of shoes could not make them much poorer than they already were. Maria did not have the courage to say that she would need a handbag as well for their trip to Piove di Sacco. So on the following market day, she took a thousand lire that she had kept aside and bought a dark suede handbag that would go well with the coat and the shoes.

By the first of February Maria had finished with the olive harvest. She returned with Giulia to the furniture store, hoping that everything would be there. Pitoni was as good as his word – the armoire had arrived. Giulia had brought 30,000 lire as a downpayment; she signed with her mark the agreement stipulating that 10,000 lire were to be paid every month for ten months. Maria and Giulia looked over carefully what they had bought – a big bed with two small bedside tables, a dressing table and chair, and a three-door armoire. Maria was thrilled with the three doors. When she first began to think about her furniture, she had always pictured one with two doors; now fashion dictated more. But she never thought that they would be able to afford more than two. Then, too, the kitchen cupboard with its glass doors was finer than what she had originally hoped for, and when she saw it in company with the matching table and six chairs, the set looked more like the furnishings of a living room than a kitchen. When she returned home that evening she thanked and embraced Salvatore, for it was his earnings in the gravel pit that would pay for the furniture. Indeed he would have to finish making all the payments before he could plan to get married himself.

A week before the wedding, Concetta arrived from Piove di Sacco to lend a hand with the cooking. They needed to prepare as much as possible ahead of time. Fortunately it was winter, and the cold prevented the foods from spoiling.

There was also the confetti to think about. Maria planned to distribute it twice: before the meal, loose, and after the meal in a little bag for each guest, as tradition dictated. Maria bought three meters of white tulle at the market for the bags and a quantity of blue ribbon for the

bows. Before setting to work on the *bomboniere*, she went over the list
again, which had grown to 125. She decided to allow for 150, because
she knew her father well – how he would go about in an expansive
mood in the piazza, after the service that morning, inviting people here
and there to his house for the wedding feast of his daughter.

X

As the time drew near, Maria found herself becoming more tired day
by day; she hardly had time to see Giacomo. One evening he came to
present her with the gold, the necklace, and the earrings that a man
always gave to his wife before they married. Maria was very happy.
Everything was just as it should be. Holding the gold pieces in her
hand, it struck her as it had not before that she was to be married in a
few days. The thought momentarily took her breath away, and she had
to sit down to steady herself.

Giacomo said that his father was slaughtering the two lambs the next
day and the dressed meat would be ready then, as well as the two large
demijohns of wine they were contributing. His suits were still not
ready, he said – the blue one that he would be married in and the brown
one he would wear on their trip. Pizzorno, the tailor, was still sewing
but promised them for the fourteenth. He still needed a pair of shoes,
and he would go to Latina the following morning to buy them. As for
an overcoat, he would just get along without one. If it got that cold in
Piove di Sacco, he would put on an extra sweater and bring an umbrella, he added. Giacomo remained for a long while in the kitchen that
night sitting and watching Giulia, Concetta, and Maria working together. He still felt embittered by the interference of Giulia, but that
would end soon, he assured himself. Besides, he could not help but
feel, as he watched the three Calabrian women working with such
assurance, that he had done the right thing by marrying one of them.
Maria was as tenacious and dedicated a worker as her mother. They
made his own mother seem flighty and indecisive in comparison. It
made him warm inside to know that he had been so wise as to ally
himself for life to such strength.

On the thirteenth Giovanni killed and dressed one of the pigs. He
was certain that the meat would be needed, for he had it in his mind to
invite one or two of his friends in the piazza who hadn't gotten onto the
list. When he was through with the pig, he started filling liter bottles of
wine from the two big demijohns that Giacomo had brought over. He
figured that there should be at least a hundred liters of wine, not only
for the meal and the toasts, but for afterward, when Maria and Giacomo had gone and his friends would still be there wanting to have just

one more glass. When he had finished with the wine, he helped Maria slaughter and dress the twenty-seven chickens. Giulia had been boiling water all morning to feather them. Later that evening Salvatore and Pasquale set to work making long tables from boards and sawhorses, and Tonino and Michele were sent to pick up chairs from around the neighborhood.

No one slept for more than a few hours that night, and all were on their feet by five in the morning. Giulia had to finish baking the last of the sweets and then start on the *zuppa inglese* that was to top off the feast. Concetta and Maria began to prepare the sauce for the noodles, which now draped over every chair and bed in the house. One hundred fifty eggs had been used in all; Maria was delighted with all the bounty that had flowed from the original thirty. Later that evening Teresa came with the wedding dress, and Maria stopped in her tracks long enough to try it on. It was decided that Concetta needed to take up the hem in two places and make an adjustment in the veil, but Maria was overjoyed. She was certain that she had never seen anything so beautiful, and she liked the way it fit when she put it on – tight around the waist.

Her only regret was that everything was happening so fast; there was no time to stop and enjoy it, and they still had so much work to do.

It was two o'clock in the morning when she and Giulia and Concetta went to bed, and they were up again at four thirty. It was cold and dark, but it was her wedding day, the most important day of her life. The thought of the hours ahead, the ceremony in the church, the feast, the going off alone with Giacomo made her feel weak. She was happy but frightened, and there were still a hundred things to do before she put on her wedding dress. Giacomo arrived at seven, looking very handsome in his dark blue suit. Concetta laid out her father's suit and those of Salvatore and Pasquale along with their white shirts, which she had just ironed. They would get ready first, and then leave the room for Maria. Giulia could not stop darting about; soon she was calling to Giovanni that the first guests were arriving. Concetta shooed the men out of the bedroom and started to help Maria get dressed. Before long the room was full of women. Maria began to let go, leaving everything to her older sister. Everyone was talking at once, giving helpful advice, but Maria did not care. In fact, everything she heard struck her as very funny, and she laughed and laughed. When Concetta had finished dressing her, word was sent that the time had come for Giovanni and Giulia to enter. Giulia clasped her hands when she saw Maria. "My daughter, how beautiful you are! May God protect you, and may San Antonio, Santa Anna, and Santa Rita see what pleasure you have brought to this mother, to this old woman," she said in a faltering voice. Giovanni put his hands to his face, held them there for a moment, and then wiped away his tears. He then blessed Maria, wishing her every happiness and a long life. Salvatore burst in and said that it was time to leave – Don Antonio would be waiting for them at the church. There was a bustling at the door as everyone lined up, Maria on the arm of her father, followed by Giacomo with his mother and Salvatore with Giulia. Everyone else fell in by twos as the procession moved off down the stairs. As they passed, people called out, "Auguri, auguri." "May God bless you," called out an old woman from her window as they walked by her house. Even in the piazza there were people at so early an hour on a Sunday morning to greet them. In fact, Don Antonio was not there when they filed in. He was old and forgetful. Tonino was dispatched to his house to remind him that Maria and Giacomo were getting married that morning.

The women knelt in the front of the church, whispering among themselves. In the cold of the church you could see their breath. The men gathered in the back to talk about the price of pigs and sheep. Don Antonio entered, still flicking bread crumbs from his stole, and told Maria and Giacomo to kneel on the hassock before him. Maria knew that she should have no illusions about the service, for Don Antonio would race through the vows as quickly as he could and then wait for the donation. Giacomo squirmed with discomfort, repeating his own vow to never set foot in a church again, except for the baptism of his first child. To his great relief the ceremony was over sooner than he had thought, due to the swiftness of Don Antonio. At the door of the church there was a sea of children all scrambling for the confetti that Tonino and Michele were throwing on the ground. Maria was sorry that there was no one to take a picture, but she did not know of anyone with a camera. As they wended their way back through the piazza, there were many more people calling out blessings and congratulations. Maria wished that she could hold on to that moment forever. She knew for a fact that such a long wedding procession had not passed through the piazza in years; not bad for a Calabrian! It was at that point that Giovanni dropped out of line, for he saw several people that he wanted to invite to his house to enjoy the wedding feast to be held in his daughter's honor.

The final count of the number of guests did turn out to be a hundred and fifty. Giulia and Concetta, with the help of several neighbors, saw that they were fed from nine thirty in the morning until five in the evening. By one o'clock everyone was seated somewhere at the table that ran from the bedroom down the hall to the living room. The feast began with an antipasto of cheese, bread, olives, and peppers, which was quickly followed by heaping portions of noodles with anchovy sauce. Then came the chicken broth with *pastina*. At this point there was a pause and several toasts were made, and shouts of "Viva gli sposi" brought Maria and Giacomo to their feet with glasses held high. Eating was resumed with roast chicken and greens, followed by lamb and potatoes, followed by the pork with more greens. Another pause occurred, which prompted people to move about and chat. In time salad was brought to the table, followed by fruit and then the *zuppa inglese*, and at the end, coffee. There were more toasts – one by the mayor, another by the vice-mayor – then someone began to play his accordion, and voices broke out in *stornelli*. The table was pushed back and Maria danced the tarantella with her father; others joined in. Later Giacomo reminded Maria that they would have to be in the piazza at six to catch the bus. But by then Maria was so tired that she could not have danced any more if she had tried. All there was to do was to pass around the *bomboniere* to each guest and receive in return an envelope with money. Maria rushed next door in one direction to change into her going-away dress, and Giacomo in the other to put on his brown suit. There was little time, barely enough to say goodbye. Salvatore went with them to the piazza to see them off.

On the train there was only standing room until they got to Rome. Then they got seats and sat next to each other for the first time without Giovanni or Giulia anywhere in sight. Giacomo took Maria's hand in his. Maria began to tell of the presents they had received. She had counted the money in the envelopes just before they had departed and it had come to twenty-five thousand lire. She had left most of it at home in the bag under the mattress but had brought some for the trip, which she handed to Giacomo. Then she recounted the pots, pans, glasses, cups and saucers, plates, spoons, washtub, bowl and beautiful knitted shawl they had received – all good and useful things. She had packed them all away in the bread chest so that they could be easily moved to where they were going to live. Then Maria and Giacomo commented on the people – how they had looked and what they had said. Maria counted up to twenty-five that her father had invited in the piazza. Yes, it had been a good day. A very good day. Everything had gone just as she hoped it would. But she was tired, very tired, and when they got to Piove di Sacco, she was burning up. Concetta, who had left by an earlier train, put her to bed with a fever, and there she remained for the whole of the honeymoon. It was a sad time, and one that Giacomo had not counted on.

6

The births of Luigi and Bruno

Maria was still weak from her bout of influenza when she and Giacomo
returned from Piove di Sacco on the fifth of February to take up their
married life in Valmonte. During their absence, Giovanni, Salvatore,
and Tonino moved the new furniture into Maria and Giacomo's rented
house on Via Virgilio. It belonged to Elena Bernini, wife of Tommaso,
owner of the inn in the piazza. Elena had made known to Maria that the
house was available as soon as she had heard definitely when they were
marrying, for she liked her and wanted her living nearby so that Maria
could keep her company. She offered it for fifteen hundred lire a
month. Maria and Giacomo accepted, delighted to find a place to live —
even though it was small, dank, and dark. In fact, the door was so low
that even Maria had to stoop when entering. But still, it seemed like a
palace to her. The kitchen was immediately filled with Maria's cupboard, table, and chairs. In the bedroom it was a squeeze to turn around
between the bed and armoire. There was a front room, but the floor
tiles had long since come loose, exposing the bare dirt below. Maria
decided that that was where she would store the wood for the fire. In
the far corner, away from the door, a hole in the floor served as the
toilet. It was the fireplace in the kitchen that pleased Maria the most,
for it drew so well. There she did all the cooking, boiling the water in a
large copper pot supported by one trivet and the sauce in a small
ceramic bowl held by another. Maria knew that Giacomo loved pasta,
but she was not aware of how profound that passion was until she
began cooking it for him herself. It seemed as if she could never fill his
plate full enough to satisfy him, nor were her efforts to vary their diet a
little with some broth or minestrone appreciated, except when she was
able to put a little chicken or pork on the table on Sunday.

The sun never touched the walls of their house. In the winter it was always cold and damp inside, except for the area immediately in front of the fire. The kitchen was lighted by a ten-watt bulb that hung from a cord directly over the table; the bedroom's faint yellowish glow was supplied by a five-watt bulb. Still and all, Maria liked her house because everything in it was hers. She could do as she wished and at the same time be free of her mother's seemingly incessant commands and directions. It was a relief for Giacomo, too, for no longer did he have to go home and listen to his mother's criticisms – nor to Maria's house where he would become angry with her because her parents did not trust him. And, when he stopped in at the bar in the piazza on the way home, it felt good to know that there was his own house to go to right around the corner when the card game was over.

It was distressing, though, that Maria's illness hung on for such a long time. She felt weak and tired all the time. Then she came down with tonsillitis and went to bed with a fever for several weeks. If that was not bad enough, she had a miscarriage on May 15, just four months after their wedding. Maria spent a lot of time crying, for it seemed as if their married life was destined to go badly. Maria knew she would have felt better after the miscarriage if she could have worked as she always had been used to before, but Giacomo made it very clear that once she had married him, she was never to work for money again; she was to be a housewife and raise their children. Maria had pointed out that what with unemployment the way it was he would probably be without work from time to time after they married, just as he had been before. But Giacomo would not hear of it; he for one did not think well of those husbands whose wives worked for wages; it was as if they were not men enough to take care of their families. Maria felt it best to agree even though she enjoyed working, especially field work. She knew that she was good at it and was always being sought after. Now, after the miscarriage, she felt even worse, as if she had let her husband down, even though there was a lot to do without being paid. As soon as she felt better, she was up and about helping her mother in the garden, hoeing and weeding; at her mother-in-law's giving her a hand; or trekking up to the mountains to collect wood for herself as well as for Giulia and Teresa. When she had nothing else to do she would call on Elena to keep her company. Elena would look forward to hearing from Maria about what was going on in the town. Maria, for her part, enjoyed the company of an older woman who did not feel the necessity of criticizing her. Elena treated Maria as if she were one of her own family. In time she entrusted the keys of her house to Maria, who could then drop in in the morning, when Elena was in the inn, and make the bed, wash the dishes, and give the kitchen floor a good scrubbing. Elena's house always looked better for Maria having been there.

By the end of the summer of 1953, Maria felt that her strength had fully returned – even though her liver continued to give her trouble from time to time. It had never felt right since the last terrible year of the war, what with all the fear she had experienced. By now she knew that it was to be her cross to bear for the rest of her life. Giacomo was beginning to develop a paunch, not that he had ever been lean and hard muscled like her father or her brother Salvatore, but now people began to notice it and congratulated Maria on knowing how to feed her husband so well. Maria wondered about herself, too, worrying whether she would be able to get pregnant again. Elena never failed to ask whether she had missed her period, and other women would appraise her stomach with a knowing eye.

II

In October of 1953 Maria began to suspect that she might be pregnant. By the following month she was certain of it. She was delighted and prayed to San Antonio, Santa Rita, Santa Anna, as well as Santa Caterina that this time she would have a live baby. Everyone assured her that she would, saying now that she had become more calm and used to having a husband, things would go differently.

Deep down inside she felt that they were right, but the money worried her. The baby would need a trousseau, or at least a few things, and with Giacomo's pay being only six hundred lire a day, there was barely enough to live on as it was. That was the reason she had wanted to work for a wage, so that they could put something aside, but she knew that it was useless to talk about that. Furthermore, word was out that the government-subsidized reforestation project would come to a halt in a matter of months. After that, Giacomo would be without work. This prompted Teresa to say to Maria, "Why not come and live with us and save paying the rent? If we live together, we can all save a little." She went on to point out that Giacomo's younger brother, Pietro, was due to leave for the military in a few weeks, so there would be room. The very idea made Maria feel all cold inside. She felt trapped, as if destiny had decreed that they were never going to have a life of their own. When Maria and Giacomo talked about it he said that the idea made him as sad as it had her, but the bare truth of the matter was that they still owed the doctor eight thousand lire for Maria's penicillin, and with the baby coming there would be more debts. At least Giacomo found now that he was married he got along better with his mother. Perhaps it was because he felt more confidence in himself, being a husband and about to be a father. He began to think that they ought to try living with his parents, at least for a while – until things got better for them. Maria agreed. So in November of 1953 they left their rented quarters in Via Virgilio and moved into one room in the house of Luigi and Teresa Rossi. Maria carried over most of the small items on her head, and Giacomo and his father brought the bed and the armoire. The kitchen furniture was stored in the old pig stall below. On her last trip, Maria stopped in to say goodbye to Elena, who cried as if she were losing her own daughter. Maria consoled her by saying that she would drop in as often as she could on her way to her mother's.

Teresa was right; living together was clearly cheaper than living separately. Not only did Giacomo and Maria save on the rent but also on food. Everything could be made to go a little further when it was a question of feeding four instead of two from the same fireplace. Maria was more efficient than her mother-in-law and showed her ways to cut corners. Little by little, Maria took over in the kitchen. Teresa, who suffered from a multitude of aches and pains and occasional shortness of breath, was gratified that Maria took charge. She found that her joints did not hurt her so much if she could sit longer by the fire. Even though things went better than she had thought they would, still, Maria found that sharing a kitchen and living in one bedroom was confining. It often made her nervous. Fortunately there were chores to do that required her to leave the house. It was Maria who went to the fountain for water, to the public wash with the laundry, and who did most of the shopping. One time she would go to the fountain in piazza Santa Anna to hear the news circulating in that part of town, another time to the fountain by the main gate to exchange further information and opinion. The hours spent at the laundry were the best, for there she could hear women telling about having babies and officiating at the births of others – stories that reverberated with testimony of pain and mishap. As her time grew near, it made her uneasy to know what might lie in store for her. She told the midwife more than once to be sure and come to her when her husband sent for her.

III

The rumor that had circulated about the reforestation project ending came true in February. It was said that there were no more funds. Giacomo, along with 120 other men, was laid off. It was then that Giacomo began to feel a sharp pain in his stomach. The first time it swept over him he thought it was something he had eaten, but when it came back the next day, and the next, he knew it was more serious. Finally he mentioned it to Maria, for it began to wake him up at night.

She told him it must be his liver. Knowing that seemed to make the pain less severe. When he went to work hoeing sugar beets in March, he did not notice it at all anymore. Giacomo hated field work, bending over the short-handled hoe all day, but he was glad to have the pay. When the sugar beets were finished in March, there was corn to hoe in April. By the end of the month Giacomo could not seem to get more than an occasional day's work. With the baby coming on in May, he felt angry and frustrated, especially since Salvatore had regular work in the gravel pit and his friend Gerardo was always busy as a mason.

IV

When Giacomo first heard that the Università Agraria was planning to distribute part of its holdings to the citizenry of Valmonte, he didn't pay attention, for he was certain that nothing could come of it for him. Two weeks later the official announcement was affixed in the piazza. It stated that 440 hectares of communal land administered by the Università Agraria were to be allocated in lots of two, three, and four hectares according to quality of the soil. All those eligible should submit their applications by June 1, 1954. To be eligible one had to have been born in Valmonte or have lived there for twenty-five years, be without real property, and be employed in agriculture as opposed to industry or artisanship. Even when Giacomo was aware that he was eligible to apply, he refused to do it, for, as he explained to Maria, he did not know anyone in the administration of the Università Agraria, and it was obvious that when the time came the officials would distribute the land among their friends. That is always what happened. Besides, he knew that he was not cut out to be a real farmer. He did not like it. Indeed, he fancied himself a mason, even though he had had very little chance to work at masonry other than assisting his friend Gerardo from time to time. But his father was adamant and insisted that he should apply. If by some chance Giacomo did get a piece, then he would help him work it – after all, he had considerable experience in farming. Maria felt that her father-in-law was right, but she knew that if she pushed Giacomo too hard he would dig in his heels. There was no more mention of the subject until one day at Giustino Cervino's store. Cervino asked Maria what Giacomo was doing about the land. When she said that he did not feel he had a chance, Cervino said right out that her husband was a fool, and he should hurry right away and make an application. In fact, he said after a moment's reflection, he would fill out the lengthy form himself, for he had practice in that sort of thing. Maria was delighted, especially as she knew that Cervino was on the governing board of the Università Agraria. She said that she would go home immediately and tell Giacomo. At first Giacomo was reluctant to even consider it, but when she pointed out again that Cervino was willing to write the application he began to relent. Before they went to sleep that night, he said that he was willing to try it. When Giacomo thought about it, he could not understand why Cervino was willing to do this favor for him, for he barely knew him – unless he hoped to persuade Maria to buy her sugar, coffee, and pasta from him rather than from Morelli. When Giacomo told his father the next day about Cervino's proposal, Luigi insisted that it was as good as decided that Giacomo would get a lot, for Cervino would not help him if he did not intend to fix things up for him. Giacomo called his father a dreamer, but when he went that evening to Cervino's to sign the form, he was impressed; you could see that it was a good application.

The following day he left it with the secretary of the Università Agraria, glad to be rid of it. It was just as well, for late that evening Maria went into labor and there was much else to think about.

V

When her first pains came, Maria sent Giacomo running for the midwife. He pounded and pounded on the door of her house only to be told by her sister, angered to be woken from her sleep, that the midwife was in Latina at the hospital with her son, who had had an attack of acute appendicitis that morning.

When Giacomo returned, Maria was stunned to hear the news. Giulia, hovering at her daughter's bedside, began to wail, invoking the names of the saints, imploring them to save her daughter. Maria told Giacomo to find the doctor as quickly as he could, for the labor was very hard and she knew that things were not going well. Giacomo found his heart pounding as he started for the door, umbrella in hand. As he left he spoke angrily to his mother, who was sitting by the fire rocking back and forth in her chair moaning, and slammed the door behind him. It had been raining hard all day and now it was coming down in sheets; the streets were flooded and in places impassable. At the doctor's house it seemed like an eternity before anyone responded to his impassioned assault upon the door. The doctor's wife opened it to tell Giacomo that her husband was supposed to have been back hours ago but had gotten delayed in the country because of the floods. There was nothing she could do, she said, except tell her husband as soon as he came home; she shut the door. Giacomo went home full of rage for the impotence he felt. He could hear Giulia crying when he came in. He felt like striking out at her and at his mother, too, to silence them. Husbands are not supposed to see their wives give birth, but he

wondered what was wrong with these women who had helped countless babies be born to become of such faint heart when their daughters
were in labor and needed them the most? It had been almost five hours
since Maria had started labor, and dawn would break soon. Giulia came
out to say that the baby should have been born by now on its own;
Maria would die very soon if the doctor did not come. Giacomo
pushed her aside and started for the door, determined to find a doctor if
he had to run to Latina to get one. It was just then that there was a
knock, the door opened, and the doctor came in. He instantly ordered
Giulia to bring him hot water from the fire and entered the bedroom to
find Maria very weak. He immediately set to work and with forceps
pulled the baby out. It was a boy. The doctor cut the cord, pulled out
the afterbirth, held it up to the dim light, and then disposed of it in the
chamber pot. Giulia rushed from the room to tell Giacomo that he had
a baby son. Giacomo felt as if his legs were going to buckle under him,
but he came and grinned at Maria and she managed a wan smile in
return. As the doctor packed his bag he told Giacomo that it was a
most fortunate thing that the rain had stopped, for he had gotten there
just in time. In another half an hour . . . Giulia wrapped the baby in
swaddling and placed him beside Maria. Then she kneeled beside the
bed and thanked San Antonio, Santa Anna, and Santa Rita for having
saved her daughter. Luigi, who had hardly slept himself, came in after
Teresa. They embraced, he congratulated Giacomo and kissed the baby
and Maria. Giacomo opened a bottle of liqueur that he had bought for
the occasion. Maria spoke up in a thin voice to say that she had known
she was going to die, so it must have been a miracle that saved her. Of
course it was a miracle that had saved her daughter and grandson,
Giulia said emphatically. Giacomo slammed down the bottle that he
had been holding in his hand and cried out that it was not a miracle but
the doctor that had saved his wife and son. "No matter, no matter,"
rejoined Luigi. "What is important is that the new mother and the new
baby are alive and well." Everyone nodded their heads and then left,
except for Giacomo, who closed the door, undressed, and crawled into
bed beside Maria. "Now we are a real family," he said, kissing Maria
and falling into a deep sleep.

The following day, and for several days thereafter, the midwife came
to wash the baby. She told Maria that she was sorry that she could not
have been there to help her, but that was life. Her son was going to be
all right. As for Maria, she was going to have to stay in bed for several
days to get her strength back after her hard labor. The baby was fine,
she said, and Maria should not worry about the elongated head – that's
what happens in difficult births when the forceps have to be used.
Before long his head would look like any other baby's. Giulia and

Teresa made chicken broth to bring in Maria's milk. But they needn't have bothered, for it seemed that Maria had plenty. She was pleased with the way the baby sucked so hard at her breast, and at the same time felt sorry for those poor women whose breasts dried up or whose milk was weak and watery.

After a week Maria got out of bed. At the end of the following week, the midwife said that Maria would have to go to Latina to the maternity clinic to be checked. Maria resented having to take the bus to Latina, leaving the baby with her mother-in-law, and being gone over by a doctor when it was obvious that she was now going to be all right. The midwife was adamant, though, pointing out that that visit to the doctor would cost her nothing more than the bus fare, since the clinic was sponsored by the State. It was the only sensible thing to do. Furthermore, she went on, Maria should not swaddle the baby for more than a couple of more weeks at the most, for everyone in the city knew that old-fashioned practices like that were not good for growing babies. On that score Maria kept her own counsel, for as far as she could tell the older women were right, and besides, if she did follow the midwife's advice and then found the baby's legs becoming crooked she would never forgive herself—nor for that matter would Giulia or Teresa.

Even before the baby was born Maria and Giacomo had decided to name him Luigi, if it was a boy, in honor of Giacomo's father. Luigi had hoped and, indeed, expected that it would happen that way, but his old eyes watered nevertheless when Maria told him of the name they had chosen. It was a name, in fact, that Maria did not especially like, and she wondered what they would call him in the family when he got older. But there was time enough for that. The first and most important thing to do was to have him baptized. Maria knew how strongly her mother felt about not waiting too long, for if something awful happened, God forbid, the baby would die a creature and not a Christian which was too terrible to contemplate.

When it came to choosing the godparents, Giacomo said that he did not care much one way or another, for as far as he could tell they didn't really do very much for your child anyway. Maria answered that even if they didn't do much, the way they used to in the old days, it was still important to have them. Giacomo answered that in that case she should do the choosing. Maria had in fact done a good deal of serious thinking about it already, knowing Giacomo's attitude. Furthermore, for her it was important to have the godmother that she wanted. She chose Marina Bassiano. Marina came from a good family, not well-to-do but respectable. Her father had been the tax collector of Valmonte for many years. Maria knew that it could not hurt to establish a connection with a family like that, and besides she liked Marina and knew that she liked her in return, even though she was from a Calabrian peasant family. They had become friends in Catholic Action. Marina told Maria right away that she would be willing to accept. She would ask her younger brother to be the godfather, as Maria had suggested. Maria immediately began to set about making a baptismal dress for the baby, buying some white tulle in the market for two thousand lire and five hundred lire worth of blue ribbon. On Sunday, just one month after Luigi was born, Maria cooked a baptismal feast for fifteen people following the service in Santa Anna. There was barely room around the table in Teresa's kitchen. Everyone complimented Maria on the baby's dress that she had sewn, and Marina presented her godson with a gold medallion on a chain with his name inscribed, just as Maria had hoped she would. It was a festive occasion, and Giovanni gave toast after toast to his grandson and their parents – so many, in fact, that Salvatore told him to stop, for he was getting drunk and disgracing himself. Maria, holding the baby in her arms, felt all warm inside. She knew now what it was like to be a real mother and not just a substitute one for Tonino or Michele. Giacomo felt better too than he had for months, sitting as a father in his parents' house. Furthermore, Salvatore had told him just two days before that he had found him a job on the construction site in Rome, where he had been working since he had left the gravel pit.

VI

For the next year and a half Giacomo did not see much of his new son except on Sundays. He would leave the house every morning at four o'clock, walk to the Portella gate to meet Salvatore, and then together they would hike down the trail to the old stone shelter at the bottom, where they kept the bikes, and then pedal to the train station. There they would get the five forty-five workmen train to the Ostia Lido station at Rome. Then bus 95 would take them to within two blocks of the construction site. They were putting up a large new apartment building. They would begin work at seven thirty and work until five o'clock, with an hour off. It was Giacomo's job to mix the mortar by hand for the masons. It was the kind of work he liked, getting just the right mixture of sand and cement and water. He was proud of his skill, and was well aware of how important it was in the construction of the great building that was climbing day by day behind his back. It was true that Salvatore earned more working on the construction itself, but Giacomo was so pleased to have a regular paying job that he did not care. The train ride back and forth every day was tiring, and he usually did not get home until eight o'clock or eight thirty, for often the train was late. By then he could do little more than eat and throw himself into bed. But still, commuting that way rather than waiting around in the piazza to be called to work made him feel a part of a whole new world that seemed to be opening up. There were times on the train when he was not playing cards that he would dream about someday becoming a mason, rather than just a laborer, and perhaps even a fore-man. Then – who knows? – they might even move to Rome and live in one of those apartments. Giacomo had bought himself a briefcase into which he placed his lunch, a large chunk of bread stuffed with greens, and he liked the figure that he cut walking down the train platform in his leather jacket with briefcase in hand.

The wage was two thousand lire a day – double the highest wage he had ever earned before. Out of that he had to pay for the train ticket as well as cigarettes and an occasional coffee or glass of wine. The rest of it he gave to Maria. Before long they had paid off the debts that had piled up since the reforestation job had ended and began to put some money aside. For the first time Giacomo was protected by health insur-ance. He coveted the little booklet that contained his policy, which covered him, Maria, and the baby from the day he started working to a period of six months after the last day. Furthermore, he received a pay supplement for the baby. It was not much, but it helped. Giacomo had never felt so prosperous. He wanted to buy a radio. Maria was against the idea. Not that she thought it immoral, as did the priest, who warned people not to listen, but rather she felt it was unnecessary – a luxury that they could do without even though she knew of a number of people who were beginning to get them. But Giacomo had his mind made up. He wanted to have something to show for the money he was making other than just food on the table. Besides, Giacomo had found out where he could buy a new one for 28,000 lire: 4,000 lire down and then 2,000 lire a month for a year. That way they would hardly notice, he pointed out to Maria. Maria agreed. Apart from Giacomo's old bicycle, it was the first thing with moving parts that he had ever owned, and it was the first real modern product that anyone in the family had ever bought. He liked the way it looked, bulky, with its dials and knobs, sitting on the cupboard. The first thing that he did every evening when he came home was to turn on the news. Maria found that she liked it, too, although she never turned it on during the day, for that would have used electricity unnecessarily; but she enjoyed listening to it with Giacomo at night. It was as if by the very act of listening they were turning their backs a little on all the hard times that they had known.

VII

In July of 1955 Giacomo's younger brother, Pietro, returned from military service. He had known even before he had left that his brother and sister-in-law were going to be living in what had been his room and he would have to sleep on a cot in the living room when he returned. He was resigned to that, but not to the baby's crying. It seemed to him that he cried all the time, keeping him awake when he wanted to sleep. Hardly a day passed that Pietro did not complain to his mother about the baby – often in earshot of Maria or Giacomo, or both. Even before Pietro returned, however, Giacomo and Maria were finding that living there was increasingly getting on their nerves. Perhaps it was the baby that made the difference; at least that is what Teresa said when she complained that Maria was doing less in the kitchen than she had before. It seemed to Maria that Teresa was getting more and more touchy, and Giacomo found himself quarreling with her again, even though he had a job and was contributing more than his share to the household. One day following a set-to with his mother, he decided he couldn't stand it anymore and immediately started looking for a house. Now that he was earning two thousand lire a day he felt he could afford to, even though he had always believed that paying rent was a waste of good money. But finding a house was difficult; it seemed as if there were not any. Giacomo did not lose hope, however, for he knew that was the way it always happened: First everyone said no, absolutely not, then later someone would say yes, they had a house to rent or they knew of someone who did. That was the way it was, although it took about a month before a man spoke up and said that he had a house for them over on Via Tarchini. Maria was delighted when Giacomo told her, for it would mean having her own place again, not having to share or worry about her in-laws. Then, too, it would mean living close to two of her best friends, Emilia and Giuliana, who both had sons Luigi's age. It came at an especially opportune time, for in September Maria knew that she was pregnant again.

The house had not been lived in for some time and was in a state of considerable disrepair. Most of the floor tiling had come up, and Maria knew how hard it was going to be to keep anything clean, especially with children playing in the dirt. But it was large with two bedrooms, a sitting room, and a kitchen. They had furniture for just one room, but the other room would come in handy to store wood in, and the sitting room they would just close off. The rent was three thousand lire a month – twice what they had paid for Elena's, but this one had a fuse box, which meant that they could have fifteen watts in both the kitchen and the bedroom, if they wanted to spend that much on electricity.

Maria again moved all the furniture on her head, except for the bed and the armoire. She was eager to move and get settled, and to try the new three-burner gas stove that Giacomo bought that very day. More and more people were buying the small white enameled tabletop stoves that ran on bottled gas. Cervino was selling the stoves in his store for eighteen thousand lire. For an additional thousand lire, you could get a container of gas, which, if you were very careful, could last you several months. Maria intended to use the stove only for making coffee and heating milk in the morning. It was so much easier than starting a fire first thing out of bed. She set the stove on a small table next to the radio, against the wall. She often found herself looking at these two pieces of the modern world that existed right in her very own house. It all seemed like a kind of miracle – Giacomo's kind of miracle.

VIII

The other kind of miracles, those that Giulia believed in, Maria found herself believing in less and less. Seldom now did she go to church, except on the important feast days. It had happened little by little, for when she was first married she continued to go to mass every Sunday morning, even though she did not attend Catholic Action functions anymore. But more and more she disliked going by herself, for Giacomo refused to set foot inside Santa Anna, and then when the baby was born, it was just easier to stay at home and not bother to change into her good dress. The strangest part was that she did not feel any remorse. She hadn't come to distrust priests the way Giacomo did. Rather, her change seemed to result from the fact that she was now a mature woman. She was not the same person she was when she had gone to Don Giuseppe to ask his advice on everything. It was just as the older women said: When you marry you have a husband to listen to and you don't need the priest anymore. The way Maria began to explain it to herself, and on occasion to others, was that there were different ways of showing your allegiance to God. Going faithfully to church was only one.

Now with the gas stove, Maria could make one less trip every week to the mountains for wood. On the mornings she did go, she would leave Luigi with Giulia. When both she and her mother went to the garden, she would leave the baby with Tonino. But on the weekly trip to the public laundry she would take Luigi with her, strip off his clothes, and duck him into the clear pool to wash him off well. Maria had never intended to keep him in swaddling as long as she did, but he would not go to sleep at night unless she bound him. Whenever she began to say "Enough," he would jump up and down and scream

"Bind me! Bind me!" For peace of mind she would. Hardly would she have the last fold in place than Luigi would be asleep.

The winter of 1956 came on unusually cold. When Maria and Giulia harvested the olives in late November and early December, their hands were so cold that they could barely make their fingers move. Maria had no gloves. She also had no boots, and when she went to the mountains in her open-toed clogs, her cold feet made her weep. Then the snow came and stayed on the ground as it had never done in the past. It usually melted rapidly in the bright sun.

In January of 1957 Giacomo's work in Rome came to an end. He knew it would happen sooner or later, but he kept thinking that he would be transferred to another site in Rome where the same construction company was about to start on another apartment house. Instead, he and many others were let go. Salvatore had already taken another job with a construction firm in Latina, but there was no call for a cement mixer, nor was there any regular work to be had in Valmonte other than odd jobs. Giacomo began to feel the sharp pain in his stomach again. This time it did not go away, even when he ate unseasoned food. To his great dismay, he began to realize that he would probably not be working when his second baby was born, just as he was not when the first came. As February rent became due, he began to wonder if he had not made a serious mistake moving from his parents' house. All during February it snowed off and on, until the snow reached across the plain right down to the sea. No one could remember anything like it before. It was too cold to stand around in the piazza in the snow, and Giacomo did not like to go into Romeo's bar to have a glass and a game when he was not working, even if there were many other men in his same situation who did. He wanted to have enough in his pocket to at least buy a glass around. Fortunately, he was covered by health insurance for six months from the last week in January, when he was let go; this made Maria, as a pregnant woman, eligible to buy bread at a reduced price from the bakery. She hated to do that, for it made her feel like a beggar. She knew from the look in the eyes of the baker and his wife that that was what they thought, too. From time to time Giulia would give her an extra loaf, but Giovanni was without work also, and Tonino and Michele had the appetites of young wolves.

By the middle of February her friends Emilia and Giuliana were telling her that she should go to Angelo Morelli, the vice-mayor, who was also president of ECA, the Valmonte relief fund, to ask him for help. They could see that she was underfed and looked peaked. Surely, they said, he would not deny money to a pregnant woman whose husband was without work and whose little boy was at home crying from hunger. Maria was reluctant to go. She had pride. No one in her family had ever gone to the town asking for help, even when things were at their worst. Besides, she knew how furious Giacomo would be if she went and he found out; he would probably beat her, although he had never laid a hand on her. But it was she who had to listen to Luigi's pleading for food, and it was she who had to think about herself and the baby on its way. She was still trying to make up her mind when quite by accident she looked up while getting water at the fountain one day to see the vice-mayor right in front of her. She could only think that God had meant her to take advantage of that opportunity. She stepped forth and found herself talking in a voice as calm as she could make it. She said that her husband, Giacomo, was not working these days and that she was expecting a baby in a month. Hardly had she uttered those remarks than she hurriedly added that she had not wanted to ask for help, and that her husband would be very angry if he knew what she was doing, but things had gotten to such a pass she felt that she had to take matters into her own hands. Even before she had finished, the vice-mayor raised his hand as if to say that he understood her plight. He told her he was glad that she should feel free to speak out that way, for that was every citizen's right. But the truth of the matter was, the fund was dry at that moment. He was sorry, but there was not even a lira. Maria felt her face blush a deep red and her knees began to shake. She wished only that the earth would open right where she was standing and swallow her then and there. Her shame and humiliation were so great that for a moment she did not know where she was; nor could she move from the spot. Then she quickly turned and walked away so that he could not see the tears welling in her eyes. When Giacomo came home she was still crying, and she could not help but tell him right off what happened. He was every bit as angry as she feared he would be. With a voice choked with rage, he told her that she should never go to anyone to ask for anything, for he was a proud man and would not permit his wife to go begging. He said he had a mind to beat her for what she had done, but he would not because of her condition. With that he left, slamming the door behind him, and she knew where he was going. Giacomo tracked down the vice-mayor and approached him just as he was finishing a conversation with the marshal of the *carabinieri* in the upper piazza. Giacomo drew himself to his full height and fastened his gaze upon the vice-mayor. "I wish to thank you," he said, "for the way you replied to my wife when she came to you a while ago asking for help. You said exactly the right thing, Mr. Vice-Mayor. It is exactly what I would have said, too, for I would never have allowed her to make that request of you. No, you did well to say that you would not help her." He paused to let his words sink in and then continued. "I know that you are a good father, and as a good father you could have said, right now we have nothing to give you for there is no money, but later when the baby has come we will make something available to you. That is what you could have said as a good father." And with that Giacomo turned abruptly on his heels and walked away.

IX

As Maria went into labor on March 22, Giacomo was without work. There was no gas for the stove, and Maria had been unable to go for wood for more than a week. The snow was still heavy on the ground. There would not even be any hot water to wash the baby with when it came. Maria had gone into labor unexpectedly and sent Giacomo to find the midwife. She lay waiting on the bed, with Luigi asleep beside her. She began to feel afraid. When the door opened she thought it was Giacomo with the midwife, but it was her mother, who had just heard that Maria was in labor. Giulia clasped her hands together in a gesture of despair when she saw that Maria was alone and that Luigi might awaken at any moment and need attention. Giulia approached the bed, squeezed her daughter's hand in hers, and with the other hand reached down to pull up the cover to keep Maria warm. Suddenly Giulia brought both hands to her mouth and screamed, for when she looked down she saw a baby's foot where the head should have been. When she could catch her breath she told Maria what she had seen and then began invoking the saints to save her daughter's life. "Get out of here as fast as you can!" Maria yelled at her. "Run, run as fast as you can, get that midwife here. She may be taking her time, not knowing anything is wrong. Hurry, hurry, or you will have something to really cry about." Giulia ran from the room, leaving Maria alone with Luigi still asleep beside her. The next half-hour was the longest in Maria's life. The fear that she felt at first gave way to a sensation of numbness, of not caring, and then the searing pain brought with it the conviction that she would die and leave Giacomo behind alone with Luigi. She was hardly aware when Giacomo returned with the midwife and Giulia. Without a moment's hesitation the midwife slipped on a rubber glove and reached right in and turned the baby around, so that the head presented itself first. When the baby was out and the cord cut, she looked across at Giulia and said, "Your daughter is lucky, I got here just in time." Giulia crossed herself and fell on her knees and thanked San Antonio, Santa Anna, and Santa Rita for having saved her daughter and the baby. Then she went into the kitchen and told Giacomo that he had a baby son. When Giulia returned with Giacomo, the midwife was examining the baby very carefully. She had noticed a hernia brought on by the strain of the birth. She sent Giulia running for hot water from her fire, which Giovanni had kept going, and then explained to Maria that the hernia she had just found could be dangerous, but that there was nothing they could do about it now. In fact, it would be necessary to wait for two years, and then an operation would be required. Meanwhile, the baby would have to wear a truss. In any event, she went on to say, things could have been a lot worse, and they should all be thankful that they went as well as they did. Maria nodded her head when she heard the midwife's voice stop. She was so tired she could hardly take in anything that had been said to her. When Giulia returned with the water, the midwife washed the baby, swaddled it, and laid it down next to Maria. Luigi, on her other side, was just beginning to wake up. Giacomo told the midwife as she was packing her bag that he was sorry he did not have a glass to offer her, but things were hard for him at the moment. She understood how that was, she said, and went on to say that she would be back the next day to check the baby, give his wife an injection to build back her strength, and show her how the truss was to be applied. Giacomo thanked her at the door and then returned to the bedroom, dropped his clothes in exhaustion on the floor, admonished Luigi to go to sleep again, and crawled into bed next to his new son.

X

Maria felt even more tired than she remembered being after the birth of Luigi and remained in bed for an extra two days. Giulia came by in the morning to get the fire started with wood she bought in the piazza. She washed and swaddled the baby and applied the truss in the way the midwife had instructed. Luigi had expressed considerable amazement at the sudden appearance of his younger brother, but his curiosity was mixed with dismay at the prospect of sharing the same bed with his mother and that creature. Luigi was accustomed to sleeping beside his mother, and in the beginning she placed the baby between herself and Giacomo. After several nights of mutual tossing and turning, she realized that the bed was too small for the four of them. She asked her brother Salvatore if she could borrow a crib. Salvatore's wife had insisted on placing her babies in a crib immediately, saying that the modern way was to accustom the child to the crib right from the start. It did not seem right to Maria – the proper place for a newborn baby was next to its mother – but now she felt she had no choice. The baby went into the crib, and Luigi continued to sleep in the place of honor next to his mother.

The first two weeks were ones of anguish for Maria. For one thing, she could not stop worrying about the hernia, and for another, the baby's nose had become bent out of shape in the course of the difficult birth, and he had some trouble breathing. Worst of all, though, was that Maria's milk did not come, despite the chicken broth that Giulia prepared for her. Maria was beside herself. One old neighbor lady who came to call said that the milk had gone away because a cat with kittens or a dog with puppies had eaten something that Maria had eaten and had thus taken away her milk. It would be necessary, the old lady explained carefully, to find a cat or a dog with milk, and "then, you see, your milk will come right in." Maria was forced to give the baby powdered milk in a bottle, even though he was peaked and not doing well. She was ashamed to feed him like that in public. One day when she was sitting in front of her door, the old lady came hobbling over and said, "Look, Maria, look, there is your dog. Quick, give her something to eat." Maria returned with a plate of minestrone and placed it down. The dog eagerly started to devour the unexpected meal. But before she had finished, Maria grabbed the plate away and forced herself to eat the rest, the old lady nodding wisely all the while. But still the milk did not come in, and Maria swore that she would never listen to one of those old wives' tales again. In despair she took the baby to the maternity clinic in Latina. The doctor brushed aside her fears and said that the baby was doing well and to continue with the milk in addition to a formula that he said she must buy. Maria did not know whether to feel thankful or not, but when she got home it did seem that the baby was getting fatter, and it warmed her heart when he smiled.

XI

Three weeks after the birth Giacomo found work again. For some time the town had wanted to hard-surface the dirt road that ran up the mountain to the village, but money had never been available. Then a request made five years earlier to the Ministry of Public Works was approved. It came as a godsend to many, most of all to the unemployed who were put on the payroll. The wage of one thousand lire a day was only four hundred lire more than Giacomo had received four years ago on the reforestation project, but he was more than thankful for it. In time he was able to pay the back rent, pay the debt to the store, and refill the gas container for the stove. He and Maria began to feel that their worst troubles were over, even though they knew that the road-paving job was a temporary one.

XII

It was some time before Maria felt like having the baby baptized, but again she did not want to put it off for too long. It was understood that the right of honoring her father should fall on either Concetta or Salvatore, as older sister and older brother, through a first or second son. Maria turned again to Marina Bassiano and asked her to be the godmother. Marina agreed and, as is the custom, suggested three names for the baby: Bruno, Sergio, and Pier Luigi. Maria liked Bruno the best, and so did Giacomo. The more they looked at the baby, now husky and compact with a crop of jet-black hair, the more they thought he looked like a Bruno. Maria invited twelve guests to the baptismal feast following the ceremony in Santa Anna. Giulia and Giovanni and Teresa and Luigi came as well as Pietro and his fiancè, Caterina; Salvatore and his wife, Dorotea; Marina and her brother; and the priest, Don Giuseppe, Don Antonio's assistant, and his mother. It was a cold spring day, so the fire in the kitchen where the table was set was welcome. Maria used the same dress for Bruno that she had made for Luigi two years before and was complimented again. Just as she had hoped and expected, Marina gave her a gold medallion on a gold chain for Bruno. She felt better than she had for months, sitting at the table with Bruno in her arms and with Luigi standing on a chair beside her and Giacomo. There was something different about having two children rather than just one. Her dream for a family was beginning to come true.

7

The births of Teresa and Caterina

The road work continued through the summer into the fall of 1957. Right before the project was to be completed in early winter, Giacomo came down with the Asian flu. He remained in bed for three weeks. It was a difficult time for Maria, with Giacomo laid up, Bruno in her arms, and Luigi ever underfoot. Giacomo was so weak when he did get out of bed that he could not return to work right away. His legs felt like rubber. It exhausted him to walk to the piazza and back. When he did finally get his strength back, the road job was completed. He was unemployed again. To add to his worries, the landlord was telling him that the house was too dangerous to be lived in. Giacomo had known of its condition when he moved in but had been willing to take the risk. He wondered why the landlord was saying those things now, when he was out of work. It was clear that he wanted to get rid of them, especially from the way he insisted on being paid on the very first day of the month. It made Giacomo furious – could the landlord not understand that he was without work right then and needed a little more time to get back on his feet?

It was Teresa who again offered a solution – why not move back in with his parents? At first Giacomo told her to mind her own business. But inside he knew that she was right. The sensible thing to do would be to move in with his family again, but the very thought of sharing a kitchen with Teresa again made Maria tense. She would assent to move, she said, as long as she cooked in their own room. It would be crowded, with the bed and the four of them and all, but with their gas stove they could do it. Giacomo answered that if they did that, his mother would feel offended, but no matter. As for Pietro, he would have to move back onto the cot in the living room

110

but, after all, he was a younger brother. As the elder, Giacomo's necessities came first.

The more he thought of it, however, the more he was convinced that there would have to be a long-range solution if they were all to live together with some peace of mind. He would talk to his father about converting the cellar underneath the house into an apartment. If he put a floor in, dividing it in half, the lower part could be the kitchen, with stairs leading to a bedroom above. The door that opened on to the old pigsty in the cellar would become their front door and would open into the kitchen. When it was all done, they could have a place of their own where they could stay forever without having to pay rent. Then Pietro could move back into his room. He was talking more and more about marrying Caterina, and they would need a place to live. Pietro was determined not to throw away good money on rent as his older brother had done. Giacomo told his father that he would pay for all the materials and do the labor himself. All Luigi said was, "Go ahead." But from things that Teresa said, Giacomo knew that both his parents coveted the plan. It would mean that both their sons and daughters-in-law would be right there to help them as they became older.

They moved their possessions as they had before, with Maria carrying everything on her head and Giacomo and Pietro carrying the bed and armoire. Luigi ran as fast as he could between one house and the other carrying small things. The gas stove was set on the small table against the wall. Giacomo drove nails above it so that Maria could hang her pots and pans. The kitchen cupboard was shoved up close against Bruno's crib. When Maria crawled into bed that night, exhausted from the day of moving, she wondered if this moving about would ever end. Perhaps that was to be their destiny, for it did seem at times that for every step forward they slipped back two.

II

Now everything depended on Giacomo finding work – regular work. No matter how they figured the costs of the materials needed to prepare the cellar, the total never came to less than seventy-five thousand lire. The work would have to go slowly, a little at a time. Maria was convinced that Giacomo was not as assertive as he should be when it came to looking for work. On more than one occasion she told him so to his face. Giacomo insisted that those who got jobs did so because they had someone pushing for them, writing letters of recommendation. The very mention of recommendations made Giacomo livid and he began to shout, saying that he was probably the only man in Valmonte who did not have a patron in a high place who could help him.

Look at Salvatore, he pointed out, who now had the protection of a powerful man in Latina. Maria flashed back that her brother worked morning, noon, and night and deserved whatever he got. Giacomo slumped in his chair. He reached for another cigarette. Maria walked behind him, stopped, and put her hand on his shoulder; with a different voice she said that she was sure something would turn up soon, for everyone was talking about the big building boom starting up in Rome.

Giacomo made a point of going on his bike more often to the employment office in Latina. There were those who said that if you waited around the office you stood a better chance. Giacomo didn't believe that, but he did find out that his name had gone toward the top of the list now that he had two children. It was merely a question of waiting, they told him; something was bound to turn up, because there was so much new construction in Rome. He wasn't in the office the day his name was called off, but he heard about it that evening. The next morning he hurried down first thing. They told him that he would start working in two weeks, the first of October. The construction was in Acilia on the farther side of Rome, so he would have to live on the site during the week. His work would be mixing cement. Giacomo went to a nearby bar and had several drinks. When he got home, Maria could see from the expression on his face that he had good news.

When Giacomo walked into the barracks on that first Monday night after work, he groaned. It brought back the painful memory of the army barracks in Gorizia that he had grown to hate so much. The only compensation for having to be away from bed and wife for five nights every week were the card games; sometimes Giacomo won and sometimes he lost, but he never bet very much. Maria knew how much he earned, how much he had to pay the mess hall, and the cost of the train ticket. His wage was three thousand lire a day, one thousand lire more than he had received working in Rome three years before in 1954. Even with the mess, railroad ticket, and pocket money, Giacomo turned over slightly more than twelve thousand lire a week to Maria, enough to live on and put some aside for materials, too.

III

While Giacomo was away during the week, Maria would laboriously chip away at the wall that had to be removed and then cart away the rubble in a bucket on her head to the large ditch at the edge of town. Every Saturday, when Giacomo came home, he would work for a couple of hours and then all of Sunday. By early spring of 1958, the work had progressed to the point where the floor separating the downstairs kitchen from the bedroom above was to be laid over three iron girders. Maria would make sure that everything was on hand, so that when Giacomo came home Saturday evenings he would waste no time. Nevertheless the work proceeded at an agonizingly slow pace. A year after they moved in, the renovation had not yet been completed.

The room in which they lived seemed to grow smaller as the boys grew larger. Despite his hernia, Bruno was an active little boy, first crawling, then running. But the more he grew, the more preoccupied Maria became, for the time was coming when he would have to have the operation. Maria groaned to herself at the thought of leaving her small son in the hospital at Latina. As the time for the annual pilgrimage of La Santissima drew near, Maria found herself wanting to go. She was afraid Giacomo would make fun of her wish, but she decided he need never know. That year La Santissima fell on the tenth of June, a Tuesday. Maria joined the sixty or so other pilgrims from Valmonte as they started off under a bright blue sky to climb to the sanctuary on the summit of Mount Bellavista. Everywhere the mimosas were in bloom, brilliant against the sky. The yellow banner of the Daughters of Maria looked splendid as it dipped and rose to the cadence of their walking. Maria took her turn at carrying it and sang with the rest chorus after chorus of La Santissima until she was hoarse. When they finally reached the top, she broke away from the crowd and entered the sanctuary. She crossed herself and kneeled before the statue of the Most Holy Mother, bowing her head for a long time.

When she looked up she made a vow that if the Madonna granted a successful operation and speedy recovery to her son, she would take him on the pilgrimage in her honor for three years. As she stared at the face of La Santissima, there was something in her expression that made Maria feel that her supplication would be granted.

After her pilgrimage, Maria found it hard to wait. She kept expecting word from the doctor. Finally, quite unexpectedly, he sent a message telling Maria to have Bruno at the hospital the next day.

Hurriedly she prepared, leaving Luigi in the care of Teresa. On the way down on the bus she reassured her young son, whose face turned questioningly toward her, that he would not feel any pain, for the good doctor would give him something that would put him to sleep; when he woke up it would be over. His mother would be right there. But in fact Maria did not know much about what would happen, and the doctor had told her nothing. Even when they arrived at the hospital, neither the nurses nor the doctor talked to her, but she was thankful that they let her sleep in the bed next to Bruno's. Early the next morning they came to wheel Bruno away. Maria's heart sank as she watched him disappear down the hall. The next three hours seemed endless. As she lay on her bed fretting, it was for a moment, as if she were again waiting for Bruno to be born, as she had on that terrifying day two years before. She moaned softly as the memory overcame her. When they wheeled Bruno back he seemed so pale that she thought for a moment he must be dead, but the nurse told her that the operation had been a success. It was then that Maria made a prayer of thanks to La Santissima. Bruno stayed in the hospital for nine days. Maria came back and forth on the bus in order to sleep next to him at night. Maria brought him home with strict instructions to keep him quiet, which she did for some time, but then it seemed as if there was no holding him back. He ran everywhere as fast as his short legs would carry him. After a while, Maria merely shook her head in mock dismay and nick-named him an earthquake. She was convinced that her prayers to the Madonna had helped to make him a little earthquake.

IV

In September of 1958, the renovation was at last completed. Maria had never moved her things with such little effort. What she enjoyed most was arranging the kitchen, putting the cupboard in its proper place, having enough space for the table and six chairs. Giacomo had built in a wood burning stove, both for warmth and for cooking, but Maria found that she used the gas burners more and more and went to the mountain for wood less and less. Giacomo had wanted to pipe in running water, but the expense was too great. He did have a meter installed, though, so that it was possible to burn more than fifteen watts at a time if they wished to.

It was a relief, too, to have their own door leading directly from the kitchen to the street so that they did not have to pass through Teresa's. That way it was easier, Maria found, to keep on good speaking terms with her mother-in-law. At the top of the short, steep stairs that led from the kitchen to the bedroom, Maria hung a piece of heavy cloth against the day when Giacomo planned to install the door, but in the eight years they lived there the door was more a dream than a reality. The bedroom was just spacious enough to hold the armoire, the large bed, and the two smaller ones that Maria had bought from Salvatore. One small window faced the narrow street, where sunlight penetrated only for a short time in the late afternoon. The low ceiling and the heat rising from the kitchen helped to alleviate some of the dampness.

V

When they moved downstairs, Maria was already pregnant with their third child. It was due in the spring of 1959. If it turned out to be a boy it would be easier, for then he could double up later with Bruno or

Luigi. If it was a girl, she could sleep with Bruno at first, but later it would become a problem. Maria consoled herself by realizing there was nothing she could do about it. She did hope, though, that this time she would have a girl. She would need one to help her.

VI

Two months after the renovation was completed, Giacomo was startled to read an announcement fixed on the wall of the piazza that the drawing for the allotments of land held by the Università Agraria would take place on the tenth of December. He had forgotten about the whole thing. For a while rumors had circulated that the allocations were to be announced the following month, but as the years went by, there were not even any more rumors. Neither he nor anyone else was surprised, for everyone assumed that the whole thing was just another trick to postpone the day of liquidation of the holdings. When Giacomo now spoke to others in the piazza they said that this time it really would happen. Pressures from high places had been brought to bear on the Università Agraria. It seemed as if the power of the local Socialist-Communist administration, which had won control of the town government in the elections of 1952, was finally being felt. Giacomo remained skeptical about his own chances, even though Giustino Cervino told Maria on more than one occasion that he had as good a chance as anyone else.

Everyone who had made an application was advised to be in the council room of the Università Agraria by ten o'clock on the morning of the tenth, a Sunday. Giacomo was of two minds about going; he was certain that he was going to be disappointed, but curious as to whether the application that Cervino had made out could do him any good. He was there along with the others at ten o'clock sharp that morning.

The drawing did not get started at ten, and as the minutes ticked by, those waiting became more tense and restless. The longer Giacomo had to stand around, the more he realized he wanted the land. Before that moment he had never allowed himself that wish. Now he owned nothing, barely more than his bicycle and clothes. Overnight he might become a landowner. It took his breath away. He could feel his heart pounding faster and faster. He had never liked working the land, but that was because he had always had to hoe someone else's. With his own it would be different. Besides, if he had land he could someday build a house. That is what he wanted more than anything in the world. He knew he had done a good job in the renovation. It was his kind of work. The waiting became intolerable. It was clear that the administration was trying to postpone the inevitable even now.

Finally the president and the secretary brought out the wire wheel used for drawing bingo numbers. The president announced that the names of the ninety-five applicants had been placed in the wheel. Destiny would decide which of those were to receive the seventy lots of land, either two hectares of the very best land, three of medium quality, or four of the least desirable. The wheel was turned and a name was called amid shouts of triumph and mutterings of dismay. The winner received an allotment of four hectares. After two hours of drawing, ten names remained to be drawn. Giacomo felt numb. He was convinced that his was not among them. He decided that he should leave. He did not want to be the last one there. He realized that he was very hungry. He lingered until only two names remained, then turned quickly and hurried down the stairs. At the bottom he heard the name Rossi. He whirled and leaped up the stairs. At the top, Giustino Cervino, smiling, shook his hand. Then the secretary handed him a certificate of an allotment for three hectares. Giacomo was so stunned that he hardly knew what to do or say. He stood rooted at the spot. Then very slowly he walked home, going over and over it in his mind. By the time he reached the door of his house, he felt as happy as he ever had in his life. That night he and Maria talked and talked about the land – where it might be, what condition it could be in, and what difference it might make in their lives. One thing they knew was certain: It would not make any difference for a long time.

It was some weeks before Giacomo found out where the land was. At first all he could discover was that it was Lot Number 1 and was located somewhere on a long strip of land that bordered a new dirt road and ran from the canal of L'Acqua Media to the main provincial road connecting Valmonte to Latina. He didn't know which end of the strip it was on.

It was fully a month after the drawing that the surveyor for the Università Agraria agreed to meet him at the intersection of the two roads. While waiting on the provincial road Giacomo noticed the new road: Via Casa Grande. The name made no sense, for there was nothing that looked like a house as far as the eye could see. It was all open land. But it made no difference what it was called – it was the road that led to his land. Giacomo hoped Lot Number 1 was going to be on the other end, away from the main highway. Giacomo began to wonder how long his good luck would hold out when the surveyor told him to follow on his bicycle. The pedaling was heavy going what with the mud, the ruts, and the holes. Toward the end the road bisected another even more primitive one that ran beside the canal, and here the surveyor stopped. With emphatic gestures he pointed out to Giacomo the boundaries of the land, identifying the stakes that marked its rectangular shape. One long side abutted on another lot, which had been won by Mario Lungo; the other side bordered on the road that skirted the canal. One of the two shorter sides faced the Via Casa Grande, and the other terminated at a driveway leading to a farm of some seven to nine hectares that belonged to Francesco Lombardo. Giacomo knew that good luck had struck again. He had known Mario Lungo for a long time. Lungo had been a foreman on the reforestation project. Giacomo liked and respected him. He had heard of the Lombardo family as hardworking and honest people. Their farm was one of the original ones allotted at the time of the reclamation of the marshes; it had been much improved since then. And he thought that if he should ever plant sugar beets it would be convenient to have the canal so close for irrigation.

Giacomo walked over his lot to get the feel of it, to savor it. Three hectares was not very much, but it was more than anyone in either his or Maria's family had ever owned. It was a great satisfaction. But as his eyes traveled the boundaries his happiness became marred, for the land was very rundown. It had not been worked for years, and everywhere it was overgrown. It was going to take a great effort to clean it up to say nothing of turning over the heavy sod. Giacomo owned no tools for that work. His father had offered to help him, and for that he was grateful, because his father had more experience with the land than he had. But his father had no equipment either. As he finally mounted his bike and began to pedal away, he found that the land looked all of a sudden totally intractable to him. He had a heavy feeling in the pit of his stomach.

Over a month went by before Maria was able to see the land with Giacomo. She had heard so much about it she felt she knew it firsthand. When she actually saw it, it was the location that attracted her the most. The fact that the Lombardo farm was nearby made her feel they had not been set down in the middle of a wilderness. Then, too, she liked the canal being so close, with its clean, swiftly running water from the springs at Sorbano. If ever they did build a house, she could do the family wash right there on its banks. But the idea of a house could only be a distant dream. The land did not even belong to Giacomo yet, for he had years and years of mortgage to pay to the Università Agraria before he could really call it his. And first of all they would have to make it render just to pay the expenses. Maria could not help but feel that what with another baby coming, the winning of the land right then did not seem the blessing that it had at first.

VII

By the middle of January, just a little more than a month after the land had been won, Giacomo was without work again. When the buildings at Acilia were completed, the construction firm let go most of its workers. Giacomo was embittered. It seemed as if he was not able to keep a regular job for more than two years. What hurt most was the realization that with Maria in her seventh month, he would be unemployed when his third child was born. He was thankful there was no rent due, but now an even heavier obligation was upon him, for he had to pay the mortgage, taxes, and a fee to the farmer's union for the upkeep of the roads and the canal. The total came to forty-eight thousand lire a year, equivalent to a rent of four thousand lire a month. There was no time to waste if crops were to be planted that year. Giacomo spoke to his father about going together on the land, dividing the expenses, plowing, and seed and the profit in half. Luigi agreed to the proposal, shaking his head at the prospect of the backbreaking work ahead. He located an extra mattock for Giacomo and they began clearing the land. By the middle of February they had it ready for plowing. Francesco Lombardo plowed and harrowed and sowed for a minimal charge. He recommended putting in sugar beets, for the local refinery in Latina would always take the crop and give a better price than one could get for wheat, though the following year they would have to alternate. Once the seed was in the ground, Giacomo and his father fertilized by hand, walking the rows with sacks over their shoulders. As soon as the plants had grown to a height of an inch or more they cultivated, clearing away all the grass and weeds between the rows. Then they turned to cleaning out the drainage ditches crossing and bordering the fields. It was hard work.

VIII

Maria's third child was born early on the morning of March 15, 1959. Angelina Ronconi from across the street also dropped over to give a hand. At the first sign of Maria's labor, at about midnight, Giacomo hurried off to find the midwife. Loud knocking brought her sister to the door. She told Giacomo curtly that she had gone to the country to deliver another baby. "That Rossi one was due later. How could she help it if it didn't wait?" she said, closing the door in his face. Giacomo struck both his hands against his forehead and cried out, "Is it destiny that we are to have babies like animals, with no one coming to help?" He ran to the house of Doctor Guido. In case of some emergency preventing the intervention of the midwife, Doctor Guido was supposed to be available. He banged on the door, but to no avail. Giacomo was certain the doctor was there, determined not to stir even if he had broken down the door. In despair he returned home. Maria's pains were coming with more frequency and intensity. She was afraid that something terrible might happen again. What if the feet should start to come first again – what could Giulia or Teresa do, or even Angelina? Angelina was standing by the bed holding Maria's hand, mopping her brow and from time to time pressing on her abdomen. The other two sat in the corner saying their rosaries, crying, praying. Giacomo left with a vow to find the midwife if he had to walk to the country to do so. He ran toward the main gate, passed through it and made the first curve when he saw headlights coming toward him. He jumped to the middle of the road and waved the car to a stop. His heart jumped when he saw that it was the midwife. The relief was so great that tears came to his eyes. He shouted in the window that Maria was in labor and God only knew what might be happening, but she must get there right away. The midwife nodded and told Giacomo to calm himself – everything was certain to be all right and she would get there as soon as she could. Giacomo called out, "Quickly, for God's sake, quickly," as the car disappeared around the corner. Giacomo ran home and told his mother, who was rocking back and forth before the fire, that the midwife was on her way. As soon as Maria heard his voice she knew that it was going to be all right. The pains were regular, and not as searing as they had been with Bruno. Angelina reassured her that she could see the baby's head, even though she could not. She instructed Giulia and Teresa to see to the hot water. It seemed to Giacomo as if it took forever for the midwife to arrive. When she did, she climbed the short steep stairs to the bedroom, without a word drew on her rubber gloves, felt inside, and declared that everything was as it should be. She instructed Angelina to continue to press and enjoined Maria to push: "Push, Maria, push just as if you were going to take a shit. There, that's right. Don't worry, Angelina will clean it up." The midwife peeled off her rubber gloves, lit a cigarette, leaned back in her chair, and tapped a foot against the floor. The wait was not long. It was approximately four in the morning when the baby girl was born. The midwife cut the cord, then extracted and examined the afterbirth. She waited until Angelina had washed and swaddled the baby and placed it in Maria's arms before she sent Teresa to tell Giacomo to come up. "It's a girl, Giacomo," said Maria warmly as Giacomo bent over her. "You see, I wanted a girl this time. A woman needs a daughter. Now I am contented." Giacomo nodded his head as he held her hand. "You did well, Maria, you did well." Beside him his mother was crying. They had told her before that if the baby was a girl they would honor her by naming it after her. At first she had been hurt when they said that they would possibly call her Teresina rather than Teresa, because they thought it was a prettier name. But now when she looked down at her granddaughter she didn't care anymore about the slight. She was too happy. Giacomo told her to fetch Luigi and his two grandsons, who had been put to bed with him. Giacomo went to the kitchen to get the bottle of liqueur that Salvatore had given them for the occasion. Teresa returned with her husband and two grandsons, both still heavy with sleep. But when little Luigi got to the top of the stairs, he looked over at his mother in bed, drew himself up, strode toward her, looked down at his little sister and said, "Well, Mama, you made a little girl this time, didn't you." "Yes, Gigi, but you will always be my first son," said Maria warmly. Bruno stood beside his mother, clutching her hand. On tiptoe he stared at the baby in his mother's arms. The small room became jammed with women as the word spread up and down the street that Maria had had a baby. The midwife closed her bag and left.

As soon as everyone had gone, Giacomo left to buy milk in the piazza to make *caffè latte* for himself and Maria. He was still upset that Doctor Guido had slept right through his knocking, which had been loud enough to wake the dead. Quite by surprise he encountered the doctor's mother in the piazza and demanded of her the whereabouts of her son. When she replied that he was at home, asleep in bed, Giacomo said, "Well, if he was at home last night he should have answered the door when I knocked. Maria gave birth to a baby girl and I came to find him and no one answered. A doctor is supposed to get up when a man comes looking for him." She could see that Giacomo was angry. She must have gone home immediately to tell her son, for when Giacomo returned home, Doctor Guido was there. Maria had rarely seen Giacomo so angry. He told the doctor that he should be glad the birth went well, for if it had not he would have had to account for it. The doctor looked startled. Maria was afraid that Giacomo had pushed him too far—he would make trouble for them some way. However, he only seemed interested in leaving after shaking everyone's hand. When he had left, Maria could see that Giacomo felt better. He stood for a long time by her side holding her hand.

Later in the morning the midwife came to check on Maria and the baby. She said that she was pleased with them both. Maria was delighted because her milk was coming in this time. Giulia had made a particularly strong chicken broth. She was determined to avoid the humiliation she had felt when Maria's milk had dried up after the birth of Bruno. The midwife sat down to smoke a cigarette while Maria recounted the story of Doctor Guido. The midwife was indignant. "What kind of tricks was he up to not answering your husband's knocking, just sleeping on? He could have endangered the lives of two persons. If things had not gone the way they had with my being here, you might have left three children behind for your husband to take care of." Maria felt comforted by the midwife's words. After she left, she slept for a long time with the baby beside her.

As she lay in bed, and later when she got up, Maria thought about who she should ask to be godparents. It was perplexing. She did not like the idea of having different godparents for each child. That is why she had asked Marina twice. But she felt hesitant about asking her a third time – she might feel imposed upon. It came as a surprise when Anna Carbone came up to her one day at the fountain some two weeks after the birth. Anna told Maria that she had never been a godmother before and that if it was all right with Maria, she and her fiancè, Enrico, would like to be the godparents. Maria was taken aback. She thanked her, saying that she needed to think it over. As she did, she found herself becoming partial to the idea. For one thing, both Anna and Enrico were young. For another, no one could accuse Maria of asking someone in order to get the present. It was Anna who had made the suggestion to Maria.

The baptism took place six weeks after the birth. The twelve guests crowded into Maria's kitchen after the ceremony in Santa Anna. Compliments were passed upon the fine dress the baby wore, the same one that Maria had used for the christening of Luigi and Bruno. It was gratifying, too, when Anna presented Maria with a gold medallion on a chain for Teresa. After she had served the coffee, Maria sat down at the table to nurse the baby. It was good having the milk come just as strong as it had with Luigi. Maria was twenty-nine, but she knew some mothers who had dried up with their third child. As for the swaddling, she would do it for six months. It was said that girls did not need to be bound as boys did. She was glad that things had worked out as they had, with two boys first and now a girl. Her mother had always said that the first should be a girl, to help with the rest as they came along. There was truth in that. Many was the time that Maria had wished to have a daughter old enough to give her a hand washing the dishes, fetching water, looking out for Bruno. But now the two boys could assist their father with the land as they grew up, and they could help Teresa when it came time for her to marry, just as Salvatore had helped her.

IX

Luigi was approaching six, Bruno three. Every morning since he was four, Luigi had gone to the Asilo and remained there until four in the afternoon. He didn't care at all for the nuns. They were always scolding him. But he liked the chance to play with his friends in the courtyard and to roughhouse in the corridors and the classroom. He would take the long way home, through the large olive grove at the far end of town, where there were constant fights between cowboys and Indians and battles between Italians and Austrians.

Bruno's world was more restricted, being confined to the street beyond the kitchen door. A loose cobblestone, a puddle of water, and a stick provided the materials with which he and like-minded children played for hours, until some altercation brought him looking for his mother. But, like his older brother, Bruno held his own against all comers. He was small for his age, but sturdy. At home he liked to watch his mother at whatever she did. It made Maria laugh to see him sitting at the table, chin resting on his hands, jet black hair standing straight up in the air, staring intently at her every move.

When the first anniversary of his hernia operation approached, Maria recalled the promise she had made to take Bruno with her to the sanctuary of La Santissima on the summit of Mount Bellavista. On the morning of the pilgrimage she gathered with the rest in the piazza of Santa Anna. It promised to be a splendid day, as it had been the year before. The women made much of Bruno as he tried to keep up with his mother. When they started the steep incline, Maria lifted him onto her shoulders, to his great delight. There he remained, bobbing up and down, until they reached the top. She felt light at heart as she placed a sprig of mimosa at the base of the statue and lit a candle.

X

For some time Giacomo's pains had been so intense that he could not sleep at night. Maria tried every way she could think of to persuade him to see a doctor, but he would not hear of it. A week after the birth of Teresa, however, the pains became so acute that Giacomo arose and held on to the end of the bed, doubled over with agony. The next day he visited the doctor. He would have to have x-rays, he was told, in Latina. Giacomo had never been admitted to a hospital before. He knew he would not die, as the old people said you would when you had to go to the hospital. But the idea bothered him, especially the x-rays. Maria kept insisting they would not hurt, but how could she know? She had never had one. At last the day came. Maria was right, there was no pain. Later the doctor told Giacomo that he had an ulcer, as well as chronic liver trouble. If he was not careful, he would get worse. It would be necessary to eat much less pasta, without sauce, and no wine, no coffee, no cigarettes. He prescribed pills. Giacomo, smitten, nodded in agreement as the doctor spoke, but he knew that he could not do without all those things, especially not the cigarettes. The pills helped, and Maria began to fill his plate with only half the usual amount of spaghetti.

Ever since the work had stopped at the Acilia site in Rome, Giacomo bicycled unwillingly to the employment office in Latina at least once a week. It was always the same story – others were deemed more needy than he. Being without work when his third child was born was embittering, but it did carry one advantage. Giacomo's name was again moved toward the top of the list.

In the middle of May 1959, two months after the birth of Teresa, a call went out from the Provincial Agricultural Cooperative for work on the canals that kept the Agro Pontino drained. It was tiresome, monotonous labor, but Giacomo accepted immediately. Owning land served by the canal system made him feel a little more reconciled to the low pay and backbreaking shoveling. He noticed, too, that after a week of work his stomach began to give him less trouble.

XI

The sugar beets that Giacomo and his father had planted in February matured well in June and July. As the August harvest approached, they speculated about how much three hectares would produce. The going price in 1959 was a thousand lire per quintal. If they received as much as a hundred quintals, the total sum to be earned would be formidable. Their forecast was close to the mark. When the final payment was made from the sugar beet refinery, Giacomo counted over and over again the ninety-five thousand lire he had received. In no time, though, the sum seemed to melt. He owed Lombardo for the plowing and harrowing, the provincial agricultural cooperative for the seed and the fertilizer. There was the mortgage to be paid to the Università Agraria, the land tax to the town of Valmonte, and his annual dues to the provincial agricultural cooperative. There remained thirty thousand lire to be divided between Giacomo and his father. Fifteen thousand lire was not much. Giacomo brought a little more than that to Maria every two weeks. Still and all, as Maria kept saying, every little bit helped.

In 1960 Giacomo and his father planted wheat, to give the land a rest. The wheat price, though supported by the state, was not as good as that for the sugar beet. He brought home ten thousand lire. In 1961 they returned to sugar beets again and received a gross payment of a hundred twenty thousand lire from the refinery. Giacomo had not realized how much prices had increased in the past two years until he began to settle accounts. That year he gave Maria fifteen thousand lire. It was clear that he was standing still rather than pulling ahead. Luigi told Giacomo that he would work with him for one more year and then stop. He was getting old. The work was hard. He was bringing so little back to Teresa that she thought he was crazy – even if it was her son's land.

In 1962 they planted wheat and corn. Hardly was the seed in the ground than Maria told Giacomo that she was pregnant. The baby was due in May. With his father leaving, Maria pregnant, and Luigi at eight too young to be of much help, Giacomo knew that he could not carry on alone. If he did not make some other arrangement, the land would become a liability.

A week after Maria told him the news, he bicycled in the evening to Francesco Lombardo's farm to pay him a visit. He explained the situation to Lombardo, how the land was not enough to support a family but too much for him to work by himself without the proper equipment. He knew that Lombardo was looking for more land for his growing herd; could they strike a bargain? Giacomo did not return until very late that night. He was tired but relieved. It seemed that Lombardo had been waiting for Giacomo to come his way for some time. He would pay him fifty thousand lire a hectare as rent for at least three years. Giacomo knew that he could not do any better. Even after he paid the mortgage, taxes, and fees from the one hundred fifty thousand lire, he would still have almost a hundred thousand lire left over. It made him wonder why he had struggled so hard for so little for the past three years. He felt a heavy weight lifted from his shoulders. The land would be in good hands, even improved, under Lombardo's care. Most important, he would not have to sell it.

XII

With her fourth baby on the way, Maria was determined to have running water in the house. With each advancing year and with each additional child the need for water mounted. She had to make two or three trips every day to the fountain. She enjoyed the chance to gossip, but she got ample opportunity at the public wash, where she spent an entire day once a week. It was not only for her family that she wanted the water, but for Teresa and Luigi as well. It was the extra trip she had to make for Teresa that she found especially onerous.

In January of 1963, Luigi applied for permission from the town to run a pipe from the main to his house, with an extension to Giacomo's apartment. The request was delayed in the engineer's office for almost two months. Because so many families were applying for requests for water. In March Giacomo and Luigi removed the cobblestones, dug a trench, and laid the pipe. The total cost of thirty thousand lire was divided equally between them. The first time Maria turned on the faucet in the kitchen sink, the water gushed out and sprayed her. Giacomo laughed as she wiped herself off. "No matter," she said, "I only have to think of all those years I sacrificed myself carrying water. Now I can just stand here and the water carries itself. What a miracle."

Giacomo, seeing how pleased Maria was with the running water, told her that there was something he wanted to have, too. When she asked what it was, he replied, "A TV." Maria was scandalized. "Who do you think we are, rich people? We are barely able to make ends meet as it is, and you want to get a thing like that – something totally unnecessary and frivolous. What's the matter with the radio – isn't that good enough?" Giacomo replied that that was just the point. When he had suggested buying the radio eight years ago, Maria had said that it was an extravagance that they couldn't afford. It had turned out all right. Getting a TV would be the same thing, he assured her. Besides, little Teresa liked to watch and was always running off to a neighbor's to find one.

It was true that Teresa had become a devoted television viewer. When Teresa was four, Maria sent her to the Asilo. She hated it. It seemed as if the nuns did nothing but scold. Her one consolation was watching television when she came home. The lady who delivered the mail had a set and charged each child ten lire to sit in front of it. Teresa was always asking her mother for another ten lire. She would sit for hours in front of the TV, until Maria had to send word for her to come home at once. Maria thought that at least Teresa must be learning something for all the time she watched – proper Italian for one thing. The announcers all sounded alike, and not one of them spoke dialect.

One day the lady who delivered the mail said that she didn't want the children coming to her house anymore, even if they paid twenty lire. They made too much confusion. Teresa was desolate and cried bitterly. It was then that Maria agreed that they should buy a TV. But when she found out the price, two hundred sixty thousand lire, she was scandalized again. Even their renovation costs had not come to half that amount. Giacomo pointed out that it wouldn't be as difficult as it seemed, for they would need to pay only fifteen thousand lire to take it home, and then seven thousand lire every month for three years. But it worried Maria that they would be in debt for such a long time. It wasn't like running up an account at the store, where Cervino or Morelli knew you to be honest and hardworking. The big companies that sold radios and televisions and motorbikes didn't care. They made everyone feel like criminals. Maria realized as she gave her consent to buy the set how easy it had become to buy things on the installment plan – first her furniture, then the radio, and now the television set.

It proved to be an immediate success. Giacomo placed it on the cupboard shelf in the kitchen. On Teresa's return from the Asilo she would be joined by her friend and neighbor, Gian Piero. They would watch until he was called home. When Giacomo came home he would take his seat at the table and watch the news while Maria prepared the evening meal. It seemed strange to be in Valmonte, where one had always been, and see pictures of people in Milan or Palermo, or even London, Paris, or New York, where no one had ever been. You could see Pope John, fat and genial; President Kennedy, tall and handsome; Jackie Kennedy smiling; and Mariano Rumor and Amintore Fanfani talking out of the sides of their mouths. At night an American movie was shown. It seemed that in America everyone owned an automobile and a refrigerator and talked on the telephone.

XIII

Giacomo's work with the provincial agricultural cooperative came to an end as the time for Maria's fourth birth approached in the spring of 1963. It was as if a cruel fate watched over him. The gnawing began in his stomach again. It was always worse in the spring. He went back to searching for odd jobs. If only he could find a permanent job of any kind, anywhere. His sister-in-law, Caterina, was lucky. She had been hired by the Accord plant in the country, where they made transistors. She wore a white smock and sat at a table inserting different-colored wires into a tiny board. But Accord didn't want to hire men and pay them more. Giacomo had dreams of being a concierge in an apartment building in Latina or Rome, where the family would be given free quarters to live in and tips from the tenants at Christmas and Easter. That dream always came up against the hard fact that without a recommendation, Giacomo didn't stand a chance. He resigned himself to making out the best he could.

Since the end of March Maria had been going to the maternity clinic for consultation. The examining doctor found her healthy but advised her to have the baby in the hospital in Latina. It was safer. If anything went wrong, as it had with her second birth, there would be someone right there to help. Maria was aware that more and more women were having their babies in the hospital, even if there wasn't anything wrong with them. In fact, it was being said that only people with old-fashioned ideas were staying at home to give birth. Maria was undecided. She did not like hospitals. The doctors and nurses made you feel like dirt. But then, there was the memory of her last two births, the fear that no one would be there in time to help. She wavered back and forth until she heard that the midwife had become seriously ill. That decided the case: She would go to the hospital. The doctor told her that she would be there for nine days, two before the birth and a week after it. "Why so long? Why do you have to be away all that time?" demanded Giacomo when she told him. "Because that is the way they do things in hospitals. Don't worry, it will be better this way. You won't have to go running around in all that confusion for the midwife or the doctor." Giacomo felt more reconciled once it had been arranged that his mother and sister-in-law would do the cooking in Maria's absence.

On May 26 Maria packed her bag. Teresa and Bruno hugged her hard around her neck for a long time. Luigi, smirking, said, "Goodbye, Mama, bring us back a beautiful baby this time, not like the last one, okay?" Teresa, bursting into tears, kicked her big brother as hard as she could. Giacomo, laughing, followed Maria to the door.

Maria's fourth baby, her second daughter, was born on the twenty-eighth. All went well enough. Maria was pleased, two boys and two girls seemed the right mixture. Giacomo was at her bed when they wheeled her back into the ward. It had been easier and less terrifying than she had thought. Giacomo had never looked as good as he did at that moment standing there. He kissed her on the cheek and held her hand as she dozed off. When she woke up she began talking about names. She had always liked the name Caterina and had prayed to Santa Caterina from time to time. She also liked double names like Anna Maria, but one Maria in the family was enough. Finally, looking hard at Giacomo, she said that she wanted the other name to be Rita, because of her devotion to Santa Rita. Giacomo shrugged and said that Caterina Rita was all right with him as long as they called her Caterina. So it was decided.

Maria found that once the birth itself was over, she enjoyed the hospital. She was not accustomed to lying in bed and having things brought to her, and it made her uneasy. But it was a relief not to worry about the children and Giacomo, as she would have done had she been at home. Giulia came down once by bus the day after Caterina was born. She brought food with her, for everyone knew that hospital food didn't give you any nourishment. She carried the chicken broth in a bottle. But Maria didn't have to worry about her milk. It came in good and strong, as it had with Teresa.

On the last day Giacomo came to bring Maria home on the bus. The children were waiting in the piazza. Teresa jumped up and down and she wanted to hold the baby right away. Bruno commented that it was too small. She should have waited, he told his mother, until it was bigger. Luigi said Bruno was a fool – all babies were small – but she certainly was ugly. Maria felt proud walking home with the baby in her arms, Luigi running ahead, Bruno holding her hand, and Teresa her skirt. It made her think of the day so many years ago when her mother's family arrived in Valmonte: She ran along holding her mother's skirt as they walked from the station to Titalo, and Pasquale was cradled in her mother's arm.

That night it took the children a long time to go to sleep. When the baby cried they woke up and hung on the end of the bed to watch her nurse and then fall asleep between their mother and father. Giacomo ordered them back to their beds, and when they had drifted off, Giacomo and Maria talked for a while before going to sleep. It was time, they agreed, to stop having children.

Maria had sensed that Marina was offended when she had not been asked to be Teresa's godmother. Maria had tried to explain to her that she had accepted Anna Carbone's offer only because she did not want to impose on Marina too many times. Marina replied that she would stop feeling put out if Maria promised to ask her next time. Maria agreed; but when it came time to ask Marina she had to refuse, for her sister-in-law had just died. Time was running short. Maria hastened to Anna Frusini to ask if she could impose upon her and Enrico again. "No matter, no matter," she said. "I would be pleased to be godmother to your baby. If you ask me what I would like to name my goddaughter, I will suggest to you the following: Cinzia, Caterina, and Antonietta. Now, which do you like the best?" Maria thought herself fortunate, for she did not have to be embarrassed for having already decided. She told Anna that while she agreed that Cinzia was a beautiful name, she knew that in Valmonte they would shorten it to Cinci, an ugly name. As for Antonietta, she already had a niece by that name. She liked Caterina the best, she said, and because the baby was born so near the name day of Santa Caterina, she would like to have her christened Caterina Rita, even though it was a little awkward.

Caterina was baptized on the last Sunday in June. It was already hot when the company gathered after the ceremony in Santa Maria. Giacomo opened the kitchen door so that a little air would circulate. There were so many in the small room – the godmother and godfather, Don Giuseppe and his mother, Giulia and Giovanni, Teresa and Luigi, Maria and Giacomo, and the three children. Maria was on her feet cooking and passing. The baby was handed about. Everyone complimented Maria on the baby's dress. Maria smiled and said it was the same dress that she had made in 1954. All four of her children had been baptized in it. She remembered that the white tulle had cost two thousand lire and that the ribbon came to five hundred lire. "Now you couldn't touch a dress like that for less than fifteen thousand lire," she exclaimed. "At *least* fifteen thousand lire," echoed the women. And everyone wondered why it was that the rest of the world was getting rich while they remained poor.

When the coffee was served, Maria sat down and nursed the baby. She was tired but satisfied. She looked around the room. All was the way she would have it: a husband, four children, a roof over their head.

Of course there was a lot to worry about, for Giacomo wasn't working and there were days when there was barely enough to put on the table. Still, there were others who were worse off than they. She was pleased, too, when Anna gave her a gold medallion on a chain for Caterina.

XIV

During the hot summer months the air stood still. Only late at night would a little breeze stir in the bedroom, where all six slept. During the day there was barely enough room to move about in the small kitchen, with the children running in and out and Caterina crying with colic. When the confusion became more than Giacomo could stand, he would bang the table with his fist and yell for silence. The first to make a noise after that got the back of his hand. Giacomo did not hold back on his blows. Screams and tears would result; Maria would intervene by trying to distract Giacomo. She knew better than to reprimand him, for a father was right to discipline his children. According to him, it was Maria's fault that the children were so unruly, so disrespectful. She was too soft. Maria knew that that was not true. She was after them all day, yelling, cajoling, threatening. But it was true she did not hit as hard as he did.

XV

By the end of the summer, Maria could hardly wait for school to start on October 1. Luigi had been admitted to the fourth grade. She was proud of him, even though he did not apply himself the way her brother Salvatore always had. Luigi at the age of nine could now read and write better than either of his parents could, but then Maria had never finished third grade. Bruno had been promoted to second grade. He liked school. Maria never heard from Bruno's teacher that he had been a problem, which was a relief, for she heard often enough from Luigi's. Teresa was dreading returning for her second year at the Asilo. For one thing, she did not want to leave her mother, especially with the baby sister in the house. And for another, the nuns would never listen to her when she said that she did not want to eat a certain thing put before her at lunch, or play a certain game in the courtyard. All the rest of the girls would crowd around the sisters while they told stories of saints, but Teresa would go off by herself to play in the corner. Yet at home she was not at all a loner. Indeed, she talked so much and so fast that her father often yelled at her to stop, for it got on his nerves. Other times, when he felt more playful, he would mimic her talk, which he likened to a machine gun.

XVI

During the summer and fall Giacomo worked in the sugar beet refinery, where the pay was always good. He was on the night shift, which meant he came home at eight in the morning and went directly to bed. It was in those days that Giacomo began to talk about buying a motorbike. It was a long way to the refinery on his bike, he explained to Maria, and he was not getting any younger. He knew more and more men like himself who were buying either a Lambretta or a Vespa. Besides, he wanted to have one before the cold rains of winter set in – when it was most miserable on a bike. Maria pointed out that you could get just as wet, if not wetter, on a motorbike. "But you get wherever you are going quicker," was Giacomo's reply. Maria could see that it would be the same as with the radio and the TV. Giacomo had his mind made up. It was best not to argue and just pray that everything worked out.

In the middle of October, Giacomo bought a Vespa in Latina Scalo for two hundred fifty thousand lire – fifteen thousand down and the remainder spread out as payments for three years. There was still money owed on the TV set. It made Giacomo nervous to sign the contract, but he felt convinced that he could manage. Besides, the motorbike was something he wanted even more than he had the TV. Giacomo felt like a new man when he sped off from the dealer. He headed for the Via Appia and then let it out to the limit for the breaking-in period. The wind rushed through his hair. He raced by the bicyclists as if they were standing still. Now he could drive right up to the village and gun it through the gate and the narrow streets to his house. A machine like that was good for a man. Someday he would get a car. He gave his bicycle to Luigi. He never rode it again.

XVII

The winter of 1964 seemed as if it would never end. Between the rain and the wind, the house was always cold and damp. All the children had colds that never went away, just as they had had every other winter. In January Bruno contracted bronchial pneumonia. His temperature shot up to 104 degrees. For days he was in bed and so weak that he lost almost a month of school. Maria was at her wit's end. In February Teresa came down with severe influenza. When the doctor finally came, he prescribed an antibiotic but said that he did not know if it would do any good. Then, after looking about, he said to Maria, "Signora, you will have to get out of here. This is no place to bring up children. As long as you stay, they are going to be sick. You will be

lucky if one or more of them don't come down with rheumatic fever."
Maria felt her face go red with anger and shame, as if she was to blame
for their illness. But she marked the doctor's words well. That evening
when Giacomo came home, she related what he had said. By the time
they had gone to bed, they were beginning to talk about the possibility
of building a house on the land. It was a dream that they had always
shared, but it was one to be fulfilled later, when somehow times had
gotten better. It was clear that things were always going to be the same
for Giacomo and Maria unless they took matters into their own hands.
Yes, they would build themselves a house on the land.

8

The house of Giacomo

I

Once Giacomo and Maria had allowed the idea of building a house to enter their imagination they could think of nothing else. Their last words at night and their first on waking in the morning were about its construction. But the thought of the cost filled them with apprehension.

Giacomo knew that he could build. For the places where he was apt to have trouble – the window frames, for instance, and the metal supports for the roof – he would call on Salvatore. But the lack of funds plagued them at every turn. For years in order to save a lira here and a lira there Maria had cut every corner, bargained with scrupulous intensity, saved every piece of string, darned every sock numerous times. Managing to put a little aside every month, the savings had grown to two hundred thousand lire by January of 1964. It seemed, until the moment they decided to build, like an astronomical sum. The cost of the materials would, however, come to ten times that amount. Over and over again the thought and talk of money brought them back to one chilling conclusion: Money was in the land, and all they had to do was sell some, enough to buy the materials. But they needed every square meter of the three hectares. They were both convinced that if they moved to the land they could live from it, between raising animals and Giacomo working from time to time to maintain the health insurance. They could not afford to sell any of it. Now that they had made up their minds to leave the village they felt despairing, helpless.

A ray of light came from an unexpected source. Giacomo had spoken several times to Mario Lungo, owner of the lot immediately to the east. He had told Lungo of his hopes of building a house if only he could find the money for materials. Giacomo admired Lungo and

132

valued his advice. He had a finger in many pies, but Giacomo never suspected that he might have the answer to his problems. Lungo told him to go to the town hall immediately and speak to Romolo Farnese, the town engineer. Lungo knew for a fact that Farnese was applying for funds from the government to subsidize the construction of farm dwellings in the territory of Valmonte. A farm dwelling was exactly what Giacomo wanted to build. If Lungo was right, Farnese might be the answer. Giacomo knew the Farnese family by name – everyone in Valmonte did.

The Farneses were landowners. Giacomo was reluctant to go, for the rich and powerful never do anything for anyone but for themselves and their friends. Giacomo knew Farnese by sight; he was convinced that Farnese did not know him. That night he told Maria about his conversation with Lungo. For a long time Giacomo sat at the kitchen table while Maria insisted that Giacomo should go to Farnese, that he would not turn him away, that it was not like going to his house with hat in hand to ask a favor, for Farnese was a town officer. He would have to be civil to Giacomo. Giacomo said very little that evening, but the next morning he put on his suit and headed for the town hall.

Giacomo was kept waiting for a half hour. He had just given himself five more minutes when the door opened. Farnese smiled, held out his hand, and led Giacomo into his office. After Farnese offered Giacomo an American Marlboro and invited him to sit in a leather armchair, Giacomo began to speak of his plans. Farnese listened attentively. When Giacomo finished, Farnese replied that he had come to the proper place. Lungo was right, he was applying to the Cassa per il Mezzogiorno for funds to subsidize the construction of farmhouses in the countryside of Valmonte. The government, he explained, wished to encourage small landowners like Giacomo to settle on the land. All that was required was a plan of a house. Since he was helping several other people with theirs, he would be happy to help Giacomo. The house must be simple, one for country people, not a villa. There had to be a stable, as a guarantee that they would work the land, not just reside in the country. The more Farnese talked, the more excited Giacomo became. The engineer was describing Giacomo's own dream. Yes, he would talk to his wife. Together they would make a plan and he would soon bring it back. He had never felt as grateful to anyone as he did to Farnese at that moment, most especially for the tone of his voice, which made Giacomo feel the vision would come true.

That night Giacomo and Maria sat at the kitchen table until two in the morning drawing different plans. At first Maria could not get beyond the idea that what she wanted was a larger kitchen, a larger bedroom for the six of them. Only at Giacomo's insistence did she imagine two bedrooms and a living room. He hastily began to sketch a plan, a square dissected by a hall at the end of which would be a bathroom with a bathtub, toilet, bidet, and sink. No member of the family had ever taken a bath in a porcelain tub – washing was done in the kitchen sink. On the left of the hall would be first the kitchen, and then the bedroom. On the right would be the bedroom for Luigi and Bruno and then the living room, where Teresa and Caterina would sleep. As Giacomo sketched the lines on the paper, Maria felt as if she were in a dream. It must be a game they were playing – a living room, a bathroom with a proper tub! She looked around the kitchen that they had worked so hard to create and it hardly seemed possible that they might actually leave this dark place, which she had come to believe destiny had allotted to her forever.

Two days later Giacomo returned to see Farnese with his plan. He explained how he and Maria wanted to have two bedrooms, for the children were growing. Farnese nodded, saying that it was not right for children to sleep in the same room with their parents as they had in the old days; parents needed privacy just as much as children do. Then he drew a sketch of the design of the basic rural home that he was submitting to the agency.

It was almost identical to what Giacomo showed him except that it included a stable in the back, as well as a storeroom for wine and hams and corn for the fowl. The construction would be of *tufo* blocks, with only the doors and windows made of wood. A composition stone looking like marble would provide the floor covering. The flat roof would be supported by iron girders. In that way, if Giacomo ever wanted to add a story or two to make a home for his married children, he could easily do so. The basic virtue of the design, Farnese pointed out, was its simplicity. Giacomo could do practically all of it himself. The costs would be limited to materials. As far as he could tell, they would amount to 2,500,000. Of that, thirty percent – 750,000 – would be given outright by the government, if all went well with the application. The remainder, 1,750,000, would have to be provided by Giacomo himself. Giacomo's confidence that Farnese's support had instilled began to ebb. It diminished even more when Farnese went on to explain that the fund would not allocate the thirty percent of costs until the building was finished and approved by them. Giacomo felt his face flush with anger. For a moment he could hardly speak, even though his thoughts were pounding inside his head. Why did those who command make it so difficult for the poor to succeed? He felt like walking out of the room but he knew too that the rules were not of Farnese's making, even though he was of the class that made them. All his life he had protected himself as best he could against the machinations of the powerful. Now that he had moved to better himself, he suddenly felt naked and exposed. "Where can I ever find that money?" Giacomo found himself asking Farnese. When the engineer answered that he must, of course, go to a bank, Giacomo thought to himself how easy it was for him to say that, a Farnese, whose worth was known throughout the province. He could walk into the local branch of the Banco di Roma, say a word to the manager, and get any amount he wanted. But what would be the reception of a Giacomo Rossi?

There was nothing to do but wait. Farnese had made it clear to Giacomo that the commission would not move until the applicants, twenty in all, gave some assurance of being able to pay the initial costs of the materials. A trip to the bank was necessary. Giacomo dreaded it. Now he would be going hat in hand to ask for a favor. He kept putting it off. Maria drew upon all her persuasive skills. She knew that if she pushed, he would draw into a corner and then lash out at her. In times like these, Giacomo's stomach pains would increase in intensity.

One morning he put on his best suit and without a word left the house. At the bank everything went as he had predicted it would. The doorman kept him waiting for an hour and a half outside the manager's office. When he was finally ushered in, the manager alternately looked at his watch and shuffled through papers on his desk while Giacomo explained the purpose of his visit. When he was through the manager looked up as if noticing him for the first time and asked, "And so, Rossi, what do you have to offer as collateral?" What indeed did he have except for the land? Giacomo hated to even mention it, for fear that doing so would lead to his signing it away. But he need not have worried, for the manager with a wave of his hand dismissed the idea before it was even proposed. "Those three hectares do not, in fact, belong to you," he said, with due deliberation, "and they will not until you have finished paying the mortgage. There are too many liens on that property to allow us to use it as collateral." It had happened just as he had expected it would. Giacomo felt there was no way out. "Well, what do you expect me to do?" he asked, his voice heavy with despair. "It is quite simple," the manager said, "you merely have to find someone who will guarantee the loan, someone who will stand behind you, vouch for your good character and stand ready to pay the loan if you should default." Giacomo almost burst out with what he was thinking: "But I don't have a patron. That is the trouble, don't you see? That has always been the trouble. I have no one to recommend me." Instead, he looked down at the floor and heard the manager say, "If I can help, if I can help you in any way, Rossi, let me know." Giacomo rose from his chair and left.

On the way home he cursed the fate that had not provided him with a powerful "friend." He compared his lot unfavorably with that of his brother-in-law Salvatore, who was now a construction foreman under the protective wing of his boss, Doctor Miore. It was not until Giacomo got opposite the land of Mario Lungo that he suddenly thought that Mario was the only person who might help; he must talk to him, at least.

A week went by before Giacomo could see Lungo, who had gone to Naples to visit his ailing brother. During that week Giacomo hardly allowed himself to think that Lungo could be his backer. After all, he was just a worker, a peasant like himself; but he knew that was not quite true either. Lungo was a man of some substance, a man of reputation. People looked up to him.

The encounter with Lungo filled Giacomo with hope again. Hardly had Giacomo finished telling of his visit to the bank than Lungo told him not to worry, he would guarantee the loan for him. He had already had dealings with the bank and knew the manager – he would even accompany him there. It would make a difference, he said. He was right. This time the manager was so much more cordial when he saw Giacomo being ushered in with Lungo that Giacomo wondered if he was the same man. After greeting Mario warmly, he said that there would be no problem in making available a loan of two million lire to his friend Rossi at a rate of six percent, a most favorable rate, he added. He would have the papers drawn up shortly, if they would be so kind as to wait in the anteroom. When they were called back for the signing, Giacomo's hand trembled so that he could hardly write. The manager and Lungo laughed, but at that moment Giacomo didn't care – he knew that he was going to have a house! With a copy of the note tucked in his coat pocket, he took Lungo to the bar next to the bank for a drink. Giacomo felt as if he were walking on air. One drink turned to two, then three. It was very late when he returned home. Maria had gone to sleep with her head on the kitchen table. Banging the table as hard as he could with his fist, Giacomo roared with laughter as she woke with a start and muffled scream.

II

In mid-July of 1965 approval for the project came from Rome. Immediately Giacomo began buying supplies from Iacinello in Latina, using first the bank loan and then the two hundred thousand that Maria had managed to set aside. Three truckloads were necessary to deposit the *tufo* blocks for the walls, the floor tiling, and the girding for the roof. Giacomo began building just after the holiday of *ferragosto* had passed. As in past summers, he was taken on at the sugar beet refinery for the harvest. When he had first worked there it had been backbreaking, shoveling the beets onto the conveyor belt, but now he had the job of operating the belt. It was tedious and he had the night shift, so he had to fight sleep, but the pay was good. As soon as he had come home and caught six hours of sleep, he would jump on his Vespa and speed to the house site. On some days his father would come to help. On Sundays his brother-in-law Salvatore gave a hand. From time to time, Farnese would drop by to see how it was going. Once the foundation was laid, the walls went up quickly. *Tufo* blocks are easy to lay, and Giacomo was in his element mixing and applying the mortar. The flooring went more slowly. It was with the roofing that Giacomo had the most difficulty. The iron support beams had to be set in sleeves of reinforced concrete laid on top of the *tufo* wall. A carpenter was called in to make the molds for the cement. Salvatore helped with the setting of the iron reinforcement rods. He even showed Giacomo ways in which Farnese's plan could be improved upon. Giacomo wanted to get the roof on before the winter rains began in November. It was a great relief when the last coat of tar was brushed on by the middle of the month. Much remained to be done – the finishing, to say nothing of the wiring and the plumbing. By the beginning of December all the money had been spent, and there were still the doors, windows, pipes, drains, and electrical fixtures to buy. There was nothing to do but sign notes for them. The mounting debt was terrifying. More than once Giacomo would awaken in the night with a start. Before long Maria would awaken, too, to lay in silence, her hand clasped in his.

Sometimes Maria would leave Caterina with Teresa in order to come down on the bicycle to help. Giacomo did not like to work alone. He felt the task went quicker when someone else was with him. Maria helped haul the buckets of cement with rope and pulley. When she was through, she walked about inside thinking how it would be like when it was finished. Over and over she imagined what the bedroom would be like, with the armoire against one wall and their bed alone against the other. The living room would be bare except for Teresa and Caterina's bed, but she knew that someday they would have furniture for it, even if they had to sign more notes. It was in the kitchen, though, that her imagination lingered the longest. It was obvious that the sink would have to go in the northwest corner, because of the water. The single window would be at her shoulder as she stood at the sink washing dishes. But Giacomo explained to her that there could not be a window in the retaining wall, along which the sink and stove would be placed. No matter, thought Maria; as far as she was concerned, their new house was perfect.

III

One day shortly after Christmas when the children were still out of school, Maria brought them all down to see the house. Luigi had been down before on his bike and had once brought Bruno on the handlebars, but neither Teresa nor Caterina had been there. Maria asked the bus driver to let them off at the beginning of Via Casa Grande. From there they walked to the land, Maria carrying Caterina most of the way in her arms. When they passed the first bend in the road, she could see the outlines of the house across the fields, for there was nothing to obstruct the view. The only other house on the road was the one being completed by Mario Lungo on the lot next to theirs. As soon as the children could make out their father working on the roof, Luigi and Bruno ran ahead, with Teresa following behind as fast as her short legs would carry her. It was a clear, cold day, and the road was dry. But Maria knew how wet and muddy the road could become after a hard rain. Suddenly she realized that getting the children to school in the winter would be a problem. It was so easy in the village, walking a short distance over cobblestones. Now they would need to walk or cycle the almost two kilometers of the dirt Via Casa Grande until they came to the hardtop. From there it was another two kilometers to school.

When she arrived at the house Maria found the children playing down by the canal, throwing in sticks and racing them as the strong current carried them toward the sea. She had been delighted that the house site was so near the canal, for she knew how convenient it would be for her to wash clothes there, the nearest public wash being four kilometers away. But suddenly she was frightened to see the children there, for neither she nor Giacomo knew how to swim. If one of them fell in, who would help? By the time help came from the Lombardo farm or the Lungo house it would be too late. And probably none of them swam, either.

As she stood there, Maria could make out only three houses: one of the original farmhouses built across the canal in the 1930s during the reclamation of the marshes, and the Lombardo and Lungo houses. Lungo was a widower. The only woman Maria's age in the immediate vicinity was Lombardo's wife. Maria had met her once, but she realized that she didn't even know her name. All her adult life Maria had lived with neighbors in calling distance. She merely had to go to the front door to see someone she knew. Many was the time she had yearned to be on the other side of the world from her mother-in-law, yet it was also comforting to have her so close, to say nothing of her own mother, just on the other side of the piazza. For the first time in her life,

Maria thought, she might be lonely. She knew she was an outgoing person, more so than Giacomo. She loved to talk. One thing was clear: Her life and Giacomo's life would become more closely intertwined. She thought of Giacomo. He was content now working on the house, but what would happen when it was finished and he had no job?

In the village he could go to the bar for a glass and a game of cards with his friends. But here, the nearest bar was five kilometers away. The more she thought, the more problems she could foresee, but there was no turning back now. It was their new destiny. They would have to make it work. She was confident of herself. In that way she was like her mother, she thought. Her parents had made the sacrifice for them in leaving the village of their birth and bringing their family to Valmonte. Now she would make a change for the good of their children. She knew she could count on Giacomo, too. They had already been through hard times together. She looked up. Giacomo was coming toward her from the house. She trembled all over as he came toward her smiling. He was building them a palace.

IV

The finishing touches were made on the house by late March of 1966. All that remained was to let it dry out through the spring. The walls needed several weeks of sun to thoroughly absorb the plaster. Maria agreed to having everything painted white as long as there was some color somewhere. She asked that the front be pink, but as Giacomo finished, she was not sure that she had picked the right color. Nonetheless she was content.

When Giacomo put down his brush he knew that there would always be other things to do here and there, but he was satisfied that he had, at least, built his own house. Next to taking Maria as his wife, it was the most important thing he had ever done. They would never have to live in rented rooms again or be dependent upon his parents to provide a roof over their heads. For so long he had felt that he didn't belong anywhere. Now, once they moved here from the village, he would never want to go anywhere again. Here in this place he would live until he died. His children and their children could go on living there after him. Now he had something that neither Salvatore nor his father or brother had, a house on a piece of land. Giacomo knew this to be the turning point. Hard times lay ahead. There was the great mountain of debt to struggle with. He would continue to be unemployed for much of the year in the future, as he had in the past. He was, after all, getting older. But he was determined that once the land and the house were paid for, this corner of the world would be his forever. His destiny had changed. Now he had a strong wall at his back. It would make it easier to face the world.

V

The move came in June, after school had finished. Maria carried all but the largest of their belongings on her head to the piazza, where they were loaded into the back of Tonino's truck. One trip was enough to bring all there was. Somehow neither the kitchen nor bedroom furniture looked quite the way Maria had expected it would when it was arranged. But she was satisfied. The other two rooms were bare except for the children's beds. The children were everywhere, but mostly in the bathroom. Everyone wanted to be the first to use the toilet and then the sink. Teresa wanted to know why there was not a seat for the toilet. She had seen a picture of one once with a seat. Her father said that toilet seats were for the *Signori* to rest their fat bottoms on but not for working people like themselves. Teresa replied that when she was all grown up she would have a seat on her toilet. It was a quiet supper that evening around the table in the new kitchen. Everyone was dead tired. When she had finished the dishes, Maria joined the rest of the family sitting on the front stoop. From where they sat they could see the village perched on its hill. It seemed so far away. They could just make out the castle, the wall around the town, and the outline of the houses. Luigi began wondering aloud what people up there were doing. Everyone joined in except for Caterina, who began to cry. She said, between sobs, that she was afraid of the wolves who would come and eat her up. Maria scolded her for being so silly and then said that it was time for everyone to go to bed. She assured Caterina that she would be safe sleeping with Teresa, and showed her how she was going to lock the front door. When she came to close the door of their own room, she realized that this was the first night in twelve years, since the birth of Luigi, that she had slept alone in a room with Giacomo. It was hard to go to sleep. She and Giacomo tossed and turned in their bed. There were so many strange new noises – dogs baying, frogs croaking in the canal. Shortly their door burst open. Caterina stood there sobbing. She was too frightened to sleep. She crawled into bed with her mother and father for the rest of the night.

9

Life in the country

I

Once the house was finished, waiting for the inspection by the Cassa per il Mezzogiorno seemed endless. Each day Giacomo expected a representative. Payments on the bank loan and the notes were coming due. Finally, in the middle of July, a message from Farnese announced that an inspector would be by the following day. The white square of a house glistened in the late afternoon sun when the inspector arrived. Giacomo was thankful that Farnese accompanied him. Farnese, after introducing the inspector to Giacomo and Maria, took him by the arm and, talking volubly, led him through the house. The inspector expressed approval at the simplicity of the design, the plainness of the interior. He gave a little speech in the hall about how too many Italians, even country people, had gotten too far away from the basic virtues of nature. "A house like this, especially when built by the owner himself, would do much, in its own way, to reinvigorate national morality." It was the stable, though, that provoked most praise. He gave another little address there, stating, "It was Mussolini himself who had stressed in his powerful speeches, delivered in these very reclaimed Pontine Marshes, the importance of farm animals in creating a strong peasant class." Giacomo was relieved when they finally departed and especially by Farnese's nod of approval as he got in the car.

Two weeks later a special delivery letter came announcing the arrival of a postal order check for Giacomo at the post office. He immediately took the check to the bank. There they told him that the next installment on the loan was due on December 20. It was made clear to him that if he forfeited payment he would be liable to lose the house.

Giacomo would have felt more hard pressed about the loan and the notes if it had not been for the fact that Salvatore had been able to find a job for him with the Miore construction firm, where he was a foreman. It seemed to Maria that God made his face to shine upon them in the person of Salvatore. She knew more about their financial condition than Giacomo did, for she handled the money. It was clear to her that they would not have made it without her brother's help. The job he got for Giacomo paid well – one hundred thousand lire a month, including small subsidies for each of the children. Still and all it would not be enough to keep up the payments on the loan and notes, as well as pay for food and other necessities.

More income was needed. The rent from Lombardo for the land paid the mortgage, taxes, and cooperative fee. The money would have to come from the stable. What could they raise that would bring in the most cash in the shortest time? Giacomo had had little or no experience with animals. Maria had raised rabbits and hens. Her father had always kept pigs. But almost everyone had rabbits, hens, and pigs. There was little money to be made with them. The answer clearly was veal. Unlike cattle, heifers should be quite easy to care for and there was always a demand for veal. Maria remembered that Farnese had mentioned the advisability of raising heifers. He had said that is what he would do if he were in her shoes. Maria asked Giacomo to call on him in his office the next time he went to the village for a haircut on his day off, to find out more about it. Farnese was emphatic with Giacomo. "If you don't start raising veal, you have no chance of making the loan payment. I will start you off with two from my farm, twenty-five thousand apiece, and you can pay me back a little at a time." Giacomo knew why Farnese was being helpful. He had a stake in proving that people like Giacomo could make a living off the land, even three hectares. He was grateful to get the heifers at such a good price. The following day one of Farnese's farm trucks came by with the young animals. Maria led them to the stall, all clean and white from its recent whitewashing, and locked them in. Then she walked down the road to the Lombardo farm. She knew that a supply of milk for the heifers was critical, and she did not have a cow. But she stopped before anyone could see her and hurried home to wrap some of her mother's olives in a newspaper. She did not want to make a bad impression right at the beginning. Angela Lombardo met her at the door and made Maria feel as if she had been expected. She felt warmed by the welcome. She left with a pail of milk to start, advice on how to get the heifers drinking by sucking on her finger, and the assurance of more milk at a reasonable price.

Once Maria felt that she had the knack of feeding the heifers, she added chickens and then rabbits. She liked taking care of animals. She realized that it was giving them food that was so satisfying, watching them grow, just as it was with her family. Not that she did not get tired and angry, but there was a feeling of well-being that came from preparing something for other mouths to eat. When she thought about it, she knew that it was because it made her feel important. She could not imagine feeling worthwhile just sitting and letting someone else provide for you. But then she never had. She was like her mother, always helping others. Here in the country it seemed that she was even busier than she had been in the village. And there she had never sat down for a moment. If she had once worried about being lonely in the country, she now laughed at such a thought. There just was not time. She was up every morning at five thirty at the latest, and she would not let herself sleep beyond six thirty even on Sunday.

As November gave way to December, Maria's worries about the weight of the heifers increased. The payment on the loan was due on the twentieth. Every evening when Giacomo came home, they would stand in the stall staring at the two beasts. It was clear that they had grown a great deal, but had they grown enough? Neither Maria nor Giacomo was familiar with the market. Maria did know that she wanted a hundred thousand lire apiece, but she did not know the dealer, or how amenable he was. She had spoken to Lombardo and told him that when the dealer came to them before Christmas, he should drop by Giacomo's too. In the last few days Maria became even more assiduous in her feeding. Then on December 19 the truck backed into the driveway. Maria felt weak in her knees as the driver strode toward the stable. She could see that he liked what he saw, but she also saw that he was not one to waste time bargaining. "I will give you seventy apiece and not one lira more. If you don't want to take my offer, I will leave right away. I have other veal to pick up." Maria froze. She had always been able to hold her own when it came to dickering. But now the stakes were too great, and before she knew, she heard herself saying, "All right." It was done. She clutched the 140,000 lire in her hand. Never had she earned so much money. A great surge of pride overwhelmed her. She sat down. She felt like crying. But it was not enough. They still needed another 60,000 to meet the loan payment of 200,000. She didn't know what she would tell Giacomo when he came home that night. When she heard his step, Maria turned away from the stove to see him standing at the door with a great smile stretched from one ear to the other. In his hand was a great wad of money. Miore had had such a good year that he awarded all his workers a Christmas bonus. Giacomo slapped down 100,000 lire on the table. It was as if a miracle had happened. Maria cried for the great joy of it all.

II

Maria had asked all the Tassoni family to the Christmas feast in the new house. Struggling with the heifers, she had hardly thought about them all coming. But now they had something to celebrate. She began to prepare by slitting the throats of four rabbits and four chickens. The day before she had made an ample amount of egg noodles. The small vineyard that Giacomo had planted the first year was now bearing. He had made wine and in October had filled a hundred liter bottles. It was good wine. You could drink as much as you wanted to; it wasn't like the kind you bought that made you drunk. He was proud, too, of the grappa he had made for the first time. Clear and strong, he knew it would taste good on such a cold day. And it was cold that Christmas. Maria started the wood stove in the kitchen early in the morning so that the house would be warm when everyone came.

Tonino was the first to arrive. He brought Giovanni and Giulia in the front seat of his truck. His wife, Emilia, and their two children rode in the back. Tonino and Emilia had been living with his mother and father in the old house in the village since they married in 1963. Tonino had made the living room and the small bedroom where Maria had slept into an apartment. Part of the space he had converted into a kitchen and a bathroom. It was crowded, but he did not have to pay rent. Giovanni and Giulia continued to live in their bedroom and the kitchen. Salvatore had partitioned off a corner of the kitchen and installed a toilet so that they did not have to use the old one outside now that they had become old. Giulia's left leg still bothered her, and it was increasingly difficult to climb stairs. With each advancing year, Giovanni's shoulders hunched over a little more. Yet he was fit for his age, except for occasional bouts of asthma. He still worked at odd jobs.

Neither Giovanni nor Giulia had seen the house before. Silently they stood at the doorway of each room, their eyes feasting on every detail. Their curiosity appeased, they came to the kitchen, kissing Maria and Giacomo each in turn. "In Stilo no one but the *Signori* had a house like this," exclaimed Giulia, "but now, thanks to God, even the poor, like ourselves, can live in comfort." "Not thanks to God," muttered Giacomo. "Thanks to *me*—God had nothing to do with it." Giovanni, smiling and nodding approval, sat down by the stove to warm himself and accepted a glass of Giacomo's grappa. After the first swallow, he raised his glass and said, "A toast to my daughter Maria, to her husband, Giacomo, to the four dear children. It warms an old man's heart to find his family in this beautiful place. We miss you in the village, but I am happy that you are making a new life here, just the way I brought you from Stilo to make a new life in Valmonte. God bless you."

At that moment, Salvatore appeared at the door, followed by his wife, Dorotea, and their three daughters. At the first sound of his new Fiat 850, Luigi and Bruno had dashed out the door to stare and later caress. It was the first car in the family; Tonino's truck did not count. A little later Michele arrived with his wife, Pasquetta, and their daughter, Anna. Maria had hoped that Concetta and Felice and their six children could have come down from Busto, near Monza, where they had moved upon leaving Piove di Sacco, as well as Pasquale, his wife Antonietta and their baby son, Pietro, from Gallarate, also near Monza, where he had set himself up as a tailor a few years before. But they sent word that they would all come down in August, when Felice, a night watchman at the Philips plant, had his vacation. Concetta could take two weeks from her duties as a porter at the factory enclosure where they lived, and Pasquale would close his shop. It would be better, for they would have more time to visit with Giulia and Giovanni. Felice could play cards with Giacomo, and Giulia could talk her heart out with Concetta. Concetta had always been her favorite. Giulia missed her. And then, too, Maria's first crop of tomatoes will have been harvested and she could give Concetta and Antonietta several bottles of tomato conserve.

It was a squeeze for all twenty to find a place around the table, but fit they did. Maria was on her feet most of the time, just as her mother had always been during meals, serving, picking up empty dishes, disparaging her food as she cajoled people into eating more. Maria knew that her mother's love for Concetta would always be deeper than for herself, but she realized as she stood there that this house, this kitchen, had become the new center of the family. Salvatore was older than Maria, and Giulia never ceased to extol the virtues of her hard-working son, but Dorotea was not like Maria. There was a lilt to Maria's eyes, voice, and gestures that made young and old feel welcome. Giacomo's house is where the family would gather. Maria would call them together. The torch had passed to her hands.

On this day Giacomo sat at the head of the table, with Luigi on one side and Bruno on the other. Usually he sat on the side, so that he could face Maria as she worked in the kitchen at the sink. These Calabrians were not his people. His mother, father, brother, wife, and nephew would come on New Year's Day. Eighteen years had passed since he had first met Maria. In that time he had become reconciled to these southerners. Indeed, he had forgiven his father- and mother-in-law for being so jealous, for having so little faith in him when he and Maria were engaged. He had felt like an enemy when he had called on her in their house. But now this was his house. They were welcome; they could no longer hurt him. He had never felt so expansive as he did then, looking about the table. He kept offering his wine until Salvatore told his father to stop drinking, for otherwise he would make a fool of himself. Giovanni replied that it was Christmas Day, he could do as he saw fit. Giacomo looked at his two sons. Perhaps someday, he allowed himself to think, he and they would build two more houses, one for each, right here.

III

It did not take the Rossi children long to feel at home. They missed their friends in the village but that first summer there were so many new things to do, places to explore, that they seemed hardly to notice. The canal was an endless source of pleasure. It never ceased to make Maria nervous to see them playing along its banks. For the most part she was successful in keeping Teresa away. Caterina went only when her mother washed clothes there. Giacomo kept saying that their children could not be protected forever. It was high time, he insisted, for them to learn to take care of themselves. Even more exciting were the places to discover on a bicycle. Luigi used Giacomo's old one; Tonino gave his to Bruno. They explored Temara, with its post office, store, and bar. Somewhat farther in the opposite direction was Latina Scalo, the railroad stop for the provincial capital. It seemed like a small city. Maria warned them over and over to be careful, not to get hurt; there was no extra money to pay for doctors or hospitals.

Teresa was seven when they made the move. She was still too young to be of much help to her mother, but Maria would always have her carry some part of the laundry across the road to the canal. When it was done, she would have her help spread the clothes, sheets, and towels on the grass and bushes. For the most part, though, it was Teresa's task to keep Caterina, who was three, from falling in.

As fall approached, Maria began to worry about getting the children to school in Latina Scalo, four kilometers away. In the village it had been so easy; even the four-year-olds could walk to the Asilo alone.

For the first week Maria rode Bruno and Teresa on her bike. Luigi followed behind on his own. Caterina was left with the Lombardos. When Maria felt certain that they knew the way and how to stop at the crossings, Maria instructed Luigi to take Teresa on his bike, and Bruno rode his own.

As far as the children were concerned, riding to Latina Scalo was the best part of going to school. When they reached the provincial road, they would be joined by others. Almost every day a race took place, either on the way to school or on the way home. Passengers like Teresa had to hang on tight to keep their seat. In the spring, they would stop to catch frogs in the ditches along the way. Hardly anyone ever caught one, but it was fun to watch them plop into the water, croaking in protest at the young intruders.

Luigi failed two courses in his last year of elementary school; he had to repeat the fifth grade in Latina Scalo. The first, second, third, and fourth grades had presented no problems, but in the spring of his last year, the teacher decided that he did not deserve to pass Italian and mathematics. Luigi was the first to admit that he had not worked hard. He liked playing with his friends better than studying. Still, it didn't seem fair to be punished in his last year for doing what he had always done.

The teacher insisted that making him repeat was for his own good. At first Luigi was so angry he wanted to leave school. By the end of the summer he had changed his mind. He would repeat the fifth, humiliating as it would be. Once promoted, he could go on to the middle school. No one in his father's or mother's family had done that. He would be the first Rossi, the first Tassoni, to attend the first year of middle school.

As Maria was about to enroll Luigi in middle school she was approached by a nephew of Mario Lungo, a young priest, Father Giorgio. He was looking for students to send to a new seminary that had recently been founded at Anguillara, near Rome. He spoke in glowing terms of the institution, stressing how new it was, how the pope had bestowed special blessings, how the teachers were the very best. Anyone who went there would receive a better education, he insisted, than at the state middle school. Besides, he pointed out, it would cost only four thousand lire a month, a saving when you considered how much it took to feed a growing boy. Maria found the Father's words convincing. Seminaries were well known for their educational excellence. It would be to their credit to have a son attend one, especially a seminary near Rome. Certainly Father Giorgio was right about the money. It would cost more than that to keep Luigi at home. Maria had heard that the Church was having difficulty finding young men who wanted to become priests; the situation must be worse than she realized. Father Giorgio finished his presentation by saying that the education at a seminary was intended for those who were to enter the priesthood. Of course, it would not be necessary for her son to have that noble desire at this time. The decision to embrace the Church would come after he had attended the seminary for a semester or two. As the young priest spoke, Maria was reminded of her own wish to become a nun, of her mother's despair. She was startled when Father Giorgio said that if Luigi became a priest, they would never have to sacrifice themselves for him again; he would be established for life. Of course, he added, he would not give them grandchildren, but . . . After a pause, Maria thanked the father for his suggestion, saying that she would need time to talk over everything he had said with her son and with her husband.

Maria was convinced that Luigi would scoff at the idea. Like his father, he detested going to church. He only made fun of priests. She would not have to worry about having grandchildren, she thought.

When she related the priest's proposal that evening to Luigi, she was quite taken by surprise to find that he was in favor of accepting. Everyone knew, he said, that boys like himself who went to seminary did better than those who went on to the middle school. He would learn more from priests, even if he did fool around. Seminaries were serious. As for becoming a priest himself, they did not have to worry. He would never do that. He would finish the three years and then tell the Father in charge he was not cut out to be a cleric. Don't worry, he added, he would give them grandchildren.

Once the decision had been made, Maria enjoyed telling people that Luigi would be attending the new seminary at Anguillara near Rome rather than the middle school in Latina Scalo. She and Luigi took a train, then a bus, to arrive there on the first of October, 1967. Some of the boys had already changed into the traditional black habit. Luigi told his mother that he would put his on later, after she had gone. Maria had never been separated from one of her children before. She began to cry, then turned away quickly, leaving him standing alone in the courtyard among the fine new buildings.

The first year Luigi applied himself more than he ever had before. He did well and got high grades. There were moments when he thought, almost despite himself, that he would become a priest. The Church would take care of him. His parents would not have to sacrifice themselves for him. His brother and sisters would give them grandchildren. In the second year, the rules and regulations began to plague him. He resented the obedience the priests expected of him. He wanted to keep to his original plan, however, and finish the three years. Besides, he enjoyed Latin. He liked showing off to his family when he was at home. It made him feel proud to converse in a different language with his friends at school. Yet the longer he stayed, the more irksome the strict life of the seminary became. He stopped going to mass. He started becoming insolent to the priests. They called him a troublemaker. One day he told a friend that he had decided not to come back the next year. Later he was sorry he had shared that thought, for the friend reported Luigi to the rector. When the rector called Luigi to his office, he told him that his relationships with the seminary had been severed. They had obviously made a mistake, he said, in accepting him, a troublemaker, into their midst. He must leave the premises at once.

By the time Luigi had arrived at home, his anger had worn off. In fact, he was elated to be free again. His mother was distraught. It was January, halfway through the school year. She was certain that there would be no place for him in the second year of the middle school. She made a large cake to take on her visit to the principal's office. It turned out that there was one opening left.

At first Luigi was embarrassed to be sitting in the same classroom with girls. It was not like the way it had been in the fifth grade. They were grown up; he hardly spoke. No one else, though, knew as much Latin as Luigi did. The teacher was so impressed that he had him help with the class. Before long Luigi was laughing and joking with his friends, getting into trouble, playing tricks on the teacher. At the end of the second year, he failed Italian. He was sent back in that subject not because he did not understand – in fact he was very capable – but because he did not apply himself. If it had not been for the fact that he had only one more year to go, he would have left school then and there. Instead, he took the remedial test in Italian in the fall and was promoted to the third class of the middle school. The final year was the best. When he concentrated he did well. He knew that if he only worked harder, he could go on. He enjoyed using his brain.

When he graduated in June of 1969 he was fifteen. At that age his father had been working at whatever he could find. If Luigi stopped his education he would be a common laborer like his father for the rest of his life. High school was out of the question. It was for the upper classes. Children of peasants and workers did not go to high school. They were needed at home, in the fields, in the factories. Besides, one of their kind would be made to feel too much out of place in high school. That summer Luigi worked in the fields during the day and at night joined the others around the kitchen table to discuss his future. Finally it was decided that he should go to the vocational school in Latina. More and more factories were being built. The need for technicians, mechanics, and electricians would be great. In the fall of 1969, Luigi enrolled in the two-year course in mechanics.

IV

Bruno started school two years after Luigi did. When they moved to the country, Bruno had already completed the third grade in the village. He entered the fourth in Latina Scalo. Although his grades were never very high, he did not have the troubled times in school his older brother had. Perhaps it was because he had become quieter and no longer like the "earthquake" he had been when younger – at least not until after school, when he would roughhouse with his friends. The part of schooling that Bruno enjoyed the most was reading. He liked books, especially adventure stories. Whenever Maria found her younger son reading it reminded her of her brother Salvatore. She remembered that he had read a book called *The Three Musketeers* four times. When Bruno was in elementary school, Maria wondered where his interest in reading might take him. He would surely follow Luigi to the middle school. Could he go beyond?

Bruno began middle school in 1968. Luigi was starting his second year at Anguillara. Bruno had missed his older brother when he had been away at the seminary. It made him feel secure to have him around; he was a person to count on if he got in trouble. Not that Bruno could not take care of himself. He was a good fist fighter. But Luigi had a way about him that won respect from other boys. Bruno was glad to see him when he returned home from the seminary in January; now they would be in the middle school together.

By the time Bruno turned twelve in 1969, he fell in love with the new American-style popular music. Turning the volume up high whenever it came on, he moved to the music the way he saw it done on TV. Names of songs and those who sung them became as important to him as soccer players and bicycle racers. Some of his friends were letting their hair grow long. He did not want to do that. Many of the "long-hairs" that he saw in Latina repelled him. But he did want a pair of blue jeans. Finally his mother relented. She gave him money to go to the American market in Latina, where secondhand clothes from the United States were sold. There he bought not only a pair of tight-fitting Levis, but a blue denim jacket to match. In his back pocket he kept a comb. Bruno gave a good deal of attention to his thick black hair.

Bruno graduated from the middle school in 1970. There was no place for him in high school, even if he did like books and history. What was needed was for Bruno to prepare himself for work. The time had come for him to contribute to the family in return for the years of sacrifice that his father and mother had made on his behalf. That summer it was Bruno who was the topic of conversation around the kitchen table in the evening; during the day he worked in the fields. It was decided that Bruno would enroll in the two-year chemical analysis course in the vocational school in Latina. There were rumors that an American company, Chemtech, was to locate a large pharmaceutical plant in Valmonte. They would need chemical analysts.

V

Teresa, like Luigi, had to repeat a grade when she began attending school in Latina Scalo; in her case, the first. She seemed to have started off well in the village school. The teacher was *simpatica*. She never punished Teresa. Instead she favored her with requests to help with this and that. Teresa felt honored to be selected out of the whole class. It was not that the teacher asked her to do the shopping, as her mother's teacher had, but rather to busy herself with little things during class time, such as removing the lint from the teacher's sweaters. By the middle of the year Teresa discovered that she could not follow the class while helping the teacher, too. Before long she was hopelessly behind. At the end of the year she was failed for general incompetence. The first grade would have to be repeated. Teresa was upset. She did not know what it was she was supposed to do to make a teacher happy. It seemed to Maria that schooling had not changed since her youth, despite all the talk about reforms.

When Teresa repeated the first grade, she was careful not to make the same mistake again, even if it meant offending the teacher. At first she was hesitant to turn aside the teacher's requests, but then she got bolder. She paid attention to the lessons and was promoted. The second and third years went well. Teresa began to enjoy school. She especially liked geography. Her difficulty lay with mathematics. Teresa felt that she never understood what the teacher wanted. When she asked for an explanation, the teacher was too busy to answer. Despite her low grades in math, she was promoted from one grade to the next. Unfortunately, the mathematics teacher in her first year at the middle school had a reputation of being a tyrant. Things went badly from the beginning. When called upon, Teresa felt so frightened that her mind froze over like ice. She couldn't even remember those few things she knew. She often came home in tears. Luigi told her to go to the principal. She was afraid to. But others were in trouble, too. One day ten of them decided to go and lodge a complaint.

The principal kindly asked them into his office. He said that he wanted to hear everything that was on their minds. Teresa, feeling emboldened, did most of the talking. The principal nodded appreciatively at all he heard. When Teresa was finished he said that he would do everything in his power to correct the situation. They must remember, however, he added, that whatever a teacher did was always for the students' best interests. The following day the teacher began the mathematics class by asking who among them had gone to see the principal to lodge a complaint. If she did not receive an answer right away, she would punish the whole class. Teresa felt as if a cold wind had blown through the classroom when each of the other nine girls pointed their finger at her. The teacher nodded gravely, telling them that she would give the matter serious thought. At the end of the year Teresa was sent back in mathematics.

If her troubles had been confined only to mathematics, her first year in the middle school would have been bearable. Unfortunately, Teresa had a severe teacher in literature as well. As the hour for literature approached, Teresa's heart pounded, her palms moistened. The teacher would begin by demanding to know who was prepared, who was not. Worse still, she would often point at Teresa, saying, "Rossi, stand up. Are you prepared or not?" Even before Teresa could make her mouth utter one word the teacher would snap, "Sit down, you get a two." At the end of the year Teresa was sent back in literature. To be promoted to the second year she would have to study mathematics and literature during the summer, taking exams in both in the fall. Teresa knew that she could not do it. It was not that she hated school. She enjoyed learning new things, especially geography and history. It seemed that to finish school was not her destiny. Remembering that her mother had not even completed the third grade made her feel better, but she would have liked to finish middle school, as her brothers had. A diploma was necessary to find a job that amounted to anything. That is what she wanted to do: have a job, earn money. Everywhere she was hearing that the Italian female did not have to be just a mother, a wife. But when she talked that way her father became angry. The woman's place was in the house. He had not allowed their mother to work. Where would they be, he demanded, if she had not stayed at home to be their mother? At that time, however, Giacomo was without a job. It was decided that Teresa would go to work for her cousin Michele in his upholstery shop.

VI

When it came time to send Caterina to the Asilo at the age of four, she had no desire to go. On numerous occasions Teresa had told her younger sister how much she would dislike it, how awful the nuns would be to her. It was necessary for Maria to half drag and half carry Caterina there the first day. She agreed to enter the door only if her mother promised to not make her stay for more than a week. When Saturday came the verdict was in: Caterina would not return, her mother could not make her go. Maria felt provoked by the stubborn determination of her younger daughter. It was both embarrassing and inconvenient to have her at home. Yet when Caterina told why she hated it, Maria could only sympathize. On the first day the mother superior had threatened to pull her hair if she did not obey. What she disliked most was the period after lunch, when everyone was told to put their head on the table and maintain complete silence for an hour. On Friday Caterina had developed a cramp in her neck. She raised her head only to have the large Sister Luisa grab her hair and push her head down onto the table. Caterina remained at home until it came time to attend the first grade of the elementary school.

VII

In the fall of 1969 Caterina was entrusted to Teresa's care for the trip to school. Maria found herself alone in the house for much of the day for the first time in fifteen years. On the one hand it was a relief. The incessant demands and chatter of the children often made her feel on edge. On the other hand she missed not having any of them there in the morning for no other reason than to entreat and reprimand. Yet with the daily round of chores there was hardly time to notice how quiet it was.

Without the aid of the two girls, Maria found laundering the clothes more tiring. And yet it was more important than ever that the clothes be fresh and clean – she did not want anyone gossiping about the children's appearance. Maria had never thought the day would come when she would begin to think about a washing machine. She had been proud of how clean her scrubbing had made their clothes. But now she wanted one. In her mind it made sense. Since they had bought two pigs to fatten for winter and added the raising of a fourth heifer, she was busier than ever. And with the children growing, there were more clothes to launder. Maria was reluctant to bring up the subject of the washing machine. Neither the bank loan nor the notes had been paid off. She felt that they could buy one and still make ends meet, but she hated being extravagant. She was surprised to find that not only did Giacomo agree, but he felt that they should buy a refrigerator as well. Keeping things cool in the kitchen had become a problem, with the flat roof absorbing so much sun. Maria had tried leaving food in the darkest corners close to the cool floor, but it spoiled anyway. Giacomo argued that in the long run it would save money, for the leftovers would not turn bad. Maria was not convinced but agreed that Giacomo should start finding out what a washing machine and a refrigerator would cost.

Giacomo had never been in a large electrical appliance store before. The two in Latina were overwhelming; there were so many models to choose from. Giacomo tried to learn as much as he could; the clerks were interested only in selling. Later he went to the small shop in Latina Scalo where he had bought the radio and the TV. The owner was from Sessa; Giacomo knew his brother. After a long conversation he made Giacomo a good offer: 95,000 for the refrigerator, 110,000 for the washing machine. Giacomo wavered. He was tempted to sign on the spot, even though he had agreed to talk with Maria first. But why should he wait? There was nothing more to know. Besides, as head of the family it was his right, his duty, to make decisions like this. He shook hands with the owner and signed the contract, agreeing to make a downpayment of 15,000 (he would bring it the next day), for the remainder in twenty-four monthly installments of 9,000 lire each. Everything had happened more quickly than Giacomo thought it would. Now they owned four electrical appliances: the radio, TV, refrigerator, and washing machine. Giacomo drove home slowly on his Vespa, thinking of the changes in his life. For so many years he had been aware that people in other places lived better than they did. Cooking over an open fire as Maria did when they were first married reminded him of the Germanic tribes of Caesar's time that he had read about in the third grade. Little by little they had inched ahead into the modern world; the gas stove he had bought in 1956, the running water he had installed in 1963, and the Vespa were all signs of this. It was a kind of catching up, he thought, catching up with the American way of life that was also becoming the Italian Way of Life. He saw it all on TV. The well-to-do in the big cities like Rome and Milan were way ahead of the likes of him – they always would be – but Giacomo knew that the gap was closing. Someday, he thought as he turned into his house, he would buy an automobile.

"So now you have put us even further into debt, you big spender you," Maria said with equal amounts of dismay and admiration in her voice when Giacomo told her what he had done. When the truck arrived the next day, Maria had the washing machine installed in the bathroom next to the bidet, so that the drain hose could run off into it. In that way she could easily take the dirty clothes piled in the bathtub and stuff them in the washer. For the first several days she waited by the machine after loading it and pushing the button. It seemed a miracle that a sloshing, whirring box could do three hours of backbreaking work in thirty minutes. She touched it lovingly as she would a good friend. She suddenly realized that with this machine she would hardly ever carry anything on her head again. She had long since stopped having to haul wood or water. She would find other uses for the big zinc laundry bucket. She wondered, though, whether it was these new ways that were making her bigger around the waist. Whenever she climbed the road to the cemetery, she needed to pause to catch her breath – but when she was a young woman she could run everywhere like a mountain goat, even with a load on her head. Sometimes she would tell Teresa what it was like to be a girl of fourteen or fifteen, hauling water, wood, laundry. "But Mama," Teresa would say, "I don't want to hear about all the sacrifices you made. What difference does it make to me what you did then? Times have changed. When I grow up I am going to have one of those machines that dry the clothes, too. How much more beautiful it would be not to have to hang them out on the line by the house." One thing was certain: Maria knew that she would never have such an appliance. It was one thing to have them washed by this wonderful box, but everyone knows how much better it is to have clothes dry in the fresh air and sun. Besides, every year the electricity bill jumped up. It was three times as much in the country as it had been in the village. Sometimes it made Maria feel guilty just to hear the machine running.

The refrigerator went between the cupboards in the kitchen. There was no room for it near the stove. It was a little awkward walking around the kitchen table to get to it, but Maria liked the simulated wood finish on the door, and it was set off to its best advantage next to the window. Giacomo asked Maria to keep a bottle of water in the refrigerator at all times. Maria insisted that ice water was bad for his stomach. He knew that just as well as she, he replied, but he liked the idea of ice water. It made him aware of how far they had come.

VIII

By December of 1969 the bank loan had been paid off with the sale of four more heifers. Six more months of payment on the notes remained. Raising and selling animals had served them well. The time had come, they were both convinced, to try their hand at milking cows. Lombardo owed the success he had enjoyed as a farmer to his herd. He had more land, but if they could start cultivating their own land again, they might make it pay. They began with three heifers. One they allowed to mature and bred with Lombardo's bull, which brought her into milk. February of 1970 saw the stable full, with two milk cows, two heifers for veal, and two heifers to be bred. Raising heifers for veal was one thing, milking cows was another. That was man's work, Maria argued. Giacomo agreed. He sent Luigi and Bruno to Lombardo to learn so that they could do the milking before school in the morning and again at night. They took turns.

In the beginning milk production was low, not more than eleven or twelve liters a day. As Luigi and Bruno became more experienced production increased, but it never exceeded seventeen liters between morning and evening. With the price of 180 lire a liter being paid to small producers like themselves, they took in between 35,000 and 40,000 lire a month. It was not much, but since Giacomo was unemployed from time to time, it was welcome. The greatest expense was feed for the animals. At Lombardo's advice, Giacomo planted alfalfa for feed in 1970, along with corn for the hens and wheat as a cash crop. It had been eight years since he had worked his own land. Renting the three hectares to Lombardo for that period had been good for them both. Lombardo had enlarged his herd, and his rent had helped Giacomo to build and establish himself on the land. But with the house built and paid for, it was time for Giacomo and Maria to utilize the land as fully as they could for their own agricultural production. Giacomo recalled the exhortations from the secretary of the Università Agraria when he had been allotted the land in 1958: "Work the land you have been given, be independent, be strong." Giacomo knew as well as anyone, however, that he would never be able to support six persons on three hectares of land. He would have to work whenever he could find a job. Yet when the young plants began to appear vigorous and green in the early spring of 1970, Giacomo felt that the goal of living from the land was coming closer than it ever had before.

The first crop of alfalfa was abundant. The second was less so. To achieve the needed four or five cuttings, irrigation was required – an additional expense. Lombardo made his cutter and bailer available to Giacomo at a minimal cost, but without equipment of his own Giacomo knew that he would always be at a disadvantage. If he could get milk production up to twenty-five or thirty liters a day, he could begin to more than cover costs.

It had seemed wisest to Giacomo to keep the animals inside; they would be safer out of sight. When one of the cows came down with pneumonia, Lombardo told Giacomo that it was because they needed to move around rather than lie in manure in the stall all the time. Giacomo built an enclosure so that they could be led outside during the day, even though there was not land enough for them to pasture. But it seemed that they had become so habituated to being inside that they bellowed constantly to be allowed back in the stall. Struggling with cows, Giacomo and Maria realized, was much harder than they had expected. Most of the fatigue fell on Maria, for when Giacomo was working he would have to leave very early in the morning or return late at night.

IX

For some time jobs had been easier to find in the Agro Pontino. In the bars and on TV there was talk of an economic boom. Whatever it was, building was going on everywhere. A line of houses began creeping up Via Casa Grande toward Giacomo's; a new apartment house was built in Latina Scalo; two small skyscrapers arose in Latina itself. American companies began coming into the area. Suddenly it seemed as if everyone wanted to work in an American factory, because the wages were good. At first it was hard to be taken on without a recommendation from a friend, but later, as work became even more plentiful, even those jobs began to show up on the employment office roles.

When Giacomo was laid off in 1968 from Miore, he remained unemployed for some months. For most of 1969 he worked for Miore again, until the apartment house under construction was finished; then he was without work for another four months. In December of 1970 Giacomo's name came to the top of the list at the unemployment office. As married head of household with four dependent children, his job eligibility was high. Two days after Christmas he received a call to take a job with an American company, Apex Black, a manufacturer of asphalt. The plant was located in Borgo San Riccardo, some fifteen kilometers away. The pay was good – 200,000 a month, with a family subsidy of 50,000 in addition, more than he had ever received before. To be at the plant by 7:45 in the morning, Giacomo left the house at 7:00 on his Vespa. Maria always packed a good lunch in his briefcase, which he strapped to the carrier. He enjoyed the ride, except for the coldest, rainiest days in January and February. On the Via Appia he could take time to stop for an espresso on the way to work and a glass on the way home. Every fifteen days Giacomo handed Maria a fat paycheck. For the first time since they had started to build the house six years before, Maria was able to put some money aside. By June the savings amounted to three hundred thousand lire. Giacomo's dream of a car filled his mind, but he knew the moment was not right; he would have to wait until Luigi found steady work.

X

Luigi received a diploma from the vocational school in June of 1971. It stated that he was qualified for employment in all branches of mechanics. Armed with the impressive document, Luigi went from factory to factory. Everywhere he was told that vocational schools were all well and good, but they did not make up for lack of experience. The only firm offer he received paid forty thousand a month; he could make as much working in the fields. Embittered, he wondered why he had wasted so much of his time and his family's funds. It was just as they said; it was not what you knew that counted, but who you knew. The trouble was that he did not know anyone, nor did his father. He thought of asking his Uncle Salvatore about work with Miore. His mother counseled him not to. Her brother had helped Giacomo on more than one occasion. It was better not to ask too many favors. Instead he should speak to her brother Tonino, who was working at a construction site in Rome. Tonino said he would talk the matter over with the foreman. For that favor Maria provided her brother with one of their best hams. After some days of waiting Tonino came by the house one evening to say that the foreman had found an opening for Luigi. It was July of 1971.

Luigi got up at five with his mother. She prepared him a bowl of hot coffee with milk into which she mixed pieces of bread, just as she did for his father. He rode to a point on the Via Appia where he could hide his bike well. There he would meet Tonino for the drive to Rome in Tonino's truck. In the back were items to be sold in the Piazza Vittorio first thing in the morning, which more than paid for the gas. At the site Luigi was assigned the job of mixing cement, a skill he had learned from his father. Pay was distributed every Saturday, rather than every fifteen days. Luigi handed his mother thirty thousand a week, considerably more than he made on any other job. It was not as much as his father was making at Apex Black, but considering his age, it was good. Sometimes Luigi and his father spoke about buying a car.

XI

In August Giacomo began suffering from stomach pains again. Neither he nor Maria could understand why. Usually it was when he was without work that it hurt the most. He enjoyed his job at the plant. Indeed, he had told Maria that if they kept him on permanently they could sell their cows and rent the land to Lombardo again; trying to live from three hectares was a dream. It was easier to work in a plant full-time for a wage than to struggle with animals and crops. The one thing he did not like at work was the black dust blown around in the production of tar; he could not avoid breathing it.

Maria insisted that it was the tar dust that made his stomach hurt. Giacomo disagreed, but by August the pain had become so intense that Giacomo went to a doctor. Tests were made. He was stunned to hear that he could not work for the American company anymore, because the fine black dust especially aggravated his condition. Giacomo left the job in September 1971.

He was at home for almost two months nursing his stomach. According to the doctor he was to eat unseasoned food with no sauces, drink no wine or coffee, and give up smoking cigarettes. He was prescribed pills to combat acidity. Maria made a special effort to cut Giacomo's heaping portion of pasta in half. She omitted the rich sauce. Abandoning the coffee and wine was not too difficult; drinking them gave him pain. To stop smoking, however, was a sacrifice Giacomo would not make. He only wished he could get hold of the American brands. They seemed less harsh. Slowly his stomach began to improve, and slowly he resumed his heaping portion of pasta, wine with the meal, and then coffee.

Luigi's wage alone was supporting the household. The savings began to dwindle.

Giacomo spoke about raising another heifer to milk to increase production and income. As it was there was hardly room for the animals to turn around. It seemed to Maria as if she spent half the day shoveling manure.

In November the employment office found a job for Giacomo in a small plant in Latina making wooden doors and window frames. The owner was besieged with orders from builders. The pay was only half of what it had been with Apex Black, but Giacomo enjoyed working with wood. He had gained considerable respect for carpenters while watching them ply their craft on construction jobs. It took him little time to learn how to use the ripsaw, the plane, the sander. In a good day the shop turned out as many as thirty frames. The boss was pleased with Giacomo's work; he would keep him on as long as the boom lasted.

XII

In December Luigi left his job at the construction site in Rome. Going back and forth every day with only a few hours of sleep was exhausting. He was determined to find work closer to Valmonte. He had been at home only a short time when Lombardo's youngest son came by to say that he was quitting his job at ILPINA, the frozen food storage plant in Latina. His family was increasing the herd on the farm; he was needed there. The son took Luigi to the plant and strongly recommended to the manager, Muti, that Rossi be taken on as his replacement. According to Lombardo, Muti was easier to get along with than most bosses. He treated his men fairly. Luigi liked him right away, and as they parted Muti told Luigi that he could have the job as soon as he obtained clearance from the employment office. Luigi was overjoyed: an industrial job with all the benefits that went with it, and only three kilometers from home! But at the employment office the clerk in charge told Luigi that he might as well go home and not waste their time, for there was a long list of job seekers ahead of him; he would have to wait his turn. Luigi pointed out that he had already spoken to the manager, who wanted him to start working at the plant immediately. Surely it would not be necessary, he said, to have clearance in that case. The clerk replied that the law was the law, to which Luigi replied that he would not go until they gave him the clearance papers. He was ordered to leave immediately, or the *carabinieri* would be called.

Luigi was determined to hold his ground. He lay down on the floor, saying they would have to carry him out. But his bravado gave way to fright when the *carabinieri* appeared in the room. They yanked him up from the floor and pushed him out the door. He arrived home with tears in his eyes, humiliated at the treatment he had suffered.

Signor Muti expressed little surprise when later Luigi recounted his story but was delighted by his courage and persistence. "Young man, what you need is someone to help you make this legal. I will write a letter of introduction to my friend, lawyer Bruno, in Latina. He will handle all the details, do you understand?" Luigi nodded. Armed with the letter, Luigi called upon Bruno. The wait in the anteroom was long. But Luigi didn't care. He was certain that he held the job in his hands. The lawyer read the letter and smiled. "I will be glad to help my dear friend Signor Muti in any small way if I can. Rossi, in a week return to the employment office," he said cordially, ushering Luigi from his office.

The week seemed like a month. Luigi was at the employment office as soon as the doors opened on the seventh day. The clerk shook his hand. He explained that there had been some misunderstanding but now the matter was cleared up; the job was his.

Luigi's first assignment was unloading trucks of frozen food to be deposited in the refrigerated warehouse. He was paid piece rate, 100 lire per quintale of weight. Unloading one truck paid 25,000 to 30,000 lire, divided among the five-man crew. In the beginning Luigi brought home an average of 30,000 a week to his mother. The work was heavy but he did not mind; he was certain he could make a permanent place for himself at ILPINA.

XIII

After he had been working at carpentry in the small plant for three months, Giacomo's stomach pains returned. At first he tried to pay them no heed. In time they became unbearable. He visited the doctor, tests were taken. He was told that sawdust was particularly bad for his condition. He would have to stop working there immediately, if he did not he would end up in the hospital. He left the plant in February of 1972 to return to a diet of unseasoned food and abstinence from wine and coffee.

XIV

This time the termination of Giacomo's wage was less distressing to Maria, for Luigi's position at ILPINA had improved. No longer was he being paid a piece rate but rather a regular wage. He had become a preparer, filling orders for clients by collecting the specified amount of frozen food. He liked his new assignment, for he liked to figure things out: how to save a minute here, cut a corner there. But there was the cold to contend with. After eight hours in the refrigerated warehouse Luigi felt frozen to his bones. He put on all the warm clothes he could find, but he still shivered. It was not until he bought a parka and insulated pants at the American market that he began to feel more comfortable. The older men on the job told him they still suffered from the cold. Some complained of arthritis and rheumatism in their joints. Maria worried for her son's health. It appeared that he had the favor of Signor Muti. His continued beneficence was to be hoped for. Maria saw to it that he received a dressed chicken from time to time. For his birthday she made a magnificent *zuppa inglese*. Signor Muti sent back hearty congratulations on her skills.

XV

Within a month Giacomo was back at work. He was taken on by an ice cream manufacturer to help out through the season. Like Luigi, he worked in a refrigerated room for eight hours a day. It was midsummer, and the demand for ice cream was at its peak. The boom was on, and people were buying as they never had before. The manager had said the job was temporary, but Giacomo hoped it would continue, for there was no dust to bother his stomach. August gave way to September, and September to October. It seemed as if there was more than enough work for everyone. People spoke of the boom as a miracle. Giacomo did not believe in miracles but was glad that people were eating so much ice cream. In November he was told that his services were no longer needed. People began to say that the boom was slowing down.

In early 1973 construction on the new Chemtech pharmaceutical plant was begun. Romolo Farnese's uncle sold two farms to the company for the factory site. An outcry resulted, for the farms bordered on the Sesto Canal and were the best farm land in the territory of Valmonte. Angry voices protested that industrialization of the Agro Pontino should not drive out agriculture. But the American company wanted access to the canal for the runoff of waste products. It made an offer to Farnese's uncle that he could not refuse. When Giacomo heard of the deal he was furious at the thought of the rich becoming richer, but he knew that the plant construction would mean jobs. In February Giacomo went to work at Chemtech laying pipes in the foundation. The base pay was low – 90,000 a month – but with overtime he brought home 120,000 to 130,000 a month. Chemtech was in a hurry to finish, but Giacomo was assured that the work would continue for a year. He was now convinced that the time had come to buy an automobile.

XVI

Whenever Giacomo talked about owning a car Maria scoffed at the idea. Where would they go? It would only be an extra expense. Besides, Giacomo didn't know how to drive and would only go running into things and cause them endless trouble. But since Luigi's work had become permanent at ILPINA she had begun to change her mind. The two men had to go in opposite directions; only one could use the Vespa. The winter rains left both cold and wet. Giacomo was pleased to have his wife finally come to her senses. The prospect of owning a car delighted him. It meant entering the new world forming around them. To be without one would be to remain country hicks forever.

At the plant Luigi heard of a secondhand Fiat 500 owned by a former officer of the *carabinieri*. He and Giacomo rode on the Vespa one day to see it. Its bright yellow shone brilliantly in the late afternoon sun. The very compactness of the tiny car was appealing; an insurance against extravagance. Giacomo had difficulty squeezing into the front seat. No matter, it was an automobile. The marshal of the *carabinieri* wanted 600,000 for it. The conversation was long and tiring. Luigi pointed out a bump on the fender, a scratch on the door. The marshal extolled the virtues of the engine, the durability of the tires. After the sun had set, a price of 500,000 was agreed upon. Giacomo had brought 250,000 lire with him, all but 75,000 of their savings. The remainder would be paid in installments of 50,000 a month for five months. Luigi drove the car home; he had just acquired his license. Giacomo followed on the Vespa.

Maria was sitting in front of the house waiting. Her face broke into a broad grin when she saw them. She ran her hand lovingly over the car's surface. It was difficult to believe that she, the daughter of peasants from Stilo, Calabria, where the donkey had been their transportation, now owned an automobile. Not that it belonged to her. It would always be Giacomo's; she would never learn how to drive, but she would ride in it next to her husband just like a lady.

Giacomo immediately enrolled in the driving school in Latina Scalo. Luigi assured his father that any fool could pass the test. Giacomo replied that it was easy enough for him to say, for he had had more schooling and knew the secret of taking examinations. It was difficult, Giacomo found, to keep all the rules and regulations straight in his head. They had to be memorized. On the day of the test he became rattled. The examiner said that he would have to take it again. That evening at the kitchen table his ire rose as he listened to their teasing. Suddenly he banged the table and demanded silence. He wished to hear no more of their silly talk. It had gotten so that a man no longer received the respect from his wife and children owed him as head of the family, he said with vehemence.

Nervousness plagued him again during the second examination. He failed. No one in the family mentioned it. Maria sensed his humiliation. Giacomo was more determined than ever. It was his destiny to drive an automobile. He knew from the bearing of the instructor that he would pass the third time even if he made a mistake. The instructor had made his point about peasants driving automobiles; the school needed to pass its students.

The evening of the day of the third test Giacomo took Maria for her first drive. She was nervous not so much for her safety but for the greatness of the occasion. Who would ever know just seeing her sitting in the front that she was not a schoolteacher or a midwife? They drove past Matera's grove, where she had picked olives so many times. When she was a girl it had taken her an hour to walk from there to the village. Now they could be there in ten minutes. Giacomo parked in the piazza. Old friends nodded, Maria smiled. She remembered how it had felt to walk through there on Giacomo's arm on the way home from the church twenty years ago on the day of their wedding. She touched his arm. Giacomo took her hand in his. They sat silently for some minutes before fetching Giovanni and Giulia and Luigi and Teresa to see the new car.

XVII

With the completion of the Chemtech plant in December 1973, Giacomo was without work. The burden of support fell not alone upon Luigi but also on Bruno and Teresa. Bruno received his diploma from the vocational school in Latina in the spring of 1972. Certified as a chemical analyst, he went from plant to plant to find employment. Everywhere he was turned down for lack of experience. Above all, he was disappointed that Chemtech did not have a place for him, for he knew they were hiring chemical analysts to work in the new plant. They told Bruno that his lack of a work record disqualified him. After several months of searching, the employment office offered him a job with the maintenance crew at Chemtech. Bruno accepted. Menial as his janitorial job was, it did mean something, working for the great new multinational company. After he had been there for a while he explained to his mother that it was run in an American way, not like ILPINA. There was no one there he could give one of her chickens to; even if he did it would not make any difference.

XVIII

Teresa worked for her cousin Michele for two years in his upholstery shop. Michele had learned the trade while he was living with his mother, Concetta, in Piove di Sacco. When Concetta moved north to Busto with Felice and their seven children, Michele returned to Valmonte. It was his opinion that with the boom there would be a demand for inexpensive upholstered furniture, what with all the new houses being built. Michele set up the shop in partnership with two others. They needed a sewer, one whom they would not have to pay too much. It did not take Teresa long to learn how to operate the heavy-duty stitching machine. The work was not backbreaking like hoeing tomatoes or sugar beets, but it was tiresome to sit there hour after hour. She was kept company by another woman sewer. When the machines were not running they could talk but otherwise they could not hear themselves above the noise. At first Teresa was paid her wage of forty thousand lire at the end of every month. As time went on there was always one good reason or another why they could not give her the money on time. Michele said that he would have to close the shop down if she insisted. He pointed out that she was a relative and therefore should understand the way things were; they had to pay the other worker because she was not family. In the end she was paid, but it always involved an argument and hard feelings. One day she came home in tears. Two weeks had passed beyond her payday. She was going to leave the shop and never go back. Her mother cautioned her to not act too quickly. They needed the forty thousand. Still and all, she thought, it was not only Michele who was trying to make ends meet with his growing family. She too had her own preoccupations, with Giacomo in and out of work. Yes, she finally agreed, Teresa should leave; Maria could use her at home. She herself hardly had time to turn around what with the animals to struggle with as well as the housework.

Hardly had Teresa left the shop than the two other partners absconded with the funds – Michele's share as well as their own. Michele was desperate; he could not carry all the work himself. He needed another partner. Tonino agreed to go into the business with him. Construction was beginning to dry up in Rome; he was looking for something else. Michele knew that Tonino would be an asset. He spoke so well. He would convince the furniture salesmen who came to the shop to make large orders.

After Teresa had been at home for two months Tonino dropped by one evening to say that they needed her back. He had drummed up a number of orders. Now there was more than their one worker could handle. He went on to say that everything was different now that he and Michele were partners; she would not have to worry about being paid on time. In fact, he added, seeing that she was still reluctant, they would let her do the sewing for one living-room suite all by herself, without help from the other worker. For that alone they would give her sixty thousand lire.

Teresa was at the shop the following morning at seven thirty. She set to work right away. It was easier than she had thought it would be; in fact she had finished all the sewing by evening. She was pleased to have worked so well and so fast. When she showed the material to Tonino at the end of the day he began to point out this defect and that. Finally he said that for workmanship of such poor quality he could pay her only thirty thousand. As soon as she heard his words Teresa told him that she could see that nothing had changed. She left the shop quickly, never to return. She felt both sad and angry.

Teresa was at home most of November 1973. Maria immediately set her to work around the house. It was not that Teresa hated housework, boring as it was, but she had her heart set on working in one of the factories. Several of her friends worked in the French-owned Accord plant making transistors. They wore long white smocks, smoked cigarettes in groups outside the plant, and complained. But Teresa was not eligible for employment in a factory; she did not have a diploma from the middle school. Even if she had, her father would not have allowed her to work in one of them. He was jealous of his daughters; there was too much loose talk and behavior in places like that for his tastes.

There was always money to be made working in the fields but Teresa hated nothing more than agricultural labor, most especially the caring for farm animals. She hated everything to do with them, the smell of the manure, the flies, the humiliation of having them so close to the house. She never went near the stable if she could help it.

In December Teresa heard of a woman living nearby in one of the newer houses who needed help with her three small children. The woman worked for Accord; she had become seriously ill. Teresa agreed to come for a short while to help the mother get back on her feet. It was understood that she was to receive ten thousand a week for her efforts; sometimes she was given nine, sometimes eight. In April the woman told Teresa that she would have to be satisfied with less money or go; she could not afford to pay her so much. Teresa returned to the housework. Maria was pleased. She told Teresa that she had been bringing her so little money that they were better off having her at home.

It was lonely, though, at the end of Via Casa Grande during the day. Caterina was away at school. It made Teresa nervous to have her mother ordering her around. She was thrilled when her best friend, Franca, informed her that the owner of the beauty parlor in Latina Scalo was looking for a helper. Teresa loved everything to do with makeup and fashion. Maria was skeptical; going to beauty parlors was a waste of time and money in her opinion, but a job was a job. Teresa went to speak to the owner, who said she was looking for an apprentice, someone who wanted to make a career of hairdressing. Teresa was uncertain, but in order not to offend the owner, she said that she was eager to learn. The pay for an apprentice/learner would be three thousand a week. Teresa could only think how disappointed her mother would be for her to bring home so little. She accepted when the owner explained that her customers were generous with the tips. Teresa found, however, that the tips had to be divided three ways. When there was a good deal of business, as there was around the holidays, Teresa brought home as much as seven thousand a week. Hairdressing in practice was not as exciting as Teresa had thought it would be. She was on her feet all day. The ladies ordered her about as if she were a servant. When Teresa complained to her mother, Maria said that if she wanted to make a career of that work she had better remain and stop complaining. Maria pointed out that her brother Pasquale had spent three years learning the tailor's trade without being paid anything.

Teresa said that she did not want to hear about how everyone had sacrificed so much in the old days; things were different now. At the end of four months she told the owner that she had decided not to make a career of hairdressing. She came home once more to the broom and dishmop.

XVIX

When Luigi returned from his tour of military duty, which he served in the northern districts of Udine and Gorizia as his father had done, he was promoted at ILPINA. Before he had left the boss had told Luigi that he would make him a forklift operator when he returned. He was as good as his word. Luigi was proud to have such a prestigious and responsible job. At first he was cautious lifting the heavy loads, as if the boxes contained china. He knew a mistake with the powerful lift would be costly to the company, and thus to himself. In time he gained confidence and enjoyed the feeling of great power that operating the machine gave him. When he had demonstrated his competence, the manager rewrote the contract of his employment. Not only was his salary increased from two hundred fifty to three hundred thousand lire a month but he was granted a cost-of-living increase every three months, a seniority increase of two percent every two years, and a month's bonus at Christmas and at the Feast of the Assumption in August. In addition to all of that he received twenty days of vacation

every year. Luigi had triumphed. Within his lifetime of nineteen years
he had secured the beachhead. No longer a distant point on the horizon,
job security was in his grasp. For the remainder of his working life
there would be an assured place for him at ILPINA. When Luigi
showed his parents the contract a feeling of well-being swept over
Giacomo and Maria. The struggle was not over – there was a long road
ahead – but another corner had been turned.

XX

For most of the winter of 1974 Giacomo remained without work. Early
in April the employment office notified Giacomo of an opening at the
Mozzi ceramics factory in Latina. Mozzi was the largest manufacturer
of toilet fixtures in Italy. Regular employment at Mozzi would be a
dream come true, better than working for one of the multinationals,
with their different ways. One had only to outlast the probationary
period at a place like Mozzi to go on the regular payroll, to be eligible
for a pension. Giacomo's younger brother, Pietro, had been working at
Accord for several years. He was already counting up what his pension
would amount to.

Giacomo drove the Fiat rather than the Vespa to the factory that first
morning. His heart jumped up when he entered the big gate with the
word Mozzi spelled in giant iron letters. The foreman welcomed Giacomo and assigned him to the sanding department. Terror struck Giacomo's heart when he saw the masked laborers wielding the electric-
powered sanders. A fine white powder was in the air everywhere.
Giacomo took the foreman by the arm and pulled him outside. He
pleaded with him to assign him another task anywhere in the plant,
carrying heavy loads, whatever they saw fit, but not the sanding department. He explained that he had certain trouble with his stomach,
fine dust of any kind aggravated it. The foreman nodded gravely and
set Giacomo to rolling empty barrels down a ramp into a truck. Giacomo realized to his dismay that he had made a fatal mistake. Giacomo
was certain that the foreman had told everything to the manager, and
the manager would decide that the company could not allow a sick man
to stay on beyond the probationary period; then they would be responsible for him forever. Giacomo continued to roll barrels until two days
before the end of the probationary period. He was called to the office.
He felt, walking across the factory yard, as if he were going to his own
hanging. The foreman was solicitous, even cordial. He said that they
were letting Giacomo go for his own good; working in a place like
Mozzi with the dust everywhere, even in the yard, would be a threat to
his health. They did not wish to be responsible, he said, for causing

him any harm. As Giacomo rode home on the Vespa that evening he felt that Mozzi had been his last chance for getting inside a factory. The boom was clearly over. It was not his destiny to be regularly employed. Fate had dealt him a double blow, denying him a patron as well as stirring up his stomach. It was fortunate for the whole family that Luigi had achieved what Giacomo himself had failed to. They would lean on him until he got married. Then it would be Bruno's turn. Lately Luigi had been talking as if the time for marrying was at hand. Then Giacomo would think of some way of building a house for them right here on his own land. It would be best for them all to stay close to each other.

XXI

Not only were jobs drying up, but Maria was finding that they seemed to be making less and less on the animals. She had not kept exact records, but as far as she could tell they had made ninety thousand lire in 1973 on each cow, not including what she spent on gas to heat water for washing out the cans, for straw, and for veterinarian bills. Most of the work fell on Maria. Teresa and Caterina did nothing but complain of the smell and the flies. The flies were bad in the summer and filled the kitchen. Maria felt that she had struggled enough. She was ready to get rid of them. Giacomo agreed that they should sell them while the price was still good. They sold the cows first, starting with the one that had had pneumonia; she was the best of the milkers. They received six hundred thousand apiece for the cows. They waited with the two large heifers until they got an offer of eight hundred thousand apiece. Later they sold the three calves for two hundred thousand apiece. Maria was sad when they were hauled away in the truck, their noses sniffing through the slats; raising the young ones had been what she had liked the most. With the stable cleared there was a proper place to hang curing hams along with the peppers and onions. It was a relief not to shovel manure; and as for the flies, most of them seemed to have left with the cows. It was good to have some money to put away now that Giacomo was without work.

XXII

Luigi and Silvia Bianchi first met in the late spring of 1973 at a berry-picking party. A cousin of Silvia's worked at ILPINA with Luigi. He invited Luigi to come along with them that Sunday. Luigi liked Silvia right from the start, especially the way she laughed. He liked girls who could joke without taking offense right away. Silvia took a fancy to

Luigi. The way he looked at her made her feel pretty. The next time they saw each other was at the beach of Latina, another outing organized by Silvia's cousin. Luigi had learned to swim when he was enrolled at the vocational school. Silvia, who lived in Sessa, had hardly ever been to the beach. Luigi enjoyed showing off, listening to Silvia's admiring laughter.

A few weeks later Luigi made a point of going to Sessa and dropping in at Standa, the department store where Silvia was a salesgirl. She blushed deeply when she noticed him all of a sudden smiling at her across the counter. She said with feigned crossness that he should not come to see her that way; everyone was a gossip in Sessa, word would get around. Luigi said that he didn't care, because he wanted to talk to her about something important. He waited until she had finished with a customer and then all in a rush he said that he knew that she was still young, that he was not yet prepared to marry, but because they liked each other and were serious they should become engaged. There was a pause. Silvia looked away. Then she said that she had been thinking about the very same thing. It was true she was still young, but her mother had already begun to collect her trousseau. It was not too early to start to think about things like that. But her mother and her father would not want her meeting someone here and there on the street. That was the way they felt about it in Sessa; so if they wanted to see each other they had better get engaged. Silvia felt that Luigi was someone she could trust. It was agreed that Luigi would call on Silvia's parents the following Sunday.

Donato, her father, was a large man, quick tempered, a lover of political polemic and wine. He had worked in Rome as a day laborer for twenty-five years, arising every morning at four thirty to catch the worker's train to the Eternal City. Sunday was his day to harangue in the piazza and then consume two liters of wine at the family table. When he had worked long enough to pay for Silvia's marriage he intended to retire to the piazza, and undertake only occasional work.

Rosaria, Silvia's mother, a retiring woman, remained most of the day in their four rooms at the top of two long flights of stairs in the center of Sessa. When she went to market or to visit she threw a large blue wool shawl over her shoulders, the mark of a respectable woman. Like most women of Sessa, she was an avid needleworker. Silvia had learned this fine art from her mother.

For that Sunday Rosaria had prepared an especially fine meal: homemade egg noodles, savored chunks of roast lamb, goat, and rabbit, and artichokes under oil and vinegar. Donato consumed only one liter of wine out of respect for the occasion. Donato and Rosaria were well disposed toward Luigi. Silvia had reassured them about his post at

ILPINA and his secure future there, of his father's talk of building a house for him and his wife. It seemed he would make an excellent choice of husband for their daughter. In Silvia, Luigi knew that he would have a wife who had been properly raised, not frivolously as they were in Valmonte, where chaperoning was no longer honored as it still was in Sessa. By the time they had finished eating it was agreed that Silvia and Luigi would be formally engaged. They would see each other only at his house or hers; in that way there would be no reason for needless gossip. Before he left Luigi announced that his parents were expecting them the next Sunday.

Maria prepared a special meal of homemade egg noodles, savored chunks of roast pork, chicken, rabbit, and greens under oil and garlic. The conversation was cordial. Donato pointed out that Silvia was their only daughter. They had always been careful with her. He told how she had wanted to take a typing course in Latina when she had finished the middle school in order to be able to get a job there, but he would not hear of it. He said that he did not want her going off every day unaccompanied on the bus to Latina, a city full of strange men who had nothing better to do with their time than to stare at young women. Instead, he was proud to say, he had made the manager of Standa find her a job in his store as a salesgirl, even though she was only fifteen. That way they had kept an eye on her. Silvia was still young, he pointed out, but then both families would need several years to get ready. He went on to say that she would continue to work at Standa so that her mother would have money to buy sheets and towels. He himself was already putting money aside for her furniture. Then Rosaria observed that she would need two years to finish the embroidering on the best sheets; she wanted to do the very best she could for their only daughter.

It seemed to Maria as she sat listening that life had come full circle in the span of twenty years. Now it was time for her first son to begin to prepare himself for the creation of his own family. He would need their help as she had needed it from her own family. Silvia seemed a serious girl – not the one she would have picked for her son, but that was his choice. She had always vowed that she would not interfere. The Bianchis were poor, but it was clear that they were going to do well by their daughter. She and Giacomo would have to do handsomely by Luigi.

10

The house of Luigi

I

For some time Giacomo and Maria had been thinking of how they were going to settle their children. Nothing was clear except that they would do their very best for Teresa and Caterina and hope they chose hard-working husbands. Maria had already begun to put away a few sheets and towels; every time the Neapolitan came by with his two suitcases of linens she would buy something. Now the engagement of Luigi made it important to plan for their son. His marriage was still three, possibly four years away, but the settling of a son was not a thing to leave to the last moment. In twenty years so much had changed in their lives. In 1953 Giacomo had considered himself lucky to find three rooms to rent for Maria, himself, and her furnishings for the bedroom and the kitchen. Now it seemed that young couples wanted the world. He had heard of cases where girls had brought television sets as part of their trousseau. One thing was certain: Neither Luigi nor Bruno would move to rented quarters when they married. To rent was to throw good money after bad. In the end, where you lived still belonged to the owner; if times turned hard a family could be forced to the sidewalk. It had happened to Concetta and Felice with their first four children in Piove di Sacco.

From the day that Giacomo had finished his house he had the picture in his mind of building two more on the land, one for each son. From year to year the vision had taken hold of him more and more. He had even chosen where Luigi's house would be: behind his own, facing the dirt road running beside the canal. Now that he was without employment he would have the time. Building for his family would be his work; in that way the costs would be cut in half. The new machinery that he saw being used everywhere would make it easier. With an electric winch one man could build a two-story house. When he had put up his own in 1966 he had mixed the cement by hand; now with an electric mixer the work would go faster. The new equipment was expensive, but with neighbors now stretched along Via Casa Grande, many of them building for their own sons, he could find someone to share the cost.

He realized that if he built a house of the kind that was beginning to form in his mind's eye, he would be breaking the law. It was forbidden on pain of fine and/or imprisonment to erect a dwelling that was not to be inhabited by those who worked the land. Every year good farm land was taken over for houses, none of them of the simple, square, one-story design of Giacomo's. Most were two stories, small villas in effect, creations of the economic miracle and transformed aspiration. The law would not deter Giacomo. He agreed with those who said it was human nature to want to provide for your children. Why should they live in shacks to satisfy strange ideas about the countryside in the heads of Roman bureaucrats?

It would not be the law that would hold him back, but rather money. After Luigi became engaged, Giacomo and his son and often Maria would sit for long hours after dinner at the kitchen table figuring. Even to build a house like Giacomo's would now cost six million lire—double what it had cost in 1966. Maria always insisted that she could not imagine wanting a house for herself different from the one she already had, but she agreed with the two men that the one to be built for Luigi would be larger, grander. It would be two stories. For months Luigi and Silvia spoke of little else. Gradually a plan developed. The ground floor would include a garage, next to it a cold cellar to store wine, oil, tomato preserve, and, to be suspended from the ceiling hooks, hams. Behind the cold cellar would be a room for the furnace. Giacomo's house was warmed by a small coal and wood stove in the hall, which heated water for the radiators in the other rooms. Now compact oil heaters were being installed in new houses. The storage tank would be placed outside, halfway between the two houses. At that time Giacomo would run a line to his house to feed a small oil heater he planned to put in the kitchen. The stove was old-fashioned; the girls complained about it all the time.

Next to the furnace and behind the garage remained space for a large room. It would be left unfinished, but one day, after the children came, it might become a "family room;" that was the way it was described in the home design magazines Silvia had shown Luigi. In the corner would be a fireplace and in front a sofa, with the stereo set next to it. The finish would be rustic, unlike the rest of the house. When Maria heard about it she had to hold her tongue. The kitchen was the proper place for the family to be. Everything important was learned around the kitchen table. From what she had heard, the kitchen that Silvia wanted would be so small there would be room for only two. Even if Silvia did come from Sessa, it seemed that her head was full of modern ideas, just like Teresa.

The second floor would be reached by an outside stair leading to a balcony. Silvia could sit there in the winter sun or in the shade of a summer afternoon to do needlepoint for her children's trousseaux. The double front would lead to a large hallway. The floor should be of real marble, not composition, preferably of a reddish hue. Luigi did not want the walls left in plaster as they were in his father's house; rather, they were to be covered with paper. He had seen an imitation brocade in one of the magazines that he liked. The marble, the paper, a chandelier would give the hallway an elegant appearance, like the house of a gentleman. To the left of the hall would be the dining room, with the small kitchen behind, then two bathrooms farther down, followed by the children's room; to the right double doors would lead to the living room, behind which would be the master bedroom. It was the living room that would make the family proud; larger than the dining room and the bedroom combined, its size alone would be a measure of Luigi's success. The same fine marble and heavy dark brocaded paper would sumptuously cover floor and wall. From the ceiling would hang a crystal chandelier. When Luigi was thirteen, his entire catechism class had been taken by bus to Terracina for an audience with the archbishop. The splendor of his waiting room had been fixed in his mind's eye forever.

Whenever his mother or father wondered aloud if Luigi was not going too far, he reminded them that it was his pay that was supporting the family; he had a right to have what he wanted. Giacomo and Maria were proud of their son. He and his wife-to-be deserved the very best; a house like the kind he wanted would reflect well upon the family forever. Nothing they had ever done or ever could do would make such a grand impression. But the costs for such a house would be staggering.

The figures were gone over many times. It would not be possible to build for less than twelve million, even with the saving of all the labor costs. Giacomo reminded Luigi that he had built his for 3 million. Luigi replied that times had changed. He pointed out two other families that his father was familiar with who were building houses for an elder son like the one he wanted.

The longer Giacomo thought about it the more convinced he became himself that constructing such a fine house would be worth the great effort. Above all it would mean that his first son, and in turn his grandchildren, would be living close by for the remainder of his life. Luigi and his wife would never have reason to move away to better their condition somewhere else, and he and Maria would never be left alone. On his land they could struggle together better than they could apart. Destiny had not seen fit to grant him the regular employment he had always sought, but it had given him the land. Now he could do something for his sons that his father had not been able to do for him or Pietro, or Giovanni Tassoni for Salvatore, Pasquale, or Tonino. Ten years had passed since he had started his own house that was to bring them all here to this place. Now Giacomo was ready to tempt the fate of the gods again and set their future forever. Giacomo always knew, too, that if dire necessity dictated, he could sell the house for twice what it was going to cost him to build it.

Now he faced the same dilemma that he had in 1964; where was he to find the money? In 1964 those in charge had wanted to help change men like himself from day laborers to cultivators by subsidizing the building of rustic habitations. Since then the Italian economic miracle had occurred, industry had taken hold in the Agro Pontino, construction was going on everywhere, land was at a premium. There was no holding back the tide. Everywhere land was being converted from agricultural to residential use. There were no funds available in 1974 to subsidize housing for the generation of skilled workers, like Luigi, that industry had spawned.

Giacomo could not go to the bank. Even if they granted him a loan, it would be for only a fraction of what he needed. He had heard, too, that banks were reluctant to put more of their money into real estate; most of them were overcommitted. And with interest rates at eighteen percent, Luigi's salary would not be enough in conjunction with what Bruno brought home to support the family and meet the loans. It was becoming apparent that Giacomo was going to have to do what he had sworn he never would do: sell some of his land. There would be no difficulty in finding a purchaser. It seemed as if everyone wanted to build. Many houses went up little by little, first the frame and the roof, then later when more money was available the walls; still later the inside was finished. At first Giacomo saw this as his solution; he would sell only a little land, enough to get the roof on. Then he would wait until he could find some more money to continue. Luigi insisted that he was fooling himself – Giacomo would eventually have to sell more land. "Where will the rest of the money come from?" Luigi demanded. "Better do it all at once right now. Who knows what the future may bring?" Maria agreed.

It was the only sensible thing to do. But she knew what it meant to her husband to part with his land. It had been their salvation.

In November of 1974 Giacomo told his neighbor Mario Lungo that he had it in his head to sell some of his land so that he could build a house for his son. Lungo advised him to let the word get around, especially up in Sora, perched high on the promontory behind them. There was always a shortage of land up there, where families huddled in tiny houses crowded along a ridge whose precipitous face once afforded protection from attack in medieval times. He had a cousin there; he could tell him. Giacomo said that he was not quite ready; first he needed a surveyor to come mark the lot to sell. He did not know yet how much he would let go – maybe as much as a hectare, but it would depend on what the surveyor said.

The surveyor came a few days before Christmas. He walked the land with Giacomo. When they had come full circle he told Giacomo that he should set aside a one-hectare strip to be divided into seven building lots. If he sold each lot separately he could receive as much as twenty million. He proceeded to show Giacomo how he would make the division and at the same time set aside a strip running in front of the lots as a right of way. Giacomo told him to drive in the iron stakes. When he went into the house later he had something of great importance to tell Maria; if for one hectare of land divided into seven lots they could receive as much as twenty million, then they could not only build the house for Luigi for twelve million but have eight million left over to start on one for Bruno. Suddenly the goal of settling their sons seemed closer; the finishing of the house for Luigi would be immediately followed by beginning one for Bruno. Giacomo felt a great surge of power as he contemplated the small familial world he was going to create in this corner of his land. That evening Giacomo, Maria, and Bruno talked at length. By bedtime it was decided that a house for Bruno would rise two stories above their own. In that way no more of the precious two hectares of remaining land would have to be used.

The following day Giacomo made a visit to his friend Lungo. The time had come to spread the word. He would himself tell the bartender in Latina Scalo and the barber in the village. He wanted Lungo to talk to his cousin in Sora.

Hardly a week had passed before a car stopped, driven by a man from Sora. He said that he heard that Rossi had a good deal of land for sale. He told Giacomo that he did not want much himself – only a thousand square meters, just enough to build a house for his son. They walked to where the iron stakes marked the lots. The man pointed to the one he wanted, the first, the one that bordered the road on one side, the right of way on the other. When Giacomo told him that the price for that piece was 3.5 million, the man threw up his hands in a gesture of despair. He cried out that he was not a rich man, indeed a poor man, who wanted only a little land to settle his son on, for in Sora there was not even a square meter left to buy. He could not pay a lira more than 2.8 million. The two remained in the field for more than an hour and a half. At the end they shook hands on a price of 3.2 million. In a week Giacomo received the payment in full. He opened an account in the Banca di Roma in Latina Scalo, where he had received the loan in 1964. In the middle of January he sold the next lot for three million.

With 6.2 million safely in the bank he decided to stop selling. From everything he saw, the price of land was still going up. He now had enough to start buying the materials for Luigi's house. If he could sell the remaining five, he would have enough extra to build Bruno's as well.

II

After squeezing himself in and out of the tiny Fiat for two years Giacomo was convinced that it was hardly an automobile at all. He now considered himself an excellent driver. He liked to push the accelerator to the floor, but even when he did every Fiat 225 and 126 sped by him. He had his heart set on owning a 124. He knew it would be hard to convince Maria. She said that she thought he was crazy when he mentioned it to her. Did they not have expenses as it was? It would be one thing if he were working regularly, she said, but as it was she could hardly make ends meet with what Luigi and Bruno brought her. He began by saying that Luigi would need a car of his own when he married. He would give him the 500. He then reminded her that he would be working in the sugar-beet refinery in the summer, as he had almost every other year. They paid well. Besides, he told her, the land belonged to him, and he could do as he saw fit with the money. When Maria heard those words she knew that it was best to hold her tongue. The following afternoon they drove to the Fiat agency in Latina Scalo. There in the window was a bright yellow four-door 124. The dealer said that he would give Giacomo an especially good price for it – two hundred fifty thousand down and twenty thousand per month for two years. He then invited Maria to sit in the front. The seat was so much roomier than in the 500. She could stretch her legs out. And when Giacomo slipped in behind the wheel, she did not have to press against the door to give him room. Giacomo was right, the 124 was a real automobile. Later in the week he picked it up from the dealer. On the way home he stopped to buy some tapes for the tape deck. Then in the late afternoon he took Maria for a ride to the village to show off. On the way he slipped a recording of a Roman *stornello* into the deck. The strong beat filled the car with music. Everywhere the sun dappled the olive groves, transforming the road into a giant kaleidoscope down which they sped. Maria threw back her head and laughed. Giacomo pressed the accelerator to the floor, forcing the car to climb at break-neck speed. The tires screeched on the first S turn. "Giacomo, you are mad, mad!" Maria screamed as she was thrown against the door. Her husband looked at her, his face breaking out into a broad smile of pleasure. Maria laughed again.

III

During March, April, and May of 1975 Giacomo worked on one of the new houses being built along the Via Casa Grande. He was biding his time on the land. Industrial employment had been falling for two years, but the price of land crept steadily upward. Giacomo felt that he was sitting on a gold mine. Agricultural prices had risen slowly. In early spring sugar beets, wheat and some corn for Maria's animals had been sown on the remaining two hectares. Since the sale of the cows Giacomo had gone to a 50-50 basis with Lombardo for cultivating the land. After all the expenses, Giacomo's half share was a little more than enough to pay the taxes and the cooperative fee. The mortgage to the Università Agraria had been paid up. The land had become free and clear in January 1974. Giacomo often looked out beyond Maria's clothesline to the yellowing wheat stretching toward the iron stakes. His eyes needed time to shorten their vision. It saddened him to realize the diminished boundaries of his domain. Already the man from Sora was pouring concrete for his son's house on the first lot. On the second, materials were being piled. But when Giacomo looked in the direction of the five lots his heart leaped. There was a great richness stored in five thousand square meters of farm land. The time was coming to harvest it all. Luigi and Silvia planned to marry in 1977. It would take a year and a half to build the house.

After the six-week turn in the sugar-beet factory in July and August, Giacomo began to clear the land where Luigi's house was to be built. One day he turned about to see a man draw up nearby and get out of his new Lancia. He was from Latina. He was looking for land. He showed Giacomo his card. He was a representative of a development corporation with headquarters in Milan. He explained that they had the capital to buy fine land like that and then sell off the lots individually at a profit. The advantage to the seller lay in saving notary fees, to say nothing of having all the money right away drawing interest in the bank. He was willing to buy the five lots for 17.5 million on the spot. Giacomo was taken aback. He had planned to sell them one at a time by the beginning of the New Year for four million a lot. If he accepted now he would get 3.5 million apiece. It was a big decision, he would need time, he said.

That evening at the table the talk was long and passionate. Giacomo was alone in wanting to hold out. The others were for selling now. Why wait, they demanded; he had done well but who knows what the future might hold. By morning he had joined them in the decision to sell. When the money was finally deposited the total came to 23.7 million!

IV

That Christmas Maria invited all of her family for the midday meal. Concetta and Pasquale sent word from Busto and Gallarate that they and their families could not join them. They would come down for the Feast of the Assumption in August instead, when they could stay longer. It was the time of the year that Giulia looked forward to most. She and Giovanni always made room for everyone, somehow, in the house. It was once again like it was in the old days – Concetta always in the kitchen with her mother, Pasquale in the piazza talking to old friends or playing cards with Giovanni.

On Christmas day Tonino arrived first, with Giovanni and Giulia, Emilia and their four children. Emilia was still feeding the baby at her breast. Michele came next with Pasquetta and their three children in his new car. The upholstery shop was doing well. Since Tonino had joined in partnership they were using new imitation synthetic fabrics. When he saw Teresa he dropped on his knees and with arms outstretched implored her in a mocking tone to return to work with them. Teresa drew back as if to strike her uncle, then turning on her heels she strode from the room. She complained of feeling nervous the remainder of the day.

Salvatore came last with Dorotea, their three daughters, and son, the apple of Salvatore's eye, "the prince" as he was known in the family. Dorotea wore a new coat with fur at the collar and the sleeves. The women gathered around to feel and admire – all except Giulia, who remained gazing at her son, caressing his face, holding his hand in hers. "Salvatore, Salvatore, my son, my son, you work too hard," she said, her voice laden with admiration, mixed with resentment. "You are always buying your wife something new. Your daughters are better dressed than the rich of Latina and you spoil Alberto as if he was the Prince of Valmonte. Your face is so thin. You will kill yourself." Salvatore smiled, patted his mother's hand and said that he knew it was a mother's fate to worry about her children until the day she goes to her grave. Then he turned toward his father, sitting silently at the table. "Why does Papa look so poorly; have you not been feeding him enough?" Giulia answered that Giovanni Battista had not been feeling well for some days. He hardly ate. She worried about him every minute. Just that morning she had lit candles to San Antonio, Santa Anna, and Santa Rita.

Maria called everyone to the table. As usual, she remained on her feet preparing, serving, cajoling. Then she joined the rest. It was tiring but exhilarating. Maria loved to talk. In time the conversation turned to politics, as it had more and more in recent years. It was Tonino's favorite subject. He had become the secretary of the Communist Party of Valmonte. Even as a boy in school he had a fascination for history. Like Salvatore he liked to read, not adventure stories, but rather Togliatti, Gramsci, Amendola. He spoke well, with conviction and feeling. He talked about the Italian working class, themselves; people like Giovanni, who had worked his whole life without proper recognition of the sacrifices he had made. It was beholden to them all, he said, to realize what their true interests were, not to be duped by the ruling classes. They had all prospered thanks to their hard work, but they must not forget that the advantages they had won could be lost. Parliamentary elections would be coming, probably in the spring. It was time for the workers to tell the governing classes that they must share their power. Maria broke in to say that she did not know anything about politics, but she knew what was right and what was wrong. It was wrong for those who rule to keep everything for themselves. It is right that all, poor and rich alike, should be treated equally before the law, she exclaimed. But that is not what happens. A peasant or a laborer steals a loaf of bread to feed his family and goes to jail. A rich man embezzles the savings of the poor and what happens? Nothing – his powerful friends get him off. It is always the same, she persisted, the priests, bosses, landowners control everything and they keep it all to themselves. "Yes, remember how it was during the war," she said, "when people with nothing to eat went to Lawyer Suza for a little flour to make some bread. He would always turn them away, he with his cellars bulging with flour and oil, he and his pious ways, saying that he was a better Christian than anyone else. But even then I did not really understand. The first time I voted for the Christian Democrats, or was it the Republicans, I don't remember. But then the next time I voted for the Socialists, for nothing was changing, even with all their fine talk. But now my eyes have been opened. I see that the Socialists didn't do anything either. They just crawled into bed with the Christian Democrats and did as they pleased. Next time there is an election, I am going to vote for the Communists."

Tonino applauded. Giacomo, smiling, pulled out his party card to show his brother-in-law. He had recently become a member. Giacomo had cast his ballot for the Socialist-Communist alliance in the administrative elections and for the Communists in the national elections from the time he was old enough to vote. At first he had shied away from becoming a member in the local section. He was afraid something might happen. It had been hard enough to find work, and if they knew you were a Communist they might tell you to go away. Since he had the land he felt more secure.

Every night on TV he could see with his own eyes what the trouble was. The same people ruled. The politicians, the priests, the bosses connived to keep everything in their own hands. Workers never got their fair share of the pie. "Things are going to change," Giacomo said when Maria had finished her discourse. "The Communists are not going to let the working classes get pushed around anymore. You wait and see Berlinguer whip those big pieces in the next election," he finished, with a note of triumphant expectation.

It was the Church that was really at the center of Giacomo's ire. "Poor Italy," he said, "we have no coal, we have no oil, just blue sky, too many people and the pope and his whole entourage to support. Why don't the Americans take him off our backs. They have all the money. Look what the priests have done to Valmonte. First they rob this church and then that one. So the archbishop gets rid of one priest and then the next one does the same thing. They had to close San Lorenzo because Don Tommaso stripped it bare. And that is because people are stupid enough to believe that God will save them. God never saved anyone. God is just an idea that people have in their heads," Giacomo said, slapping his fist down on the table.

A strangled moan escaped from Giulia's lips. "Don't talk that way, you are blaspheming. It is a crime to talk that way about God." The words rasped, one rapidly after the other, from her clenched throat. "God created everything. God is everywhere. God makes miracles every day. You can say what you like about the priests; once they were real priests, now they are just men like everyone else. But there is nothing without God. Who is there to help us poor creatures if it is not God?" Giulia's dark eyes flashed at Giacomo and fixed on him.

Giovanni pulled on her sleeve to make her desist. He had heard those words so many times. Giovanni, like his wife, always voted for the Socialists. The Socialists believe in taking away from the rich to give to the poor; that is the way it should be. Giulia vowed that she would never vote for the Communists because they don't believe in God. Giovanni was not certain. As long as he could remember, he had been a Socialist, even though he had not always carried their card. There was the time he had enrolled with the Fascists in Stilo to get a job in Rome, and it did not do any good. Since then he had not had much faith in parties. But they were right. There was still no respect for the worker. The struggle had to go on. But it was up to them – to Tonino, to the others. It was their struggle now.

V

Christmas day was the last time Maria saw her father. Giovanni died suddenly on January 16. He had been feeling poorly for some time but it did not seem serious. It happened in the late afternoon. He was sitting in the kitchen with Giulia when he got up to get something from the cupboard, staggered a few steps and fell to the floor. Giulia remained as if paralyzed; she tried to scream but no sound came. For a moment she could not move. She had always known that Giovanni Battista's day might come before her own. But she was not prepared. She ran to the door calling Tonino's name, down the stairs, up the street, clutching the wall for support as she went. As she turned the corner she ran into her son; collapsing in his arms, she cried, "He is dead, he is dead." Tonino helped his mother back to the house, his face clouded with tears. Giovanni was still breathing but unconscious. Tonino gathered his father in his arms and carried him to his car. Giulia in back leaned forward to cradle her husband's head in her arms. "My Giovanni Battista, my dear, dear Giovanni Battista," she cried. At the bottom of the hill his head slumped to one side. He was dead. From Giulia came a sustained wail that carried all her grief, despair, and love born of fifty-four years of living with her beloved Caicala. Tonino continued to drive helplessly toward the hospital. In a piercing, wailing voice Giulia began the lamentation that a southern woman sings on the death of her husband. At the hospital she continued while a crowd pressed in to stare at the Calabrian until her husband was removed from the car.

The funeral was held two days later in Santa Anna, to give Concetta and Pasquale time to come down from the North. The church was full, Calabrians filling the first seats, Valmontesi in the rear. Long black shawls draped Giulia's, Concetta's, and Maria's heads. They sat with the family on either side of the coffin. Their cries of grief intermingled with the voice of the intoning priest. As the bell signaled the end of the service, Pasquale and Tonino supported their mother and helped her slowly from the church; then Salvatore, Pasquale, Tonino, and Michele bore Giovanni aloft on their shoulders and began the procession toward the main gate of the village preceded by the priest, an altar boy swinging the thurible, amd another one carrying the cross. Giulia, Concetta, and Maria with the help of Giacomo, Luigi, and Bruno walked behind followed by Dorotea, Emilia, Pasquetta, Teresa, Luigi, Pietro, and all the rest. At the gate the procession stopped. The coffin was placed on the back of a truck for the steep, bumpy ride up to the cemetery of San Antonio. Giacomo, Salvatore, and Pasquale followed in their cars, others walked. The long path through the cemetery to the new burial wall was lined on either side by large wreaths supported on metal stands. The procession regrouped, then stopped again as if Giulia, Concetta, and Maria could not allow the last final steps to be taken. Their wailing filled the air. Salvatore, Tonino, and Pasquale consoled, despaired, cajoled, reprimanded; they must move on, the time had come. The opening was in the bottom tier. The wheel of fortune had assigned Giovanni Battista to the abyss. The coffin was slid into the aperture. The wailing flowed, ebbed, ceased entirely. The priest uttered the words of the internment and with his blessing everyone slowly moved away except for Salvatore, who remained to watch the sacristan wall up the aperture with brick and mortar.

Afterward, the family gathered in the old house in the village. It seemed as if there could be no end to the mourning. There was so much to grieve about, to remember. It was said over and over what a good father he had been, struggling and sacrificing for them all. They would remember him every day of their lives. Maria would see to it that fresh flowers were placed on his grave every week. They agreed to divide the expenses of the funeral. First one then another spoke of ways in which respect to Giovanni had been shown. They told how the church had been full; the names of Valmontesi at the church were recalled; the messages on the twenty wreaths that lined the path in the cemetery were lovingly recited. Salvatore spoke for all of them when he said how proud it had made him feel as a Calabrian to see the whole town turn out to pay respect; everyone knew Giovanni as a good husband, a good father, and a good worker. But it still made him angry, he said, to think about all those years of humiliation he and Mama had suffered because they had come from the South.

For days afterward, Giulia was not to be consoled. Life for her was finished, she repeated over and over again. She should have died when Giovanni Battista did so that she could lie next to him in eternity; now when her time came who knows where in that wall she would rest. Fifty-four years together. None of them could understand, she insisted, how alone she felt. It was finally Concetta who persuaded her to leave the house, to move in with Maria. Only a daughter could properly care for a mother. Concetta and Pasquale brought her down on their way to the train. Everything in the house was left the way it was when Giovanni died. Giulia brought with her only a few clothes, an extra black dress, her shroud, and her oxygen tank and mask to help her through her asthma spells. Maria made up Bruno's bed for her; she would share that room with Luigi. Bruno slept on a cot in the hall.

Giulia remained in bed for two weeks, her hands clutching a rosary. She cried that she had no will to get up. She wanted to be left alone to die. When the first of February shone bright and clear with a warm sun, Maria placed her mother's chair outside and entreated her to take a turn sitting. Giulia only moved her face toward the wall, but later she rose, dressed, and slowly walked outside to meet the sun.

On the first of March a pension check arrived. Tonino brought it down from the house, where it had been delivered and where he continued to live. It was for a hundred eighty thousand lire. The enclosed notice, which Tonino read to his mother and Maria, said that the same would be sent to her every three months. Maria said that it was none of her business what her mother did with the money, it was hers, but what with all the expenses and Giacomo out of work, the money should be turned over to her, just as Giacomo, Luigi, and Bruno gave her whatever they were paid. Maria could see the anger in her mother's face. She said nothing more about it. Later Giulia told Maria, "I have no use for that money. Take it, you need it, but you have to put some away each time it comes for my funeral, and leave enough for the oxygen and every once in a while a box of sweet cookies."

VI

In March of 1976 Giacomo began to build Luigi's house. Luigi had had a blueprint made by a friend in Latina Scalo who had taken the engineering program in the vocational school. The beginning was simple enough; the problems would come with the stairs and the roof. Giacomo was out first thing in the morning and worked straight through until Maria called him for the noonday meal. As soon as he finished his coffee he rose from the table, retightened his loosened belt, and returned to placing one *tufo* block by another, making cement in the xower mixer, tapping the blocks with a trowel, squinting along them to see if they were straight. He liked what he was doing. It was work for a man, not like hoeing sugar beets or cultivating tomatoes. Every day he could see that the wall had crept higher. In the early evening and on Sundays Luigi and Bruno would help him, and the walls would advance more rapidly. Still, it was slow and fussy work, especially building in the window and door spaces. Giacomo had wanted to have the roof on before the winter rains started.

VII

In June Caterina graduated from the third and final year of the middle school. She never had the problems in schooling of Luigi and Teresa, and she got better grades than Bruno. At the end of her second year there was talk around the table of her going to high school. Maria was of two minds about her going. On the one hand Caterina was the last chance they had. If she went she might become a schoolteacher or midwife – a lady. On the other, Maria needed her in the house. Giacomo was at home most of the time and Luigi back from ILPINA every day for lunch; eating sandwiches at work was just not the same as taking a good meal around the table. Giacomo did not like the idea of her going. The way he put it was that all they heard on the television was that high school students, even university students, could find no work when they graduated. It was not right, he said, for parents to sacrifice for their children to get all that education for nothing. That was part of it. The rest he did not put into words. He felt possessive of his daughters. He wanted to know where they were and what they were doing all the time. He felt jealous as well. If Caterina got more education, she would put on airs. It was difficult enough now when they teased him because of his Sessa dialect or for Italian words that he mispronounced. Caterina teased her father by saying how far behind the times he was. It was difficult to maintain his authority without flying into a rage that Maria would criticize him for. It was decided that Caterina would stay at home and help her mother. Caterina said that it did not make any difference to her; she didn't want to go to school anyway. When she had finished her chores by midmorning she would get in the front seat of Giacomo's car, turn on her favorite rock tape, and sway to the music.

VIII

In June Teresa met Giuseppe Campagna. She had not had many chances to know anyone before. The country was different from the village, where during the late afternoon promenade opportunities existed. Several times Teresa's friend Franca had invited her to come along for an outing. Franca had a car. Giacomo had refused to allow her to go. Maria had said nothing out of respect for his rights. But the fourth time she asked him how he expected his daughter to meet a man if he kept her at home like a nun. "You have to keep up with the times, Giacomo. If you don't, you will be sorry – something worse will happen," she said. Giacomo relented with a shrug. "Go ahead, go on, go," he said.

There were six altogether in the car. Franca had agreed to take her friend Lidia, who had invited her friend Pietro. Pietro had said he would go as long as he could invite two of his friends, Mario and Giuseppe. When Giuseppe was introduced to Teresa he said that he knew her even if she did not know him. He had gone to school with Bruno. It made Teresa feel better that at least one of Franca's friends was not a stranger. She liked Giuseppe right away. They drove to the beach in Latina for an ice cream and then returned. Teresa said that her father expected her back before dark. On the way home Giuseppe told Teresa all about himself. He said that his father raised sheep, that he himself drove a tractor plowing fields, and that he was going to have to do military service soon. As she was getting out of the car he said that he wanted to see her again. That night she lay awake for a long time wondering how she could like a man so much whose father was a shepherd and who was happy being a tractor driver. During July and August Giuseppe came by every Sunday afternoon to visit Teresa. Teresa could see that her father liked him. He was serious, a hard worker, not the kind of person to take advantage of a man's daughter. Twice Teresa went off on her bicycle to meet secretly with Giuseppe for a ten-minute conversation in his car. When she returned Maria guessed what had happened. "This situation cannot continue," she said, "because you know how your father is. You either have to get engaged or let him go."

Teresa and Giuseppe became engaged in September. On the first Sunday of the month Giuseppe was invited by Teresa for a noonday meal. It took a while for him to find his courage. After a glass of Giacomo's grappa he asked for their daughter's hand in marriage. Giacomo replied that Teresa was still young, but if she wished to become engaged he would not stand in her way. "If you have any intentions of taking advantage of my daughter you should leave right now," Giacomo said sternly. He then told Giuseppe that he could call on Teresa in the evening three or four times a week and on Sunday. Giuseppe said that he understood and had no intentions of taking advantage of their daughter. His only desire, he said, was to make her happy. Before he left he invited Giacomo, Maria, and Teresa to take the noonday meal the following Sunday with his parents.

Angelo and Natalia Campagna lived on the far end of Valmonte that borders on Sessa. Their house on a dirt road surrounded by fields reminded Giacomo and Maria of how Via Casa Grande had looked when they first moved. They liked it. It was country. In the back seat Teresa moaned audibly. "They are in the sticks, not a house around and this dirt road. I would hate to live here." Angelo was herding his sheep into the pen when they arrived. Natalia was removing loaves of bread from her outdoor oven. Giuseppe jumped down off the tractor. There were apologies for not being more prepared, but in a short while they were around the table. Giacomo and Maria immediately felt at home. Angelo spoke at length about his sheep, how devoted he was to them,

how his devotion had paid him rather handsomely. With the sale of
sheep at the right time he had bought some land here and there. Now
he had twelve hectares in all, something to leave his three sons. As for
the sheep, "None of them care about the sheep the way I do," he
explained. "Mario has his automobile repair shop and Giuseppe has his
tractor. And young Matteo – all he does now is fool around and listen
to that crazy music. Who knows what he will do? Yes, better that they
sell the herd when I die." Giuseppe, he pointed out, had a head for the
land, so he could handle the cows. "I am going to build a house for him
over there behind the cow shed when he has done his military service,"
he said, "so that he and his wife will have a decent place to live."
Giacomo said he was pleased to hear about the house. "Now that our
daughter and your son are engaged it is not too early to begin to make
plans to settle them." Maria said that Teresa was still young, so it was
just as well everyone needed more time to get ready. "I have started, of
course, on Teresa's trousseau, but I still have a long way to go. You
know how it is with a husband out of work much of the time and the
marriage of our first son approaching. I think that I will need at least
another three years before I am ready." Natalia nodded understandingly. She said that she did not know how long it would take to build
the house. "My husband has not worked with houses the way yours
has. He is not so handy with tools. It's the animals that he is good at."
After dinner Angelo, Giacomo, and Giuseppe played cards while the
women cleaned up.

On the way home Giacomo and Maria talked about how they felt in
good company with Angelo and Natalia. Giacomo liked the stories that
Angelo told. They made him laugh. Maria held a loaf of Natalia's bread
in her lap. She wished that she had an outdoor oven. It would be good
for roasting pork, chicken, and rabbit, as well for making bread. Teresa
sat in the back seat without saying a word. The more she saw Giuseppe
the more she liked him. He was gentle, he was serious. He was tall,
handsome with a moustache. But it was the animals, the dirt road, and
the house behind the cow shed that her future father-in-law planned on
building for them that gave her pain.

IX

By the beginning of November Giacomo was ready to raise the roof on
Luigi's house. He wanted it on before the rains set in and before Bruno
left for the army. Being peaked, it was a more complicated construction
than his flat roof. Salvatore helped set the supports. One Sunday five
men, including Tonino, worked all day. By the following week it was
completed. Giacomo felt relieved. The heaviest task had been done, but

already the six million lire had been spent and costly work lay ahead. The red marble tile floor alone would cost 1.5 million, and the wooden doors and window frames another 1.3 million.

The interior work – wiring, plastering, papering, tiling – moved slowly. Giacomo had had less experience with finishing. After he had laid the tiles in the kitchen and bathroom, Maria pointed out that he had made a mistake; the lines formed by the edges of the tiles were intended to meet, not separate. They had to be reset. It was already spring. Luigi and Silvia had planned to marry in the summer of 1977, during Luigi's vacation. But the house was not finished, nor was Silvia's furniture yet complete. The big bed, side tables, armoire, and bureau had already been paid for, as well as the highboy, table, divan, and armchairs for the living room. Donato had spent 5.5 million. He still had to provide the kitchen and the dining room, the china, the silver, the crystal. The style chosen was heavy, baronial, expensive. Silvia was his only daughter. Giacomo was building a handsome house for his son and Donato was determined to uphold his honor. By the beginning of October he would be ready. All would be in hand, he could retire. The total for the furniture would come to 7.5 million. Rosaria had finished embroidering the last of the sheets. The trousseau occupied six large boxes and two battered suitcases, which contained thirty sheets, fifty towels, three bedspreads, six tablecloths, and thirty six napkins. Then there was her personal wardrobe. The wedding was reset for the thirtieth of October.

X

In the middle of July Giacomo stopped working on the house in order to work at the sugar-beet refinery. He was given his assignment as conveyor belt operator. He was glad to be taken on. Each summer employment at the refinery became more critical; without regular work it was the only way to get health insurance. Now he and his dependents would be covered for another eight months. His stomach still caused him discomfort, especially in the spring. Maria nagged him to have tests in the hospital. "They don't hurt you," she said. "Italia's son had it done. You just have to swallow some stuff that tastes like chalk. Stop being a sissy. All our married life we have had to struggle with your stomach. Enough!" Finally he promised Maria that he would go if she would stop talking about it – not this year, because he had the house to finish, but next summer, after the refinery turn was finished.

Maria often thought that she should go to the hospital for tests. Every year her liver bothered her more and more. It had never been right since the war. From time to time she would eat unseasoned food.

Her liver pained her less, but then she felt nervous. She enjoyed eating as much as she did cooking. Teresa kept telling her mother to stop eating what other people left on their plates. Teresa herself was a finicky eater and left food on her plate, complaining first of a stomachache, then of her nerves. Maria attributed it to her high-strung nature. Sometimes she had to confess that she did not understand what Giuseppe saw in Teresa; Luigi was probably right, Giuseppe actually liked her flightiness.

XI

Giacomo returned to working on the house early in September. He installed a sliding door on the garage and jalousies in the windows, and dug the leach field. Then he stopped. He had done enough. Luigi could finish the cupboards in the kitchen and install the ornate flowered ceramic towel holders, soap dish, and mirror. Around the table final calculations were made. The house had cost fifteen million lire, a million more than they had estimated. There was still 8.7 million left in the bank to start Bruno's house with in the spring, but there was the wedding to pay for.

XII

The burden of organizing the wedding was Maria's. Giacomo had built the house. Maria had had several conversations with Rosaria. Luigi had brought his future mother-in-law and Silvia in the car for noonday meals on two Sundays in August. Both Rosaria and Silvia were relieved when Donato pleaded some excuse. Silvia only hoped that her father would not disgrace them all at the wedding by drinking too much. Maria made it clear that Luigi would give Silvia the traditional gold wedding ring and bracelet in addition to the engagement ring he had already bought her. It was the clothing that concerned her, she said. She knew that Sessa custom was like Valmonte; the man should buy both the bride's white wedding dress as well as a going-away dress and coat. But, as she pointed out, the costs for the house had been great. It was not necessary for Maria to pay more. Rosaria told her that she understood very well; Maria should not concern herself. They would buy Silvia's clothes.

On the next occasion the conversation turned toward the feast. The wedding service would take place in the church of San Giuseppe in Sessa. Rosaria had already fixed everything with Don Natalino. He was more broad-minded than most about Donato being a Communist and his blaspheming the Church every day in the piazza. Better that the Church make a place for such a black sheep in its ample bosom and infinite wisdom, Don Natalino argued. As for the restaurant, Luigi had selected one in Sonnino, near Sessa. The owner was a client of Luigi's boss. He would give the best price of all the places that he had been to – eighty-five hundred a person for thirteen courses, including wine. Not only that but the restaurant was located behind the medieval Abbey of Fossanova, where Thomas Aquinas had died. The owner told Luigi that his wedding couples found it convenient to go there between the pasta and meat courses to have their pictures taken in the cloister. The conversation made Maria mindful of how much had changed since she and Giacomo married twenty-four years before. Whoever thought of having a wedding feast in a restaurant in those times? She still didn't like the idea, but now no one would think of going to all that work – not even she would – but she did want to have a reception in her house before they went to the church. She would not feel right if she did not prepare something for her family and friends.

Maria had been working on her guest list for some time. It had grown to 130 names. She had tried to cut it down but found it impossible to leave off a single name from her side. Rosaria said that there would be seventy from theirs. Maria could not help but be gratified that even though the wedding was in Sessa more of their side would be there. But the cost alone, as she figured it in her head, would be over one million for her share, and they had not even talked about the confetti. It was still the custom, as it had been when she was married, for the bride and groom to pass confetti from a basket. She remembered how she had handed out loose confetti as well as some wrapped in bags to every outstretched hand. Now it was the custom to wrap all the candy in little bags of tulle, tied with a ribbon. Maria reasoned that it would not take too long for her, Teresa, and Caterina to make the 200 *bomboniere*. It was agreed that she would buy the confetti, tulle, and ribbon, if Rosaria provided the large basket.

Later that week after she and her daughters had prepared the candy, Maria started making up thirty-three favors, one for each family she had invited. She had already selected three miniature replications – an automobile, a telephone, and a balance. Maria had almost decided upon the airplane instead of the balance, but she wanted to include one old-fashioned thing.

Each favor was wrapped in a small plastic box with a ribbon. She left until the last the special task of filling a basket with artificial flowers and confetti and covering it with cellophane. This would be for Luigi's boss. Later, a few weeks before the wedding, Luigi would deliver one favor to each family they had invited. At that time she was surprised and pleased to hear that most people had liked the balance the best. She had thought they would prefer the automobile or even the telephone.

In September Maria turned her attention to clothing the family for the wedding. Both Teresa and Caterina needed new dresses. Twice she went with them to Latina, first to the stores, then to the open markets. Nothing pleased until Maria threatened that they would have to get along with what they already had. If they disgraced the family it would be their fault. Caterina chose a two-piece beige dress, Teresa a black one. She agreed to buying them matching shoulder bags too, even though she said it was ridiculous to throw away good money on such a detail.

For Giacomo and Bruno's suits she was able to save by sending their measurements to her brother Pasquale. He had the suits made up for half of what they would have paid in a store. That made her feel better about spending more on Luigi's suit and her own dress and coat. "They are going to have to last me the weddings of Teresa, Bruno, Caterina, as well as Luigi, so they had better be good," she said emphatically. Even without new shoes for everyone, Maria had spent 300,000; the shoes would come to another 50,000 at least. Counting the feast, clothes, favors, and reception, Luigi's wedding was going to cost at least 1.5 million lire. There was nothing to do but continue to take money from the bank. That would mean less to start building Bruno's house with, but Maria knew they were doing the right thing. At that moment Luigi's wedding came before everything else.

Two weeks before the wedding Maria began laying plans at a midday meal for the reception that she wanted to have before the wedding; everyone would come to their house, she explained, have something to eat and drink, and then drive to Sessa. In that way everyone would have a ride, no one would get lost, and the day would start pleasantly for their family and friends. At first she planned to have it outdoors, in front of the house, with a big table made of boards and sawhorses. The more she thought about it, though, the more convinced she became that it was going to rain that day. "When Luigi was baptized, it rained torrents, while houses were swept away in the valley. On his communion there was a downpour again. No, I know it will rain. I will have it indoors, even though no one will be able to move for the crowd. But who cares on a wedding day? What matters is that everyone is together," said Maria. She began a list of what there would be to eat: four kinds of sweets, maybe five, and liqueurs. She was thinking, too, of sandwiches of ham and cheese and hot chocolate. Giacomo could contain his irritation no longer. "What is all this business about sandwiches here and hot chocolate there?" he asked angrily. "All people want to do is have a glass or two, and coffee. Enough is enough."

"You leave this reception to me. It's my business—my business! Do you understand?" Maria answered tartly. "I know what I am doing.

There are people who like a bite of a sandwich in the morning, a cup of hot chocolate to carry them over through the service. It will be late before we sit down to eat. I have never made a bad impression yet in any of the baptisms or communions that I have prepared in this family and I do not intend to start now with the wedding of Luigi." Giacomo knew it was better not to protest further; Maria did know what it was best to do for her first son's wedding.

In the last week there was much to do to make everything presentable; the yard had to be picked up, the old bedspring and tires placed out of sight, the hall whitewashed, the pigsty cleaned. There was hardly a moment for anyone to sit down. On the Thursday before, Giacomo drove Maria, armed with baking tins, flour, oil, eggs, and sugar, to the house of Natalia, Teresa's future mother-in-law. Natalia had invited Maria to use her outdoor oven. When they arrived, they met Natalia returning from the hills with a bundle of olive wood on her head gathered early that morning from their grove. Maria remained to bake for two days. The smell of the burning olive branches and the glow of the ashes inside the oven evoked strong memories of her childhood, standing as a little girl by her mother's side. Could it have been that she was recalling the oven at Stilo, or was it the one in Titalo that her mother first used when they came to Valmonte? The work touched her deeply. As she stood there pushing in the blobs of dough on the long-handled paddle and pulling out pastry baked to a golden brown, she was overwhelmed with a deep feeling of mingled sadness and joy. All of a sudden, and for the first time, she realized what it meant to have part of her life finished. Her children were leaving now, and yet it seemed that it was just yesterday that they were born. She remembered with piercing vividness how it was the day that Luigi arrived. She was startled by a quick pain deep down inside; then it passed. In her reverie she burned a batch. Her breathing began to quicken as she removed the next; they were done perfectly. Her first son was to marry, she thought with joy. Everything seemed to be coming around in full circle, generation following generation. That is the way it must be, she said to herself. During her time at Natalia's, Maria baked six different kinds of pastry.

On Saturday, the day before the wedding, the sun shone brightly as it had all during the week of October. In the late afternoon Concetta arrived with Felice and two of her sons-in-law; her oldest daughter was expecting in three weeks, her next suffered from kidney disease and could not travel. The rest of the children stayed at home, for there was no room for them in the car. Their young husbands, a mechanic and a bus driver, came in their place. Giulia was overjoyed to have Concetta at her side. "Mama, you look so good," Concetta said. "Living here

with Maria must suit you, like I told you it was the right thing to do."
Giulia said nothing, but later out of earshot of Maria she told Concetta
that it did not always suit her, but what could she do, she had to hold
her tongue. "Teresa and Caterina fight all the time and they are disrespectful to me. Giacomo is a heathen and Maria takes my pension
money," she whispered hoarsely. Concetta patted her mother's hand
and told her that Maria had much to contend with, with her husband
out of work most of the time, the preoccupations about the houses,
Luigi's wedding, and still a son and two daughters to settle. Her
daughter's sympathetic caressing made Giulia feel better. "Yes, Maria is
good, she is a good daughter," she said.

Just before the evening meal Pasquale, Antonietta, their two young
sons, and Pasquale's partner, Tall Giovanni, as they called him, and his
wife arrived. Until Pasquale married he had lived with Tall Giovanni
and his five married brothers in a building owned by their widowed
mother above the tailor shop. Giovanni was welcomed and treated like
a member of the family, as if he were a brother.

After the meal the men went to Michele's house to play cards, leaving the house for the women to prepare. Teresa complained that she
was tired of washing dishes; it seemed to her that is all she did. Her
spirits rose considerably when Giuseppe dropped in later. They sat by
the window holding hands. Bruno called on his girlfriend, Luisa, a
worker at Accord. He had been paying her visits since he had come
home from the military. It was past midnight when the men returned;
Felice and Luigi were singing *stornelli* at the top of their lungs, and
Giacomo started running around the kitchen slapping Maria on her
behind until they both collapsed in chairs spent with laughter. Giulia
had taken to her bed from the excitement hours ago, her oxygen mask
clutched to her face, but as Concetta promised, they aroused her and
drove to the old house in the village for the night. It was like old times,
Giulia kept saying. It was one o'clock when Maria went to bed. The
rain had begun to fall.

She was on her feet by four the next morning. The guests had been
invited for eight thirty. There was much to do. She started preparing
the sandwiches. By six she had everyone else up with instructions to
make their beds right away so that there would be room to lay out the
clothes. Then Maria, assisted by Teresa, spread Giacomo's suit and tie
on the large bed, leaving room for Luigi's and Bruno's. The suits of the
two sons-in-law were arranged on Giulia's bed. Teresa ironed their
shirts, Caterina shined their shoes. While the men dressed, Maria fed
the animals.

By the time she was done, the invasion had started. The arrival of
Pasquale, Tonino, and Michele brought nine children into the kitchen.

The sandwiches were discovered, and Maria had to hurriedly make some more. When she turned from the table she saw Giacomo, Luigi, and Bruno standing in the door. Her heart jumped; how handsome they looked in their dark blue suits and white shirts!

Maria went to get dressed. She liked the way she looked; the blue dress with the stripes made her seem taller. So did the shoes, although she could barely squeeze her feet into them. Teresa and Caterina dressed and came for their mother's approval. While Concetta fixed her hair, Maria could hear Giacomo complaining loudly that he had been in the kitchen for ten minutes waiting for coffee and no one had prepared it. "Teresa, run quickly," she ordered, "and make coffee for the men."

By nine the house was full. It did not seem possible that it could hold any more and yet they came, wiping their wet feet at the door, leaving their umbrellas outside. Maria tried to be everywhere at once, seeing to the sweets, the liqueurs, the coffee, the sandwiches, the chocolate. She was gratified by the number of people who took chocolate. Giacomo was ebullient, serving drinks, offering his Marlboros. Maria could hardly believe it when Luigi told her it was eleven and they would have to leave.

He had to be there in time to talk to the priest – to confess, he said, making a wry face. Maria laughed. "All right, my son, let's go, the time has come," she said, kissing him warmly on both cheeks.

Maria was the last to leave; she locked the house. The rain had stopped, the sun shone brightly. Maria got in the back seat with Luigi, and Giacomo and Bruno sat in front. Teresa and Caterina rode with Concetta, Felice, and the sons-in-law. Now the moment was at hand that Maria had waited for, the ride to the church in the back seat of her husband's car with her son, the groom. "It is not possible, it is not possible," she said to herself as the car climbed toward Sessa. She was thinking back to her own wedding day with the man in the front seat. She leaned forward and put her hand on Giacomo's shoulder. "Hey Gia, we have pulled ahead a little since you and I did this, haven't we?" Maria said. "Yeah, a little," he replied, nodding. She could see his smile in the mirror.

The church of San Giuseppe in Sessa was larger than Santa Anna in Valmonte. There was plenty of room for the guests to move about in the back, to chat, to stop and read memorials. Don Natalino paced the service to meet the needs of the photographer, who flashed his bulbs first from one side, then the other, first in back and then in front. The four parents sat to the right of the altar in isolation on a long pew. Giacomo and Donato stared straight ahead, Maria and Rosaria prayed for a long time on their knees. Maria beseeched San Antonio, Santa Rita, and Santa Caterina to watch over and protect her son and his new wife and whatever children God might see fit to bless them with. She looked over at her mother, who knelt through the entire service with her rosary clutched in her hand, and knew that Giulia was doing the same thing. At the end, Maria prayed that her father's soul might rest in peace. As she sat back up on the pew she knew that it did not make any difference that she had voted for the Communists in the last election; those were all things apart.

As Maria predicted, several people got lost between the church in Sessa and the restaurant in Sonnino, but after much milling about everyone was seated and the thirteen-course feast was begun. In Maria's opinion, the antipasto was too small a portion, the broth was too watery, the pasta was overcooked, the chicken tough. She knew that she would have done better. She pushed off her new shoes under the table and downed another glass of wine. Tonino offered a toast, and then Pasquale, Michele, Felice. Cries of "Viva gli sposi" echoed from the right of the hall and then from the left. Luigi and Silvia rose to their feet at every "Viva." By five o'clock Felice and Tonino were singing *stornelli*; an accordion took up the beat. Tonino was like a top, wound up. He rushed over to where his mother was sitting next to Concetta and, throwing himself at her knees, sang "Mamma" with arms outstretched. Giulia covered her mouth with her hand as her body shook with laughter. Quick as lightning he was at Maria's side singing, teasing her for raising such good pigs. Hardly had he finished than Maria answered in a high staccato voice, teasing her brother for being so short and talking so much. Back and forth they went until they were laughing so hard they had to stop. Tonino slipped away momentarily. To Maria's left Rosaria was trying to free the wine bottle from Donato's grasp. Tonino returned and approached the head table with an air of great expectancy bearing two plates held firmly face to face. He stopped in front of Luigi and Silvia; children pressed round him, adults behind. In his most stentorian voice he announced that in the plates he was bearing the gift of life, the secret of the universe, the panacea for old age, the blessing of the young. Then with a great sweeping gesture he removed the top plate and pushed the bottom one toward the newly married couple; it bore a pear with its center hollowed out, into which was nestled the stem of another. The roars of laughter were deafening, the children jumped up and down with glee.

The time had come to pass the confetti. They had been seated at the table for five hours. It was dark outside. Maria turned toward Giacomo. She realized that he had been looking at her for some time. He smiled. Maria trembled all over.

11

The house of Bruno

I

After the wedding, Luigi and Silvia drove north with Pasquale, Antonietta, and their two boys. Apart from a day's trip into Switzerland from Busto, they spent half of their two-week honeymoon with Pasquale, the other with Concetta. That way they saved most of the eight hundred thousand lire they had collected in envelopes when they passed the confetti. There were still a refrigerator and a washing machine to buy.

When they returned to Valmonte, Silvia went back to work at Standa; it would be lonely in the house all by herself with nothing to do but dust, she said. Luigi had agreed to let her work until she became pregnant, then never again. The announcement came in the first week of March 1978: The baby would be born in September. Silvia stopped working; now she spent most of the day at home dusting, sleeping, and when the weather was fair sitting on the balcony embroidering the baby's trousseau. If Silvia did not drop in Maria went every day to visit – not that she wanted to interfere, she said, rather just to help if she could. Now Silvia had plenty of time to practice her cooking. She had not learned much from her mother, for Rosaria, forbidden from working by Donato, was jealous of her kitchen. Silvia would often come by mid-morning and say to Maria, "Hey Ma, how do you cook greens that way that Gigi likes?" or "Do you put anything on the chicken wings before you roast them, Ma?" On many days Silvia would eat the big midday meal with the rest of the family when Luigi returned from ILPINA; then there would be eight around the table, including Giulia.

Like her father-in-law, Silvia spoke in a Sessa dialect. From time to time Luigi would correct her, repeating the proper Italian word. Indeed, Luigi maintained a watchful attitude toward his wife, suggesting this, disapproving of that. He thought she ate too much, observed that she was getting fat, tried to restrict her to two glasses of wine a meal. One day after her third glass Silvia rested her head affectionately on Luigi's shoulder; annoyed, he pushed it away, saying that he wanted to eat. "What's a matter with you, Gigi, you're crazy! What kind of a man did I marry?" said Silvia, taking offense. Luigi angrily took her hand and twisted it. Silvia bit his. "Stop it, stop that right away!" yelled Luigi. Silvia persisted – she was not to be bullied by her husband. "I can eat and drink what I like, thank you very much. Besides, look at your stomach," she said sharply. Giacomo, sensing that it had gone far enough, put his arm around Luigi to prevent him from grabbing Silvia's arm again. "That's enough. Stop it you two. You have to live a lot of years together," he said. Giulia nodded vigorously across the table. Luigi and Silvia stared at each other for a moment in anger; then Silvia, smiling, took her husband by the hand and said, "Come on, Gigi, come on, I want to show you something that came for the baby this morning while you were at work. Ma, I'll come back later and you can show me how to make the sweet."

As soon as they were beyond the door Teresa said, "I can't stand Sessa dialect. Of course, I know Silvia can't help it because she was born there, but it sounds awful. How come she never learned Italian? Well, one thing I am thankful for, Beppe speaks Italian." Giacomo, raising his hand, slapped his daughter across the face once, twice. "If you think you are so smart, why didn't you finish the middle school? Tell me that!" demanded Giacomo. Teresa dropped her fork, leaned across the table toward her father and screamed, "I will tell you why, because you are so backward! You don't know what's going on, you didn't help me ever. All you ever want to do is control me." Bruno, pushing back his chair, said that he was going to leave, he couldn't stand "all the rubbish flying around." Giacomo turned away from Teresa and recommenced eating. Teresa, fidgeting before her half-eaten plate, said, "Ma, I can't eat a mouthful more, my stomach aches. This morning I woke up with a headache. I feel so nervous, I don't know what I am going to do. Beppe hasn't written in two days. Last time he wrote he said that they were going on maneuvers and then I won't hear for ever so long." Maria, between mouthfuls of bread, told her to take one of her tranquilizing pills from the cupboard. "Oh, I don't want to. I took one this morning and they don't do anything." Bruno returned for a drink of water before leaving to look for work. "Oh, there is Bruno, the most beautiful brother in the whole world," cried Teresa, jumping to her feet. She rushed to hug and kiss her brother. He pushed her aside and left. Giacomo, looking at his older daughter with incredulity, shook his head. "Poor Italy," he muttered, "poor Italy."

"Hey Ma, hey Ma," said Caterina, trying to get her mother's attention, waving a fork with a piece of tomato in her face. "I need a new pair of jeans. These are getting too tight." Maria continued eating, looking at her daughter. "Yes they are, Ma, they are. Besides, last week you gave money to Teresa for a pair and I didn't get anything." "Oh, shut up, you talk too much," retorted Teresa. "And you shut up," said Maria to her older daughter. "Get over there and start washing the dishes." With a dramatic sigh Teresa moved toward the sink. "You wait and see, when I get married I am going to live in a villa and have a dishwasher," she said with feeling as she wearily turned on the faucet. "Oh no you're not, you are going to live on a dirt road behind the cow barn," taunted Caterina. Teresa stamped her feet in rage. "I am not going to stand here and be insulted by my idiotic sister," she said, and swept from the room, striking out at her sister as hard as she could as she went by. Caterina expertly dodged the blow and persisted. "But Ma, all the girls have new jeans but me. You are so stingy." Giacomo picked up a glass of water to hurl its contents at his youngest daughter. Maria raised her hand just in time to prevent him. "You shut up and get over there and make the coffee," Giacomo yelled at Caterina. Caterina rose and walked tauntingly by her father. He raised his hand. She laughed and jumped away. Giulia pulled at Maria's sleeve until she got her attention and whispered that Caterina took three peaches, pointing at the pits on her plate. "Well, so what, Mama, what is so bad about eating three peaches?" demanded Maria. Giulia replied, "They are badly brought up, these girls, they know no shame; first they want this and then they want that." "Oh, I heard you," said Caterina, standing by the stove. "You look like a viper when you talk to Ma that way. You don't know anything, you are just an ignorant Calabrian." The muscles in Giulia's neck and throat tightened. "You have no respect. In Calabria people are brought up properly to have respect, to honor their grandparents. In Valmonte everyone does as he pleases and that is the truth." Giacomo picked up Caterina's refrain. "You are not even Italian, Giulia, you are African, all Calabrians are Africans, black Africans. And who can understand you when you talk? You never learned Italian, anyway." Giulia shrugged. She had heard the taunts many times. Giacomo persisted. Giulia turned to her tormentor. "You should talk, look at your skin, dark as an African." "And as for dialects, what about Sessa?" interjected Maria, coming to her mother's aid. Giacomo tried another tactic. "One thing is certain, I will never go to Calabria. It is full of mafiosi and kidnappers. Everyone is poor and backward." Giulia, enraged, jumped to the defense of her native land. She pointed out that in Stilo there were more noble families than in Valmonte. "There were people there who owned thousands of olive trees and hectares of pasture land. There was a courthouse and a barracks for the *carabinieri* and besides in the main piazza there was a large statue of Thomas Campanella. So there." Giulia sat back exhausted but satisfied with having once more saved truth from its enemies.

Teresa returned to her dishes and cheerfully sang a popular tune. Caterina, waiting for the espresso machine to gurgle, stood provocatively near her father. Suddenly she said, "Hey Papa, let me go to a movie. Hey Papa, why don't you let me go to a movie?" "I will movie you, that's what I will do," he said, grabbing her by the arm and twisting it up her back until her face was within striking range. He hit her in the face. She pleaded to be let go while he laughingly continued to strike her. When he let up she laughed triumphantly but he forced her to submit again. Maria watched while she ate, smiling at the familiar scene, but as Caterina dropped to the floor she said, "Hey Gia, enough, enough," and then began to tickle him until he relented. Caterina stood up red in the face, shaking her head. "Why do you always do that to me? Why are you so mean? Why can't you be nice to me?" "Shut up and pass the coffee. It must be ready." Caterina did as her father ordered. Teresa left the sink and came and leaned on her father's shoulder. "Hey Pa, do that whistle again," she said. Giacomo complied by demonstrating how her future father-in-law calls his sheep dog. Immediately Caterina exclaimed, "Hey Pa, listen to this." She stuck two fingers in her mouth to make an ear-piercing whistle. Giacomo roared with laughter. "Well listen to that, will you. I never knew you could do that," he said, his voice full of admiration. "Hey Caterina, listen to this, can you do it this way?" he asked, curling his tongue back in his mouth and emitting another powerful whistle. Caterina, with a triumphant nod of her head, bettered her father's in volume. Giacomo's face was alive with adoration. "Well, I never heard anything like that before," he said, his laughing eyes caressing his daughter. "I guess you got that from me along with your brains and your looks." "Oh, shut up, you Sessese, you artichoke head," said Maria, laughing at her allusion to Sessa's major crop. She took her husband's head in her hands and caressed it. She moved closer to him and rested her head on his shoulder. Caterina, alive with interest, stretched her body halfway across the table on her elbows until her face was close to her mother's and father's. "Hey Pa," she said, "why did you marry Mama? She's ugly, isn't she, Papa, isn't she?" Giacomo placed his hand gently on Maria's head. "No, my daughter, your mother is beautiful, very beautiful."

II

In the middle of March Giacomo began to build a house for Bruno. Plans had been drawn up by the same friend who had helped to design

Luigi's. Six million, nine hundred fifty thousand lire were left in the bank. It would be enough to get the walls up and the roof on. The interior would have to be done little by little. In some ways, building Bruno's house would be easier than Luigi's, for Giacomo's would serve as a foundation, but the long exterior stairs and the mansard roof would be more challenging. The plan called for stairs with a half-landing rising to a balcony and the front entrance. The first floor would contain a living room, kitchen, dining area, three bedrooms, and a bathroom; the second floor would be a large "family room" under the eaves of the mansard, with a fireplace in one corner. Bruno planned someday, when his family grew, to have a sofa in front of the fire with the stereo next to it and a place for his children to play. Since the construction of Luigi's house the mansard roof had become popular. Bruno argued that it would be a waste of money to build a house that would finally be three stories high without having the right kind of roof on it. Giacomo agreed, but he knew that he would have to have a lot of help from Salvatore.

The stairs consumed both time and money. They were made of reinforced concrete, and a carpenter had to be called in to construct the forms. Maria thought that Giacomo could handle the wood himself, but he was less confident; Giacomo had respect for carpenters. The work progressed, but Giacomo and Maria worried more and more about the money.

III

Luigi's wage no longer supported the family; he had his own household. When Bruno was discharged from military service, he enrolled in the employment office as a chemical analyst. With the service behind him, he thought he now stood a better chance of being hired by Chemtech. But there and everywhere he was told the same story: Without work experience he was not qualified for employment. Furthermore, they informed him, there were thousands, hundreds of thousands of young men like him all over Italy looking for jobs. So there was no money coming into Maria's hands apart from Giulia's pension, a little from the land, and some that Bruno earned from odd jobs.

Everywhere there was an air of uncertainty. The television carried only bad news – kidnappings, strikes, bloody street demonstrations, terrorist raids. In March Aldo Moro was kidnapped. It seemed as if no one was safe. Even the Communists, who had always been clear about what was wrong when they were in the opposition, did not seem to know what to do now that they were "in bed" with the government.

Giacomo didn't feel sorry for Moro. He was going to get what he deserved, he said. The Red Brigades were right; Moro was just a tool of the multinational corporations. He helped to bring in all those American industries where there was no place for Bruno. It was the same old story, Giacomo argued. There was only one solution; Luigi would have to get Bruno into ILPINA. Maria killed and dressed a chicken and made another *zuppa inglese*.

IV

Giulia's pension payment was still one month away. Maria was surprised when Tonino came striding into the house one day bearing a check, crying out, "It is a miracle, folks, a real honest to goodness miracle. God has seen fit to perform a miracle for Giulia Tassoni, one of his greatest admirers. Hey look, Ma, look at the bundle they sent you." He held the check in front of her face and read the figures: six hundred fifty thousand lire. It was the liquidation of his father's pension, Tonino explained. "Tonino, my son, you blaspheme, but it is truly a miracle. This is God's doing," she said, kissing the check. Giacomo could not contain himself. "God had nothing to do with it. You get a pension because men struggled for the rights of workers." "Oh hush, Gia, don't start that again," said Maria, putting her hand on her husband's arm. Teresa grabbed the check from her grandmother. "Six hundred fifty thousand for Grandma. It is incredible." Both she and Caterina looked at their grandmother with respect.

Tonino ordered Teresa to return the check to Giulia and then said, bending over with a solicitous flourish, "Now Mama, we must take good care of you. This pension business is wonderful. We have to think of a way of keeping it going. Ah, yes, I have the answer." Tonino bent double and slapped his knee in anticipation of what he was about to say. "Yes, this is the answer, Ma. When you die we will quickly stick you in the freezer there that Luigi gave to Maria and keep you nice and fresh. Then when the day comes to go to the pension office to pick up the money, I will come down, take you out of the freezer and walk you to the office on my arm just as if nothing had happened. Then when we get the money I will just pop you back in the freezer until the next time. Look, Ma, stand up, see," he said, grabbing her arm and dragging her along as if she were a dead weight. Giulia put her hand over her mouth while her body shook with mirth. When the laughter died Giulia said, "Maria, take this money, put away two hundred thousand for my funeral, keep some for the oxygen and the sweet cookies and keep the rest." Maria felt a surge of relief pass through her body.

V

In May Bruno was given work at ILPINA. It was not permanent, but with the help of a friend the boss had said that it could be cleared eventually with the employment office, Luigi reported. Bruno's job was to check off merchandise as it was loaded from the trucks at the refrigeration plant. Being outdoors he did not have to wear heavy clothes, and with overtime the pay came to three hundred fifty thousand a month. For the first time since November enough money was being given to Maria to allow her to put some aside for Teresa's trousseau.

VI

In June Bruno and Luisa became engaged. Maria had known that her youngest son would take that step too, but it seemed so soon, everything was moving so quickly. As she told Giacomo, Luisa was not the girl that she would have picked out for Bruno, but as she always said, she would never interfere; enough that they were happy with their choices. Luisa was so different from Silvia. She seemed distant, serious, and often critical, but that was because she still did not know her, she thought to herself. She worked at Accord, drove a car, and sometimes arrived wearing her white smock. From what Bruno said, she planned to work after they were married. Luisa was a modern woman, Bruno explained. As far as he knew he would not try and stop her. "You have to keep up with the times," he said. "Well, I'm like Luisa," said Teresa, "I'm a modern woman, too. I'd like to work, but probably won't because I couldn't get a job, so I'll stay at home just as I do now. But the first time that Beppe says, 'Teresa, do this for me because I am working to support you,' I'll go out and get a job, any job. But that's not going to happen – Beppe isn't that kind of a man. He even said that he'd help me with the housework. Of course, I would never let him wash the dishes and I'd help him as long as it had nothing to do with the animals."

When Luisa came with her mother and father to a Sunday noonday meal in the middle of June, her father said that Luisa was still young to be married, but if she and Bruno were happy together then he would not stand in her way. Giacomo said that it was proper that their marriage was still several years off, because it would take some time for him to finish the house. Luisa's mother said that she knew what a costly thing it was to build a house like that, and she would do her very best to provide her daughter with a fine trousseau. "I have been laying aside things for some time," she said, "but I will need several years before I am ready." After they left Maria remarked to Giacomo that they probably would not be seeing as much of them as they would of Angelo and

Natalia. Giacomo nodded. But Maria knew that in the years ahead she would see a great deal of her daughter-in-law Luisa, for she would be living upstairs for the rest of her life.

VII

During June Giacomo hurried to get the roof finished before he went to work in the sugar-beet refinery. For two weeks Salvatore came over late every afternoon and all day Sundays to help lay the supports. By the end of the month all was done except for the laying of the tiles. At first it gave Giacomo a start when he drove home to see a three-story house towering where for so long there had been only his flat roof. Styles of houses and ways of building them would change in the future as much as they had in the past, Giacomo thought, but one thing was certain: He had built to last.

For the next two weeks Giacomo and Salvatore helped Tonino raise the roof of the house that he was building on a small piece of land given by his mother-in-law to his wife, Emilia. Emilia's two brothers-in-law were building houses only a few yards away. Emilia's family were from Carpineto, where it was the custom for the bride's family to provide the house or the land upon which to build.

Ill fortune had been dogging Tonino and his wife. The town of Valmonte had found Emilia guilty of building illegally and fined her two hundred thousand lire and sentenced her to twenty months in jail. Tonino knew that she would not have to serve her sentence, yet he was furious that she had been singled out for punishment for doing what was common practice. He was convinced that it was an act of revenge on the part of the Christian Democratic administration against him as a Communist; they did not like it that he spoke up so often in the piazza.

If that was not bad enough, Emilia's sister, Giuliana, died in child-birth three days after Easter. It was not convenient for the widower to keep the infant, as he would have to start looking for another woman. The burden fell on Emilia. She was already working eight to nine hours a day on one of the two sewing machines. She, Pasquetta, and the older children in the shop would share the mothering.

With Tonino leaving, the old house in the village would be empty for the first time since 1946, when Giovanni moved his family there from the wooden shack in the country.

VIII

For most of July and August Giacomo operated the conveyor belt at the refinery. He wished he could work there regularly. He had spoken to the boss many times, but there was always some new excuse. Now they told him that with his children growing up there were other, younger men more needy than himself. In fact, this year they had made it uncertain that he would get the summer work until the very last minute. He had the night shift; he came home at four and slept until noon. He didn't like it, but at least it extended the health insurance for another eight months. Maria reminded him of his promise to go to the hospital to have tests made on his stomach. Reluctantly he agreed. He would enter the first of October.

IX

On September 16, 1978, a baby girl was born to Silvia in the maternity wing of the hospital at Latina. She weighed 4.200 kilos at birth. It was Giacomo and Maria's first grandchild, and Giulia's sixth great grand-child. Giulia was glad that Silvia had had a baby girl, for a woman should always have a girl to help with the others as they came along. Giacomo said that he had been certain that Silvia would give Luigi a son, but Luigi said that he didn't care. "Sooner or later we will have one. I feel proud to be a father." Silvia and Luigi had already decided to name the baby Maria if it was a girl. Maria had secretly hoped they would. She hugged the young couple warmly when they told her of their decision.

The baptism was held in the church at Latina Scalo the third Sunday after the birth. Giulia, as usual, advocated an early baptism, so that if something happened the baby would die a Christian rather than a crea-ture. Silvia said that that didn't bother her but still there was not much point in waiting too long.

Maria helped her prepare the noonday meal. The table was spread in the dining room. There was hardly room for two of them to turn around in the kitchen. Finally Maria told Silvia to go sit down with the rest, she would finish. She moved back and forth between the kitchen and the dining room, thinking that this was not her way. She liked to have everyone whom she was preparing food for right there to talk with them. After the meal they sat in the living room while Teresa and Caterina washed the dishes. Luigi served everyone digestives from an antiqued cart that a friend had given them for a wedding present. Giacomo leaned back in one of the armchairs, saying with a laugh, "This is the way the pope must feel when he sits down after a meal."

Maria sat next to her mother on the overstuffed sofa. Giulia fingered her beads. Maria looked around the room, her eye taking in the crystal in the highboy, the chandelier, the brocaded walls, the marble floors, and her family. "Who would know that we are not gentlefolk?" she thought. "Yes, this woman and I have come a long way. She was wise and married a good man. He brought us here from nothing in Stilo. I married a good man, too, and he brought us here to this place. My mother has almost finished her journey, but Giacomo and I still have a ways to go. There are times when I wish my life could be different. I would like to ease away from the struggle, rest, maybe even go somewhere with Giacomo, although heaven only knows where we would go. He gets so nervous in the car as soon as we leave these parts. He is afraid that he won't know the way and he is too proud to ask. But we can't stop. I still have Teresa to marry and I won't be ready for two years. Bruno can't marry until he has helped his sister. Then after Bruno there is still Caterina. I have so much work to do for her; I have hardly begun. Sometimes I feel so tired I would like to lie down and die. There are so many preoccupations, Giacomo without work, my brother, and now this news that Concetta is very ill with high blood pressure and has been taken to the hospital. That's why Mama won't stop saying her beads. Perhaps someday things will be easier, but now there is a long struggle ahead. I have always struggled, like this woman beside me, it is our destiny. I would not know any other way. And now it has brought us all this. Best of all this beautiful baby, the daughter of my dear son and his wife. I truly am one of the fortunate ones. Before me lies, God willing, years of joy with our blessed family that we have created in this corner of the world."

12

Conclusion

It is common knowledge in the United States that it is Americans who have created the contemporary modern world, an opinion shared by most of the rest of mankind. Like all myths, it contains a measure of truth. It is true that much technological and organizational innovation is American in origin, just as our popular culture serves as a model for persons all over the world who wish to express modernity in song, dance, and life-style. The creed that spurns the old and venerates the new is as American as apple pie. Apart from the sanctity of private property and the individual, the dyad of our faith, nothing else in substance or meaning is sacred. The wrecker's ball is ever ready to sever our ties with the past in order to point our vision toward the future. We have won the right to be the purveyors of modernity, we have dedicated ourselves to its cause. Indeed, we have no close competitors. It makes no difference that the tread on New World modernity is wearing thin in places, that problems are omnipresent. And yet even though other industrial societies seem to manage their modernity better than ourselves, we still hold center stage.

Just as we take credit for having broken the tyranny of the past and having affirmed the way of a better tomorrow, so too do we accept responsibility for the profusion of consequences for person, family, society, as well as nature that our chosen course has brought about. We accept the figures that tell us of a drastic increase in acid rain fallout, single-person households, the incidence of divorce, toxic waste, child abuse and wife battering, groundwater pollution, and the number of unwed mothers as if they were the battle scars won from leading the vanguard, the price we must pay for an open society, for the privilege of being American.

The conviction that the family is in crisis is a commonplace in American thought. Alive in our imagination is the vision of the once extended American family, which included under one roof an assortment of relatives surrounding the core conjugal family as well as boarders and hired hands if not servants – a large residential kin group which functioned as a unit of production as well as consumption back when America was still largely rural. Recent research in family history suggests that that vision is wrong on at least one count. The American preindustrial family, like the English, was for the most part not extended.[1] The modest size of the houses precluded the formation of multiple-family households, and the abundance of land stimulated a shift from the custom of impartible to partible inheritance and the creation of independent households at the time of marriage.[2] But though not extended, the family did provide a wide range of "functions" – educative, religious, medical, welfare – which in the course of time were usurped by bureaucratically organized institutions. The transformation occurred over several generations, but a feeling of contraction and a sense of loss of control still prevail. In the process our individualism has been secured, our privacy achieved, but at the cost of an enhanced feeling of separateness and vulnerability.

Certain as we are about what has happened to ourselves, so are we certain about what is happening to other people exposed to the forces of industrial capitalism; their experience will be ours. But comparative cultural analysis tells us that modernity is not monolithic. There are as many ways of being modern as there are separate cultures experiencing it. Anyone who has traveled internationally knows that all air terminals are uncommonly and even depressingly identical; an international jet-propelled subculture has emerged. But the same traveler knows how much of traditional life may be preserved within the shadow of the airport if not within the terminal itself. These observations are superficial but indicative of the actual complexity in societies undergoing modernization.

Against this background it may seem incongruous to American readers that persons exposed to the forces of rapid social change would choose to invest so much in building the foundations of a strong family for the future. But what appears to be one man's meat may be another man's poison. Giacomo and Maria do not feel themselves to be exceptional in their undertaking and indeed they are not, for the houses that Giacomo built are similar in intent, if not in design, to other houses other fathers are building for their sons in the Latina area.

There is, after all, a cultural precedence in what they are doing. As discussed in the Introduction, we know to what extent familial extension is a convention in central and northern Italy. Valmonte is on the border between central and south, and traditionally it partook more of the southern inclination toward nuclearity than the central proclivity toward extension. Before the post-World War II industrialization of the Agro Pontino most Valmontesi were agricultural day laborers like Giovanni and existed in nuclear families. Kin supported each other in the struggle to survive, and resources were never sufficient to permit the foundation of extended families. The exceptions were those families that were allocated farms following the draining and reclamation of the ancient Pontine Marshes in the 1930s. Now in possession of a patrimony, a significant number of these families made room for married sons, built an extension for them or constructed a separate dwelling nearby.[3] The resulting households were similar to those described by Douglass for Agnone, by Silverman for Montecastello di Vibio, and by Angeli and Belletini, and Kertzer for Emilia Romagna, although the Valmontesi did it on a somewhat smaller scale. The retention on the land of one or more married sons not only ensured the perpetuation of the patrimony but also produced sufficient labor for its maintenance.

When Giacomo won his three hectares of land in the lottery in 1958 the industrialization of the Agro Pontino was already well advanced; agriculture was on the wane as a source of livelihood. The three hectares were not sufficient to support Giacomo, Maria, and their four children without the supplement of wages from Giacomo's other work. With each passing year the capacity of the land to effectively produce support for a growing family decreased while its value as real estate increased. As industrial use drove out agriculture, small plots like Giacomo's became increasingly attractive as residential sites. And as the economic boom of the sixties got under way, residential building increased dramatically as more and more people realized the opportunity to exchange modern housing in the countryside for cramped quarters in medieval towns like Massano, Sora, and Valmonte. This dramatic transformation of land use from agricultural to residential was marked by Giacomo's resolve to sell one of his three precious hectares of land to other housebuilders in order to allow him to build for his own sons. But although Giacomo's and Maria's behavior was consonant with a venerable Italian convention for extension, it was no longer imposed upon the traditional material base of agricultural productivity. And it is that among other things that makes it appear all the more striking.

Not all of cultural convention is instrumentally comprehensible, however. It was the tradition in Valmonte, even for the many who owned very little, for the man "to bring the house" and for the woman to provide the furnishings. What this meant was a considerable outlay on the part of the woman and her family in exchange for the small rent the husband was obliged to pay for their meager quarters.[4] Implicit in the bargain, however, was the expected work capacity of the man, who would toil in the landowner's fields while the woman bore and raised their children.

When it came time for Giovanni and Giulia's three sons to marry, Salvatore, Pasquale, and Tonino moved in turn into rented apartments in the village with their wives, just as Giacomo had done when he and Maria married in 1953. Even when Giacomo and Maria were living with his parents, the tradition of "his house" was still retained. Giacomo has maintained the spirit of that cultural expectation and even deepened it by the construction of the two houses that relieve Luigi and Bruno of the necessity of finding rented quarters. For them to have done so would have taken them not just a few doors or streets away, as it had always been the case in the village, but rather several kilometers distant to Latina Scalo or to Latina itself, beyond easy reach for visiting and sharing.

The basis for linking kin in a cooperative network is to be found not in the cultural norms of Valmonte alone but in the larger universality of strategies for survival among working-class families. Sharing, pooling, "huddling" among kin has been eloquently testified to by Young and Willmott, Komarovsky, Stack, and others, as noted in the Introduction. Living within a few yards of each other provides opportunities for conserving and avoiding redundancy. The sharing of a common oil tank to service Giacomo's and Bruno's as well as Luigi's is a case in point. The single telephone that was eventually installed in Giacomo's house is another, as is the common use of fruit trees, vineyards, and vegetable garden, as well as the distribution by Maria of the products of her pigs, rabbits, and hens. But these concrete examples are only a few of the more tangible advantages that emerge from cooperation. The stronger adhesion flows from the daily visiting between Maria and her daughters-in-law, the shared tending of Luigi and Silvia's baby, the exchange of support and advice, the many meals taken together, the conversation in the parental kitchen, and the joining together for ritual and festive occasions. There is every reason to believe that they enjoy each other's company, and that enjoyment is a strong centripetal pull. It would be wrong, though, to think that peace and tranquillity always prevail among them. It does not.

Few days pass without some anxiety, often acute, about some eventuality or perceived calamity: the recurrence of Giacomo's ulcers that have bedeviled him for so long, the prospect of his not being hired at the sugar-beet factory for the harvest and thus losing their health insurance coverage for the year, the exhaustion and severe headaches that Maria often suffers from as she prepares one more meal for her expectant husband and children, the knowledge that she should have her gallbladder removed, the need for long and intensive dental work if Giacomo and Maria hope to retain some of their remaining teeth – even though they know that attention will never be forthcoming. These ailments and physical liabilities weigh upon them as so many wounds received in the trenches of class struggle.

Like all working-class families, the Rossis are articulated with the marketplace through the production of their own labor power. For Giacomo that link has been a veritable bridge of sighs. Found too young or too old or too independent by one capricious boss after another, for not having armed himself with the protection of favoritism, Giacomo has suffered silently with the knowledge that his considerable skills have rarely realized their true exchange value. As for Maria, her travails are the price she has to pay in a lifetime of domestic work for the reproduction of labor costs as well as her dues to a system of patriarchy that prevents her from working outside the home.[5] But to see the Rossi family as merely a location where production and redistribution take place, as some might suggest, is, I think, wrong.[6] It is more than the basic unit for transfer of labor costs from capital to the working-class. It is an entity in its own right, albeit not one formed by nature but by generations of social struggle. For only in this way may one appreciate the faith the Rossis have in themselves as family, understood not as complicity with bourgeois hegemony but of a piece with working class commitment to family ideology.[7] That ideology as articulated by Giacomo and Maria centers on the Italian verb *sistemare*, the primary goal in life of any married couple. Implicit in that imperative is the recognition that the best and most worthwhile things in life are to be realized only through the formation of a family. But inherent in that ideal is the political truth that for working-class people, only the family provides the means by which they can attain control over areas of vital interest and responsibility for their own nonworking members.[8]

The alternative to supporting the old, the infirm, or even the young is to lose them to alien institutions, thus depleting the family and strengthening the power of the State at the family's expense. It is true that Giulia brought her pension with her when she moved in, for which Maria was most grateful, but there is no doubt that a place would have been found for Giulia even without the pension, just as there will always be a place for Caterina, if for some reason she should not become engaged. And although belief in family may exact a heavier price for some members than for others, it also enhances the ability of a working-class family to control its own labor power. Giacomo's persistent unwillingness to allow Maria to work for money outside the home is consistent with the traditional resistance to woman's wage work on the part of Valmonte men, fired as it was by the perceived threat to their authority. But with the introduction of industry in the late 1950s, the barriers to female employment crumbled as employers drove the wage down. Justified or not in terms of his own motives, Giacomo's actions are commensurate with a larger struggle to prevent the lowering of the wage through the exploitive use of women workers.

In his much-commented-upon book *The Moral Basis of a Backward Society*, American political scientist Edward Banfield located hostility toward Italian community life in the southern Italian family, with its suspicion of the world beyond its door.[9] But Banfield has the picture wrong. The problem does not reside in a mentality of "amoral familism" found in poor families but in the malgovernance of the ruling class. To perceive the problem as emanating from below rather than from above is merely to blame the victim. If much of Italy is badly governed, it is not because of its "bad" families but because of the hostility of the governors toward the governed. Government at all levels is seen by many Italians as oppressive, exploitive, and self-serving. Every member of the Rossi family has harrowing tales to tell of encounters with officials, schoolteachers, doctors, to say nothing of bosses. The often harsh and nonreceptive cast of the public domain has as a consequence sustained the family's continued monopolization of available sentiments of trust and interpersonal affection.

I have been attempting to indicate how the structure of this new familial arrangement reflects local and regional cultural expectations and, even more important, how it responds to the needs of working-class people in their struggle to control their own destiny. But other questions remain that are not so directly structural as attitudinal, that do not pertain directly to organizational matters as to those of mentality. As I have said before, the ideology of family as put forth by Giacomo and Maria is based upon the belief that an individual's interests are best realized within the familial setting. These interests are recognized for what they are, those of mutuality. The ethos of individualism, so deeply entrenched in the United States, is fundamentally at odds with familism, although the two societies partake of differing degrees of both. The creed of individualism holds that the fundamental need of a person is to realize independence. Acting on that belief, the raising of children in the United States has as a main goal the acquisition of proofs of independence at the earliest possible age. Evidence of dependency beyond an acceptable time of development generates confusion, dismay, and parental as well as filial embarrassment. Much interparental communication concerns exchange of proof of and mutual celebration for acts of independence among offspring: toilet training, the task performed without mother's help, the first overnight stay away from home, the summer job, the car purchased, the apartment rented.

In *The Pursuit of Loneliness*, Philip Slater makes that very point, stating that in American society independence training begins almost at birth and continues largely unabated throughout childhood and adolescence. Parents may experience some regret in watching their children sever one tie after another, but they participate in a mutual pursuit of the fantasy of total self-reliance. For as the parents become older and enter that population for whom dependency needs are existentially palpable, again they will be expected to continue to fly the banner in the cause of independence or else suffer the consequences of experiencing the very rejection they meted out to needful others. For Slater the compulsive equality of the pursuit of independence/loneliness lies in its function as a frustrator of deep-seated dependency needs among Americans: "the wish to share responsibility for the control of one's impulses and the direction of one's life."[10]

The issues of independence-dependency on the one hand, and control and expressivity on the other, are experienced and expressed differently in cross-cultural settings. In striking contrast to the American cult of independent self-reliance is the Japanese idea of *amae*, best translated as dependence. In his foreword to *The Anatomy of Dependence* by psychiatrist Takeo Doi, John Bester states that within the context of *amae*, which pervades all of Japanese society, "the individual may deliberately act in a way that is 'childish' as a sign to the other that he . . . wishes to be dependent and seeks the other's 'indulgence.' "[11] In the Rossi family the tolerance of manifestations of dependency are also present, although perhaps not to the same degree as in the Japanese family. Teresa is allowed her attacks of nerves and sudden outbreaks of tears, Caterina her outbursts of temper, Giacomo his moods of petulance, Giulia her moans of self-pity. These are not viewed as healthy emotional releases but rather are greeted with shouted invectives, a mode of expression in which everyone eventually joins. In the bedlam that ensues consistency of response is not a virtue. To be capricious is everyone's right. Acceptance, however, does not mean approval. The needy one's claim provokes castigation more often than not. Maria screams at Teresa to stop whimpering. Luigi raises the back of his hand to hit Caterina for her impudence. Yet the railing against specific dependencies nurtures at the same time an acceptance of dependency as a whole.

I think that in such family settings dependency and expressivity are linked in a dynamic that stands in contrast to the dyad of independence and control mentioned by Slater and more fully explored in the works of Nancy Chodorow and Dorothy Dinnerstein. In their respective ways, Chodorow and Dinnerstein discuss how the gender arrangements typified by families of advanced capitalist societies produce mother-centered personalities. In a chapter entitled "The Sexual Sociology of Adult Life" from *The Reproduction of Mothering*, Chodorow moves the analysis to an explanation of the root causes of independence, especially among men. In a statement informed by Talcott Parsons, Chodorow writes,

> This close, exclusive, preoedipal mother-child relationship first develops dependency in a son, creating a motivational basis for early learning and a foundation for dependency on others. When a mother 'rejects' her son or pushes him to be more independent, the son carries his still powerful dependence with him, creating in him both a general need to please and conform outside of the relationship to the mother herself and a strong assertion of independence. The isolated, husband-absent mother thus helps to create in her son a pseudo-independence masking real dependence.[12]

It is in the ambience of isolation of the nuclear family that the dynamic of which Chodorow speaks is most fully developed and where the concomitant need for internalized systems of impulse control are most fully realized; for to be independent necessitates being in control of one's self. If control is a defense against the kind of terror that Dinnerstein speaks of, "the terror of sinking back wholly into the helplessness of infancy," then independence is a flight from that terror.[13] What is important to remember, however, is that a strong mother-son relationship in itself does not instill a final motivation for separation; as in the American case, the mother pushes the son to be more independent, thus stimulating the submergence of powerful dependent needs and the unconscious formation of a reaction against them in the form of a "strong assertion of independence." Italy would seem to offer a quite different outcome, for the mother indulges those needs and thus avoids their repression and their satisfaction, which leads to the making of, in the words of Anne Parsons, "a very strong centripetal tendency."[14]

Indeed, the issue of dependency would seem to be a source of sharper gender distinction in American upbringing than Italian. Carol Gilligan has made the point in her book *In a Different Voice*. She writes, following a discussion of Chodorow: "Consequently, relationships, and particularly issues of dependency, are experienced differently by women and men."[15] She goes on to say that the outcome of the confrontation with dependency among American boys is eventual separation and individuation, whereas for girls it is attachment and responsibility. If the project of separation and individuation is less compelling for Italian males than for American males, to what can this be attributed? It is not that Italian boys get brought up the way American girls do, to realize in their maturity the ethic of caring for others. Rather, the dependency satisfactions that an Italian mother affords her son do not polarize the issue for him in such a way that he needs to repress his ambivalence about dependency in order to assert his manhood.

For Italians the American belief in "being on one's own" is bewildering. It was not easy for Giacomo and Maria to accept the fact that when I came to Italy in the fall of 1977 my son took himself to a midwestern college as a freshman and we remained separated for the year. Although they did not say it, their feeling was clearly that I was callous in regard to my son's best interests. Being an American and trained in the ways of independence I could not agree, but I was able to recognize that I, like other Americans and Northern Europeans, experience myself differently in Italy, as if I were free to feel a part of myself that I do not allow to be expressed at home. Although Italians are more realistic in indulging their own dependency needs, so are they more adept at recognizing them and meeting them in others; consequently we from the North discover that it feels good in contrast to the "uptightness" that comes from the level of control we experience in our American lives.

Nothing of this sort is discussed around the kitchen table, but an implicit awareness of it prompts Giacomo and Maria to do what they are doing and for others among them to confirm it. The necessity for Luigi and Bruno to remain in the familial ambit is more than the need to leave it – for them and for their parents. Both sons will benefit from their parents' preoccupations about them, just as Giacomo and Maria will benefit from the concern of their sons and daughters-in-law for them as they grow older. Not that Giacomo will expect either Silvia or Luigi to clean him, as Giulia had her father-in-law out of respect, but they will be cared for as they understand it; that is as it should be.

And Teresa and Caterina? It might be asserted that culturally attuned satisfaction of dependency needs is more male than female oriented. That is true insofar as men are more openly catered to by women. It is expected that Caterina will do her father's bidding, not only because she is his youngest child but because she is a girl and thus available for service in a way never demanded of Bruno. It is probably accurate to say that Giacomo, Luigi, and Bruno have never washed a dish in their lives and will never be expected to. In fact, it is in the serving of men that women gain a measure of control, at least in the domestic realm, which may compensate for their lack of formal authority in public life. The social psychology of subservience has brought us to the conclusion that the server gains control over the master. But given the contemporary realities of Italian life and the constitutional equality of men and women before the law, the paradigm of subservience must be only suggestive. Closer to the point is the recognition of the extent to which the Italian family is matri-centered. The role of *Mamma* is at the very affective heart of the Italian family. Giulia in her time and now Maria have constituted the significant other for their children, the object of assured constancy whose love has been unqualified. First from breast and then from fireplace and stove has come an often meager but unceasing flow of food (their attention to the alimentary needs of all has been unremitting) – a constant reminder that it is the mother alone who gratifies the most primitive need. Oral dependency is but one aspect of a much larger configuration, but its primacy in survival and psychic well-being ensures power to she who satisfies it, for in being fed both husband and children are subordinate to her. The amount of time spent in the daily rituals related to the preparation and consumption of food, as well as the cleaning up afterward, is impressive, and the priestess of this cult of food is the mother.

The centrality of the kitchen table symbolizes another aspect of Maria's influence: the control of the purse. With money, as with food, the dynamics of dependency are elaborated, but with money there is attention to the mutuality of need. As we know, Maria has never been allowed to work for wages. By this taboo Giacomo made a formal statement of her dependency upon him, just as Luigi did with Silvia and Giuseppe intends to do with Teresa.[16] Apart from the actuality of Maria's life of unremitting work, her need to be taken care of has been formally addressed, if not in fact affectively satisfied. But at the same time she is the dispenser of that second most important commodity – money. It had been Giulia's way to give to Giovanni an exact sum every day, which he could use for a cigar or a glass of wine. Maria is less exacting in her role as distributor, but the principle of allocation is the same, as is the perception of her as the ultimate source of security. Not only does the wife's control of the purse enhance her power in the domestic realm, which balances her husband's domination of the public realm, but the allocation of his wage to her and her distribution of these funds to him, as well as to the others, dramatizes their state of mutual dependency.[17] In this regard my understanding of the Rossi household brings me closer to Belmonte's description of the Neapolitan family of Fontana del Re as mother-centered than to Ann Cornelisen's perception of her Lucanian families as being matriarchal, even though I sympathize with the intended corrective borne by the polemical power of that word.[18] Matriarchy connotes an asymmetry between husband and wife that does not correspond to my observation of Maria and Giacomo and the circumstances of relative prosperity in which they now live, nor does it correspond to the relationship between Giovanni and Giulia in much more economically depressed times. Maria and, in her time, Giulia, have been energetic and strong persons, constantly engaged, constantly on the move, but their formidable power has not been achieved at the expense of their husbands' personhood, even when Giovanni and Giacomo were unable to support their families as they wished.

The answer to the question about the dependency needs of Teresa and Caterina becomes clearer. It is Giuseppe, who after marriage will care for Teresa, and it is her future father-in-law who will build Teresa a "nest." Teresa wishes for a more urban setting, a house among others along a paved road out of sight of animals, but she is deeply aware of the extent to which Giuseppe's love will mean her security. Indeed, as Maria understands, much of the fascination that her daughter holds for Giuseppe is the anticipation he has for indulging her. Endowed with confidence by his parents, Giuseppe is happily reconciled to settling down in his own house, to be located only a few yards from theirs, with a wife who will care for him as he indulges her.

Teresa and Caterina, children of their time, rebel at their father's controlling ways. They castigate him unabashedly for being old-fashioned and tyrannical, and they appeal for understanding to their accepting mother; yet they obey him. (This is a paternal-filial situation thus quite different from that depicted in the film *Padre, Padrone*, where the father is indeed a tyrant.) In his possessiveness, his jealousy, they feel secure. In his refusal to let them wander off on their own, to have their own adventures, they sense the depth of his caring, even though it is to a great degree designed to avoid the ignominy of scandal and gossip, the kind of experience suffered by Giulia and Giovanni in wartime when control was difficult to exert.

The father's ritualistic admonition to a suitor that if the young man has intentions of taking advantage of his daughter he should drop his suit immediately masks a father's physical feelings toward his daughter. In her essay "Is the Oedipus Complex Universal?" Anne Parsons, writing of the Neapolitan family, says, "the incestuous impulses in the father-daughter relationship are quite close to the surface."[19] The observation fits closely the almost daily play indulged in by Caterina and her father. Her seductive proximity to Giacomo, the demand of his attention incessantly flaunted, always provokes the desired playful physical response. On occasion Teresa may participate, but then Giacomo's interest is less intense; she is already spoken for. His "passion" is saved for Caterina, whose paying court confirms his still virile attractiveness just as her father's aggressiveness reassures Caterina of her growing desirability as a woman. They are audience to each other's fantasied needs. Maria smiles vicariously at the scene, as do Giulia's sparkling eyes, but at a certain point Maria monitors the play so it does not become excessive. The time will come when Giacomo must release his daughter to a real suitor, whom he will admonish not to take advantage of her and whose father hopefully will in the bargain build for her a "nest," as Giacomo has done for his two daughters-in-law.

Indeed, it is in the explosive idiom of teasing that both the father and the daughter's sensual needs are indulged, just as in the catering of the mother to the boy dependency needs are satisfied. But the two modes of behavior bear different consequences for family organization. As Parsons put it, "while the mother-son tie acts primarily as a centripetal one, in that it maintains itself in such a way as to make for an unbroken continuity of the primary family, the father-daughter tie acts in the inverse sense in that the incestuous tension, being much closer to the surface, has to seek an external outlet."[20]

The marriage of the daughter ends the drama of courtship involving the dual attention of father and fiancè and begins her confrontation with the responsibilities of marriage and motherhood. For American working-class women the transition from single to married status carries an additional significance: the promise of autonomy in the founding of a family. For those who have been forced to postpone gratification, it means the fulfillment of love and achievement of independence.[21] But as the young working-class women in Lillian Rubin's *Worlds of Pain* discovered, "the freedom they had sought in marriage was a mirage, . . . they had exchanged one set of constraints for another perhaps more powerful one."[22] For people among whom the ideology of family does not promise the ideal of autonomy, however, marriage would seem to suffer less the injuries of spoiled expectations.

The recognition that, in the Rossi family, members' needs are engaged and met at many different levels assists us in understanding the powerful centripetal pull that life around the kitchen table in effect has. In the idiom of today, "this is where the action is," albeit not exclusively, for Caterina would love to dance at the discotheque in Latina Scalo, and Teresa would rather pore over clothes in the better stores in Latina. But the level of gratification is high, partly because constraint creates a tension that in itself is satisfying.

A concern felt by those who live according to the ethos of individualism is that familism inhibits the sovereignty of its members. It is true that one may be called upon to renounce what is desired for one's self in the interest of what is regarded as good for the household; the postponement by Salvatore and now Bruno of their own marriages to help their sisters marry first are cases in point. Subordination of personal gain to the welfare of the larger whole on which one is dependent is a central expectation of a familial ethos. For the persons we have encountered in this history it is not an expectation rigidly met, but it is a norm that prevails. Giacomo gets his way and buys a car at the expense of other goals. Maria gets her way and has a wedding reception. But it is not expected that members of the household would deny giving Maria their earned money on the grounds that it belonged to them and they could do with it as they saw fit. The individualist might then ask of the familist whether such renunciations constitute an undue repression of self-interest. The familist would answer no, pointing to the assertiveness of members of the same household. What is at stake is not the danger of a surrender of self, which can happen in a variety of social circumstances. Rather it is the recognition of the provenance of the question that masks the fact that uninhibited self-serving behavior proves to be good business in a consumer society.[23]

II

I have attempted to provide some answers to the question of why an extended family is in the process of formation at the end of Via Casa Grande among the Rossis of Valmonte. The response has been largely synchronic, as anthropologists would say – that is, identifying general economic, sociopolitical, and attitudinal conditions in existence at this time in Italy that I regard as determinate.

But part of the answer must be looked for in diachrony, that is, history. Indeed, the apparent anomaly of the situation is pointed up immediately when we realize that when our story started both Giovanni and Giulia were born into nuclear, not extended, families in the highly traditional community of Stilo, Calabria. The all-female composition of Giulia's small family of orientation was a rarity but not unique. In the territory of the former Kingdom of Naples, where poverty was endemic, it was not unusual for all-female households to exist; in this instance it was the result of violence in the service of honor, illegitimacy in the service of privilege. Households of the peasantry which comprised the great majority of the population of Stilo were vulnerable to the vicissitudes that inflicted on them high rates of infant mortality, death of the mother at childbirth, and death of the father/husband from disease or accident, and that assaulted the family stability created by the direct economic and sexual exploitation of the peasants by the gentry.[24]

In the case of Giovanni's family of orientation, its equilibrium was shattered by his mother's death when he was three and reorganized again when his father took his mother's sister as his new wife. When the time came for Giovanni and Giulia to marry, neither Giulia's mother nor Giovanni's father could provide them with more than the most minimal resources to establish a new household. Giulia was not even able "to bring a house" in keeping with Stilo custom, but rather only the most essential furnishings purchased with money given to her by her grandmother after she was constrained to sell her one-room house. The young couple began their married life in a rented room divided by a curtain to provide Maria Luisa and themselves with privacy. Their first child was born and died in Giovanni's absence. The second infant died as well. Giovanni wondered whether they could create a family. Giulia simulated one by providing foster care to a child born out of wedlock to a peasant girl, sired by her master. Their third child, Concetta, survived; she was born while Giovanni was in Argentina earning money to buy a house of their own. The relative well-being that followed Giovanni's return was shattered when he contracted malaria and was incapacitated for more than a year. The full burden of support fell then on Giulia, mother of two more children, Salvatore and Maria. Even when Giovanni returned to work their circumstance improved little; no future was seen for them in Stilo.

The monumental decision to migrate, after the birth of Pasquale, was made in the hope of changing their fortune in Rome. The eventual settling in Valmonte was fortuitous. But even there the search for a firm base upon which to build a family eluded them. They shifted from rented house to rented house. Finally, through Herculean efforts (Concetta's supervision of the other children, freeing her mother to glean in the fields, was crucial), Giovanni purchased a one-room wooden shack in the country. Removed from the discrimination they had suffered from the Valmontesi in the village, they hoped to find a sanctuary in that rural setting. But first the terrors of war and then the shame that befell them from Concetta's ill-fated marriage disrupted their lives again. The country was abandoned in favor of the village once more. The sale of the shack allowed Giovanni to buy a house, their first habitation to contain more than one room. The seven years from 1946 to 1953 constituted the final phase in the life cycle of Giovanni and Giulia's family of procreation. It was the epoch when the remaining children, including Michele, came of age, approached and passed through adolescence, and moved toward marriage. For the first time since Giulia stopped working with the birth of Tonino in 1938 the burden of support was shared by Giovanni and Salvatore and the others to varying degrees. These were also years of a severe economic depression in Italy, remembered as *La Miseria*, when Giulia made every lira count to feed and clothe her family the best she could and at the same time to assemble a respectable trousseau for Maria. The time was at hand to systematically settle the children still at home, Concetta's dilemma having been resolved by her second marriage. The only real property Giovanni owned was the house. Necessity dictated the adherence to a neolocal rule of residence; the process of dissolution began. First Maria, then Salvatore, and then Pasquale left. (Michele had moved to Piove di Sacco to be near Concetta.) Tonino alone remained living with his parents, even for a short while after marriage. The pattern of household growth followed by household dissolution in the service of forming other new households constituted the only adaptive strategy for those who, like Giulia and Giovanni, lacked the resources upon which to build a more enduring familial structure. In time each child left, but not to fulfill the goal of achieving an esteemed independence; fission was inevitable, not necessarily desirable.

The household formed by Giacomo and Maria in 1953 was scarcely more secure than the one established by Giovanni and Giulia in 1922. Beset by low wages, unemployment, and the anxieties that these wants created, especially once they had children, Giacomo and Maria were constrained to make a residential alliance twice with his parents in the interests of economy, an instance of co-residence homologous to the one formed by Tonino with his parents. In both cases a kind of terminal extended family was created under the stress of scarcity.

The Rossis' quantum leap toward an expanded household organization established to endure was simultaneous with the surge of Italian prosperity that followed the depression of the fifties, with Giacomo and Maria's particular fortune in acquiring land, and with the higher wages brought by the capitalistic industrialization of the Agro Pontino. The creation of such an extended family, anomalous from the viewpoint of American experience, becomes understandable within the framework of an Italian family experiencing the process of modernization without the compulsions of an individualistic ethos.

III

There remains another developmental trend in the present Rossi experience that is as seemingly contradictory to American reasoning as the relationship between affluence and familial solidification: the progressive radicalization of their politics. In a sense it requires discussion only in the light of American perspective about political choice not in terms of Italian political consciousness. Being a client state containing the Vatican and an overwhelmingly Catholic population with close ties of kinship involving millions on both sides of the Atlantic, it is bewildering to Americans why the largest Communist Party in the West should exist in Italy. There are, of course, historical reasons why this is so: Some of the more crucial ones are the critical role assumed by the Communists in the resistance to Fascism, assuring them a crucial patriotic legacy; the tradition of intelligent and adroit party leadership, stretching from Gramsci through Togliatti to Berlinguer; the mobilization of the venerable Italian tradition of anti-clericalism and the creation of a militant mass party capable of expressing the discontent of millions outraged by the inequities of a class society.[25] They all touch upon Rossi consciousness.

Giacomo and Maria were adolescents during the war; memory of it is still searingly vivid. For months in 1945 they were surrounded by German soldiers and the embittered Fascists of Mussolini's Salò Republic. It was a time of continuous anxiety, at times outright terror. Now a kind of watershed in their consciousness is marked by the demise of that holocaust, the establishment of peace, the end of Fascism, and the emergence of democracy, symbols of a better future.

Integral to that history was the recognition that the Church in Valmonte, dependent for its existence upon large landed holdings, was inevitably aligned with the rich and the powerful. For Giacomo as for many others (later for Maria), it seemed obvious from their earliest reflections that the Church was the enemy of people of their class with their aspirations. Becoming a member of the local Communist Party may have for Giacomo some of the dimensions of religious witness, but it would be facile to say that Communism has become Giacomo's religion, since he is a skeptic. He does, however, feel supported and energized by being a member of a vast organization whose leaders for the most part articulate his deep-seated resentments and hopes. Its size alone imparts respectability. When Caterina told her father that she wanted to join the youth section of the local branch of the Movimento Lavoratori per il Socialismo, an extraparliamentary party to the left of the Communist Party, Giacomo dismissed her suggestion curtly. For him small ideological parties have no significance, nor indeed do ideological issues. It is enough to be against things the way they are. When Giacomo's brother, Pietro, a worker at Accord, told Giacomo that they should not be Communists because they have all benefited from the fruits of industrial capitalism in the area, Giacomo answered that the Communists for years have run Bologna, where industry thrives. "Nor should you worry about them collectivizing this and collectivizing that. We Italians are not good at collectivizing anything, we won't stand for it," he said, laughing.

Giacomo, like his two employed sons, is of the working class. Neither Luigi nor Bruno aspires to transcend his status as a laborer at ILPINA. Their goals involve familial responsibility, not mobility. Yet although the trappings of the bourgeoisie are in their possession, they are not exposed to a mythology of equality that obscures their class interests. They are secure about their working-class identity and the political responsibilities attached to it.

Giacomo is a Catholic in the same sense that he is an Italian; baptized to the faith, he expects to receive the last rites of the Church as his right. Around his neck on a chain hangs the cross that Maria gave him. In his wallet he carries his party card. When Don Virgilio comes to the house once a month to hear Giulia's confession, congratulate her on the tenacity of her faith, and console her in her suffering, Giacomo receives him cordially in the kitchen if he is there, and chats, jokes, and offers him a glass as he would any other guest. For Giacomo there is no conflict; his Catholic and Communist identities arise from different circumstances of his life. He had no more choice in becoming a Catholic than in being born; what is done is done. He chose to be a Communist and is proud of that decision, for to him it reflects his understanding of how his interests and those of his country can be best served. And for a man like Giacomo who has never enjoyed the protection of a boss, the party serves as his *gran padrone*.[26]

For Maria the course to her present understanding has been more difficult; it is a position hard won. When I first knew Maria she was assiduous in her expressions of the faith. She attended evening service and Sunday mass. She was a loyal member of the local Catholic Action. She enjoyed the company and confidence of Don Antonio's assistant, Don Giuseppe. His gravity and youth touched her. At that time she found the socialism propounded by her father and brother disrespectful, disloyal. Engagement and then marriage to Giacomo had their consequences for her faith – not that she immediately or blindly identified with his views, but rather she slowly found that the Church, priest, and rites had less and less relevance for her.

She herself recognized that increasing preoccupation with family, children, Giacomo's unemployment, and their poverty left her little time and inclination for matters of faith. Nor did the Church have acceptable answers to her problems. She experienced anger, not solace, when the priest told her that it was her fate to bear children for God, to suffer in this world for the redemption that would come in the world hereafter. Disinclined to be patronized, Maria reacted with increasing bitterness to every tale of nepotism that circulated about the successive priests of Valmonte.

Maria no longer goes to church functions or to mass; after all, she points out, living in the country makes it inconvenient. She says that she has her own way of believing in God, of being religious, through her continuing struggle for her children, support of her mother, and loyalty to the memory of her father. It is Maria who decorates his grave with fresh flowers every week, crossing herself as she enters the cemetery, dusting the small marble statue of the Pietà that she placed there. Maria is impatient at times with her mother's unswerving faith (even donkeys recognize the sanctity of Christ, Giulia argues, for when pawing the ground with their hooves they are really making the sign of the cross), but she understands as well and shares some of her devotion for San Antonio of Padua, Santa Anna, and Santa Rita. Indeed, Maria never tires of telling the story of Rita's suffering and redemption. The tale of the miracle of the roses blooming in winter becomes as immediate in her relating as if it were a piece of news broadcast on TV.

Maria does not hold party membership as does Giacomo, but she does vote for Communist candidates. The most crucial underlying factor in that political act has been the history of increasing affluence enjoyed by the Rossi family. Maria herself exemplifies that contention better than anyone else in the household. It is not that their new and relative prosperity has awakened in Maria a large reservoir of material wants. If anything, that is truer of Giacomo and certainly of her children than of herself. It is rather that her expectations and critical judgment have developed in the past several years in consonance with a general wakening of consciousness among women of her class who, freer from drudgery, reflect, talk, argue about their lives, their futures. Maria rarely and barely reads. There are no newspapers in the house. But everyday TV brings topics for discussion and rediscussion. Maria finds many of the arguments made by the various women's liberation movements understandable. They are compatible with her own sense of justice. She holds her own against Giacomo when he inveighs against the movement and in turn criticizes him for not being more critical of terrorism, for she recognizes its fundamentally undemocratic and anti-proletarian aims. Maria has not stopped gossiping as she did around the fountain when they lived in the village, but now she gossips less and argues and criticizes more. And she has not stopped believing in the hand of fate, but more and more she believes in the course of history and the possibility for people to shape their own destiny. For Maria, more than for Giacomo, to be both a Catholic and a Communist is to be for two goods, for both Christian compassion and social justice.

IV

When I left the Rossi family in August of 1978 with the understanding that I was to write their history I wondered, as I returned to American life, if I would be able to retain in my mind's eye the vision of their lives. It has been easier than I thought, aided as I have been with copious notes and tapes. I owe this to the fact that in the twenty-six years that I have known them, something of them has always been close to me. It is simply the recognition that on one level their history has been the story of an ongoing romance, first that of Giulia and Giovanni and then that of Maria and Giacomo. It is – how can I say it without being cloyingly sentimental – a love story. That has become clear to me as I have written. To identify it as a love story, however, involving only husband and wife is to fall prey to my cultural bias, which sees love as an expression of the process of individuation, creating for itself a private space where two people know each other alone. It is difficult to see love other than in those isolating, transcending terms. Knowing the Rossis has helped me to come some of the way toward perceiving love differently, as the expression of lives lived collectively in struggle.

In much of the Western world love is pursued as solace to the isolation imposed by a driven search for autonomy. As such it constitutes a continuous rendezvous with failure, lacking as it does the morality of a profound commitment to ends other than self-realization. Both the detachment exacted by the imperatives of career and the exclusivity imposed by the American nuclear family mask the real social interdependencies that exist in the workplace and in the neighborhood. Increasingly Americans are searching for social arrangements that will allow them to realize those very interdependencies that constitute the meaningful base of their lives.

Unfortunately the family in America is caught in a cross fire; it is seen on the one hand as a regressive institution and on the other as a project for returning us along some sentimental lane toward a past that never existed. But in a society, however, in which the individual is destined to become ever more vulnerable to political mobilization and economic crisis, the family is desperately needed to protect us all. It is within this context that we need to imagine a familism, a moral familism, that will both shelter us from the world and open us up toward it. Such a familism would take upon itself the dissemination of love, a love now made impotent by its exclusivity, in such a way as to help regenerate those ties that can commit us to each other.

The Rossi family is, of course, a special case, specific as it is to a particular time and place. It is firmly articulated with a past, with that "convention" of extension we have discussed at the same time that it is responsive to the exigencies of today. Essential to its core is the kin tie based upon marriage and procreation. Like Italians, Americans will continue in large numbers to marry and have children. As Mary Jo Bane says, the family is here to stay.[27] Only in rare cases may it assume the complex form of the Rossis. Organization and composition, however, is not the point. What is important and what can be learned from them is the way they have engaged their energies, their intelligence, their emotions in a common effort to shape their future. It is my distinct feeling that the kitchen of the Rossi family is on the growing edge of Italian culture every minute of the day.

On the Via Casa Grande where the road and the canal meet, Giacomo and Maria are architects of a developing community in which men and women, young and old, parents and children, grandparents and grandchildren, great grandparents and great grandchildren, sisters and brothers, uncles and aunts, and nieces and nephews will have the experience of living together for years to come in a manner that maximizes the advantages of both autonomy and interdependence. This communal enterprise has been made possible by those economic and social changes that in other cultural contexts have been identified as the fashioners of detachment, isolation, and alienation. Here in this corner of the world the Rossi family in conjunction with many others is bending history in another direction.[28]

Notes

Introduction

1. This is not to overlook the extent to which scholarship in social history, family history, and women's history has in recent years become more responsible to those formerly unrecognized. One should note, too, the increasing interdisciplinary dialogue between social historians and anthropologists. See Carlo Ginzburg, "Anthropology and History in the 1980s: A Comment," *The Journal of Interdisciplinary History* 12 (1981), pp. 277-278.
2. Ronald J. Grele, ed., *Envelopes of Sound*, Chicago, 1975, p. 135.
3. Clifford Geertz, *The Interpretation of Cultures*, New York, 1973, p. 14. I would like to add here that Luisa Passerini sees in oral history's dedication to discourse a larger significance evocative of Marx and Engels's perception of language as practical consciousness (K. Marx and F. Engels, *The German Ideology*, New York, 1970, p. 51). Luisa Passerini, "Conoscenza Storica e Storia Orale: Sull' Utilità e il Danno delle Fonti Orali per la Storia," *Storia Orale: Vita Quotidiana e Culturale Materiale delle Classi Subalterne*, Torino, 1978, p. viii.
4. See Peter Friedlander, *The Emergence of a UAW Local, 1936-1939: A Study in Class and Culture*, Pittsburgh, 1975, pp. xx-xxxii. It would be naive to think that what I brought to that narrative was inconsequential to the final outcome; needless to say it is overdetermined. What is apparent to me, though, is the feeling of well-being I experience in their company and the pleasure I take in their affection. They extend to me and mine the status of relative, and I feel familial with them, my other family. That they are as generous as they are with their time and information and as patient with my persistence is indicative of the satisfaction they derive from being the subject of my concern. If they are anxious about what I may write they have not revealed it to me. My motive to learn from them I can only account for as a personal desire to know in depth the story of another family. I am also aware that there are old ties between Giacomo, Maria, and myself that always have included a place for the memory of Emily,

who died in 1964. It is my memory of her love for them that fires my persistency.

5. Richard Sennett and Jonathan Cobb, *The Hidden Injuries of Class*, New York, 1972.

6. Dorothy Gallagher, *Hannah's Daughters: Six Generations of an American Family, 1876-1976*, New York, 1976.

7. P.G.F. Le Play, *Les Ouvriers Europèens: l'Organization des Familles*, 6 vols., Tours, 1877-1879.

8. Louis Henry, "Historical Demography," *Daedalus* 97 (1968), pp. 385-396.

9. See Michael Gordon, Introduction, *The American Family in Social-Historical Perspective*, 2nd ed., New York, 1978, p. 4.

10. William Goode, "The Theory and Measurement of Family Change," in E.B. Sheldon and W.E. Moore, eds., *Indicators of Social Change: Concepts and Measurements*, New York, 1968, p. 321.

11. Peter Laslett and Richard Wall, eds., *Household and Family in Past Time*, Cambridge, 1972, p. 126.

12. Ibid., p. 73.

13. Jacques Dupâquier and Louis Jadin, "Structure of Household and Family in Corsica, 1769-71," in Laslett and Wall, eds., Cambridge, 1972, pp. 283-297; A.M. van der Woude, "Variations in the Size and Structure of the Household in the United Provinces of the Netherlands in the Seventeenth and Eighteenth Centuries," in Laslett and Wall, eds., pp. 299-318; Étienne Hélin, "Size of Households before the Industrial Revolution: The Case of Liège in 1801," in Laslett and Wall, eds., pp. 319-334.

14. Lutz K. Berkner, "The Use and Misuse of Census Data for the Historical Analysis of Family Structure," *The Journal of Interdisciplinary History* 4 (1975), p. 727.

15. Ibid., p. 726.

16. Ibid., pp. 729-738.

17. Peter Laslett, "Family and Household as Work Group and Kin Group: Areas of Traditional Europe Compared," in Richard Wall, Jean Robin, and Peter Laslett, eds., *Family Forms in Historic Europe*, Cambridge, 1983, pp. 516-530.

18. Aurora Angeli and Athos Belletini, "Strutture Familiari nella Campagna Bolognese a meta' dell' Ottocento," *Genus*, 35, 3-4: 1979, pp. 155-172; L. Morassi, "Strutture Familiari in un Comune dell' Italia Settentrionale alla Fine del Secolo XIX," *Genus*, 35, 1-2: 1979, pp. 197-217;

19. Laslett, "Work and Kin Groups," p. 517.

20. Michael Anderson, "Family, Household, and the Industrial Revolution," in Michael Gordon, ed., *The American Family in Social-Historical Perspective*, 2nd ed., New York, 1978, p. 43.

21. George S. Rosenberg and Donald F. Anspach, *Working Class Kinship*, Lexington, 1973, pp. 144.

22. Sydel F. Silverman, "Agricultural Organization, Social Structure, and Values in Italy: Amoral Familism Reconsidered," *American Anthropologist*, 70, 1968, pp. 1-20.

23. Jane Schneider and Peter Schneider, *Culture and Political Economy in Western Sicily*, New York, 1976; Constance Cronin, *The Sting of Change: Sicilians in Sicily and Australia*, Chicago, 1970; Edward Banfield, *The Moral Basis of a Backward Society*, Glencoe, Ill., 1958; John Davis, *Land and Family in Pisticci*, New York, 1973; Ann Cornelisen, *Women of the Shadows*, Boston, 1976; Tullio Tentori, "Social Classes and Family in a Southern Italian Town: Matera," in J. G. Peristiany, ed., *Mediterranean Family Structures*, Cambridge, 1976, pp. 273-285; Thomas Belmonte, *The Broken Fountain*, New York, 1979; Anne Parsons, *Belief, Magic and Anomie: Essays in Psychosocial Anthropology*, New York, 1969.

24. William Douglass, "The South Italian Family: A Critique," *Journal of Family History* 5 (1980), p. 351.

25. Ibid., p. 354.

26. Ibid., p. 354, n. 16.

27. Sydel Silverman, *Three Bells of Civilization: The life of an Italian Hill Town*, New York, 1975, p. 180.

28. The household configuration noted by Silverman is analogous to that discovered by Frank McArdle for Tuscany in an earlier time. Frank McArdle, *Altopascio: A Study in Tuscan Rural Society, 1587-1784*, Cambridge, 1978, p. 132.

29. David Kertzer, "European Peasant Household Structure: Some Implications from a Nineteenth-Century Italian Community," *Journal of Family History* 2, 4 (1977), p. 338. Kertzer also comments that "Contrasted with household structures in other Western European communities recently summarized by Laslett . . . , the Northern and Central Italian communities stand out for the frequency of extended and multiple family households. The high proportion of multiple family households in Bertalia, as in Tuscan villages, appears especially noteworthy." P. 339.

30. Ibid., p. 347. For a further elaboration of this theme see Kertzer, *Family Life in Central Italy, 1880-1910*, New Brunswick, 1984.

31. Laslett, "Work and Kin Groups," p. 548.

32. R.R. Ring, "Early Medieval Peasant Households in Central Italy," *Journal of Family History* 4 (1979), pp. 18-19. See especially David Herlihy, "Family Solidarity in Medieval Italian Society," in David Herlihy, Robert S. Lopez, and Vsevolod Slessarev, eds., *Economy, Society, and Government in Medieval Italy*, Kent, Ohio, 1969, for more about the family in Italy during the Middle Ages. Herlihy concludes his article by saying, "As shown by the spread of family names, a consciousness of family unity penetrated deep into Italian urban society during the late Middle Ages. As shown by the domestic chronicles, the importance of the family to the individual, and the individual to the family, were strongly felt. As shown in all sorts of literary works, the family acquired a new kind of solidarity, as a source of cultural and spiritual satisfaction, consolation, encouragement, *diletto e piacere*, for its members. The Middle Ages passed on to modern Italy not the 'autonomous nuclear family' of our own society, but one strongly tied together by bonds of mutual self-interest, mutual help,

and mutual appreciation." Pp. 181-182. For more about the past see also Christiane Klapisch, "Household and Family in Tuscany in 1427," in Laslett and Wall, eds., *Household and Family in Past Time*, p. 279; and Diane Hughes, "Domestic Ideals and Social Behavior: Evidence from Medieval Genoa," in Charles E. Rosenberg, ed., *The Family in History*, Philadelphia, 1975, p. 118.

33. Laslett, "Work and Kin Groups," p. 559.

34. Michael Young and Peter Willmott, *Family and Kinship in East London*, Glencoe, Ill., 1957; Mirra Komarovsky, *Blue-Collar Marriage*, New York, 1962; Carol B. Stack, *All Our Kin: Strategies for Survival in a Black Community*, New York, 1974.

35. Sylvia J. Yanagisako, "Woman-centered Kin Networks in Urban Bilateral Kinship," *American Ethnologist* 4, 2 (1977), pp. 207-226.

36. Stack, p. 122.

37. Yanagisako, pp. 218-222.

38. Chiara Saraceno points out that in Italy the working mother inevitably gives her small children to grandmothers or other female kin to look after. Chiara Saraceno, *Anatomia della Famiglia: Strutture Sociali e Forme Familiari*, Bari, 1976, p. 105.

39. Talcott Parsons, *Structure and Process in Modern Societies*, Glencoe, Ill., 1960; Phillip Aries, *Centuries of Childhood: A Social History of Family Life*, New York, 1962; William Goode, *World Revolution and Family Patterns*, New York, 1963; Edward Shorter, *The Making of the Modern Family*, New York, 1975; Lawrence Stone, "The Rise of the Nuclear Family in Early Modern England," in Charles E. Rosenberg, ed., *The Family in History*, Philadelphia, 1975, pp. 13-57; E.A. Wrigley, "The Process of Modernization and the Industrial Revolution in England," *The Journal of Interdisciplinary History* 3 (1972), pp. 225-259.

40. Goode writes in the final paragraph of *World Revolution and Family Patterns*, "I see the world revolution in family patterns as part of a still more important revolution that is sweeping the world in our time, the aspiration on the part of billions of people to have the right for the first time to *choose* for themselves." P. 380.

41. Christopher Lasch, "The Family in History," *The New York Review of Books*, November 13 (1975), pp. 33-38; Joyce Appleby, "Modernization Theory and the Formation of Modern Social Theories in England and America," *Comparative Studies in Society and History* 20 (1978), pp. 259-285; Tamara K. Hareven, "Modernization and Family History: Perspectives on Social Change," *Signs* 2 (1976), pp. 190-206.

42. Lawrence Stone, "Family History in the 1980s: Past Achievements and Future Trends," *The Journal of Interdisciplinary History* 12 (1981), p. 75; Carl N. Degler, *At Odds: Women and the Family in America from the Revolution to the Present*, New York, 1980; Mary B. Norton, ed., *Liberty's Daughters: The Revolutionary Experience of American Women 1750-1800*, Boston, 1980.

43. What is in fact traditional and what is modern in regard to the family is in itself somewhat problematical. Phillip Aries has written convincingly that

evolution in the past few centuries has led not to the triumph of individualism but to the triumph of the family. Aries, p. 406.

44. Mariarosa Dalla Costa and Selma James, *The Power of Women and the Subversion of the Community*, Bristol, 1972, p. 41.

45. Tamara K. Hareven, ed., *Transitions: The Family and the Life Course in Historical Perspective*, New York, 1978.

46. From a more theoretical than methodological perspective I find useful the distinction that Rapp makes between household as the actual material entity in which persons live–the material base–and family as the "normative, correct way in which people get recruited into households." Rayna Rapp, "Family and Class in Contemporary America: Notes Toward an Understanding of Ideology," *Science and Society* 42 (1978), pp. 280-281. It is within this understanding then that we can speak of family as ideology that both "reflects and masks the realities of household formation and sustenance." Rayna Rapp, Ellen Ross and Renate Bridenthal, "Examining Family History," *Feminist Studies* 5 (1979), p. 177.

Conclusion

1. J. Demos, *A Little Commonwealth: Family Life in Plymouth County*, New York, 1970, pp. 62-67.

2. D. Pitkin, "Partible Inheritance and the Open Fields," *Agricultural History* 35 (1961), pp. 65-69.

3. D. Pitkin, "Land Tenure and Family Organization in an Italian Village," *Human Organization* 18 (1959), pp. 169-173.

4. D. Pitkin, "Marital Property Considerations among Peasants: An Italian Example," *Anthropological Quarterly* 33 (1960), p. 36.

5. The Italian feminist Mariarosa Dalla Costa's call for women to "get out of the house, . . . reject the home," remains one of the most powerful assertions of the subservience of women in capitalism. It was her work that initiated the debate on the economic value of housework. Mariarosa Dalla Costa and Selma James, *The Power of Women and the Subversion of the Community*, Bristol, 1972, pp. 21-56. It is true, of course, that feminist analysis, both radical (patriarchy) and Marxist (capitalism), has moved beyond Dalla Costa's perception that women are subordinated first and foremost by capital and dominated only secondarily by men. Accordingly in those terms the solution lies primarily in altering the relations of production, which determine familial forms and the woman's place in it. Natalie Sokoloff, *Between Money and Love: The Dialectics of Women's Home and Market Work*, New York: 1980, pp. 127-128. Thus radical feminist theory stressing the role of patriarchy as the cause of woman's oppression opts for a transformation of the family and the female-male relationships within it. Dorothy Dinnerstein, *The Mermaid and the Minotaur: Sexual Arrangements and Human Malaise*, New York, 1976.
At the same time that there has been an attempt to overcome the dichotomy between the domestic and work spheres marked by earlier feminist

thought, an effort has been made to see how the dialectical relationship between patriarchy and capitalism makes for oppression of women in both realms. See Joan Kelly, "The Doubled Vision of Feminist Theory: A Postscript to the 'Woman and Power' Conference," *Feminist Studies* 5 (1979), p. 225.

6. The view of the family as a locus of struggle and a location where production and redistribution occur is forcefully presented by Heidi I. Hartmann in "The Family as the Locus of Gender, Class and Political Struggle: The Example of Housework," *Signs* 6 (1981), p. 368. The extent to which the family reflects the larger society touches upon an issue of considerable moment: the derivation of cooperation as opposed to conflict. If capitalism and patriarchy shape primarily the nature of familial interrelationships, as some would have it, the relationships cannot help but be tense and dissonant. But from whence comes solidarity if children are socialized by the expectations of class and gender conflict? It seems unlikely to believe that class solidarity springs full-blown from the sudden recognition of common interests by isolated individuals. One could argue with some merit that dialectically, differentiation creates interdependence. But there is a quality of solidarity that pervades the Rossi family that emanates not just from the instrumentality of divisions of labor but from years of life experiences shared together. And in that way the mutual dependencies of family life can generate community. In thinking about this point I was helped by Jane Humphries, "The Working Class Family: A Marxist Perspective," in Jean B. Elshtain, ed., *The Family in Political Thought*, Amherst, 1982, p. 218.

7. I am indebted to Rayna Rapp for her insights concerning the importance of ideology for working-class families. "Family and Class in Contemporary America: Notes Towards an Understanding of Ideology," *Science and Society* 42 (1978), p. 294.

8. Humphries's analysis provides, I believe, a useful corrective to those Marxist feminists who see the family primarily as epiphenomenal to capitalism. Humphries, pp. 197-222. For an excellent summary of the arguments among Marxist feminists see Sokoloff.

9. Edward C. Banfield, *The Moral Basis of a Backward Society*, Glencoe, Ill., 1958.

10. Philip E. Slater, *The Pursuit of Loneliness: American Culture at the Breaking Point*, Boston, 1970, p. 5.

11. Takeo Doi, *The Anatomy of Dependence*, with a forward by John Bester, Tokyo, 1973, p. 8.

12. Nancy Chodorow, *The Reproduction of Mothering: Psychoanalysis and the Sociology of Gender*, Berkeley, 1978, p. 187. I do not wish to leave the impression that the drive for independence is to be understood primarily as a psychological phenomenon. Economic and social variables certainly impinge significantly as well. Nor is woman-mothering typical only of industrialized societies. See Phillip E. Slater, *The Glory of Hera: Greek Mythology and the Greek Family*, Boston, 1968.

13. Dinnerstein, p. 161.
14. Anne Parsons, *Belief, Magic and Anomie: Essays in Psychosocial Anthropology*, New York, 1969, p. 48.
15. Carol Gilligan, *In a Different Voice: Psychological Theory and Women's Development*, Cambridge, 1982, p. 8.
16. According to Virginia Yans McLaughlin, working-class Italians in Buffalo "retained a cultural bias against female employment even among the second generation." McLaughlin, "Patterns of Work and Family Organization: Buffalo's Italians," in Theodore K. Rabb and Robert I. Rotberg, eds., *The Family in History: Interdisciplinary Essays*, New York, 1971, p. 122. For affirmation of McLaughlin's findings, see Elizabeth H. Pleck, "A Mother's Wages: Income Earnings among Married Italian and Black Women, 1896–1911," in Michael Gordon, ed., *The American Family in Social-Historical Perspective*, 2nd ed., New York, 1978, p. 502.
17. One might argue that the convergence of distribution of both food and money by the wife to the mother implies an asymmetrical component to the relationship: the wife playing mother to her husband-son. Insofar as this is true the structure of the three-generation family affords the proximity for its continuous realization.
18. Thomas Belmonte, *The Broken Fountain*, New York, 1979, p. 87; Ann Cornelisen, *Women of the Shadows*, Boston, 1976, p. 219.
19. Parsons, p. 49.
20. Ibid., p. 52.
21. Rapp, p. 285.
22. Lillian B. Rubin, *Worlds of Pain: Life in the Working-Class Family*, New York, 1976, p. 80.
23. It is possible, of course, to romanticize such an arrangement as the one created by Giacomo and Maria, to be seduced by its evocation of communalism. Herbert Gans, Elliot Liebow, and Carol Stack have pointed to the costs and pressures that may flow from such parental support. But in this instance and in others visible in the area, cooperation does not seem to have leveled personal advantage. Rather it has maximized it for everyone. It is not that they lack individuality but that it is expressed differently, more in regard to the skills of responsiveness than in the assertion of rights. To be *simpatico* is more important than to be correct. Herbert J. Gans, *The Urban Villagers: Group and Class in the Life of Italian-Americans*, New York, 1962; Elliot Liebow, *Tally's Corner: A Study of Negro Streetcorner Men*, Boston, 1967; Carol B. Stack, *All Our Kin: Strategies for Survival in a Black Community*, New York, 1974.
24. For additional information about Stilo see Luigi Cunsolo, *La Storia di Stilo e del Suo Regio Demanio dal Secolo VII ai Nostri Giorni*, Rome, 1965.
25. David I. Kertzer, *Comrades and Christians: Religion and Political Struggle in Communist Italy*, Cambridge, 1980.
26. In this respect the Communist Party serves the same supportive function for Giacomo as it does for Mario Cecchi as described in "The San Vincenzo Cell." Jane Kramer, *Unsettling Europe*, New York, 1980, p. 11.

27. Mary Jo Bane, *Here to Stay: American Families in the Twentieth Century*, New York, 1976.
28. A direction toward which some Americans are also moving. The high cost of housing linked with unemployment is causing some young couples to co-reside with one set of parents or the other. Furthermore, the increase in life expectancy means that most people will have parents until they are well into their forties, with the consequence of increasing cross-household family relationships. George Masnick and Mary Jo Bane, *The Nation's Families: 1960-1990*, Boston, 1980. Bell makes a similar point for nineteenth-century Italy, stating that "a substantial improvement in the life expectancy of those who reached adulthood . . . created an increasing number of extended families." Rudolph M. Bell, *Fate and Honor, Family and Village: Demographic and Cultural Change in Rural Italy since 1800*, Chicago, 1979, p. 112.

Index

aggregate analysis, 8–9, 11
amae, 211
America, 66, 205, 219, 223
  "catching up," 154
  influence of fashions, 150
  multinational companies, 156, 200
Anderson, Michael, 10, 226n20
Angeli, Aurora, 10, 207, 226n18
anger
  Caterina, 198
  Giacomo, 78, 93, 105, 120, 134, 152, 163
  Giovanni, 36, 47
  Giovanni and Giulia at Domenico, 62
  Giulia, 36, 183
  Luigi, 149, 196
  Maria, 131, 221
  Silvia, 196
  Teresa, 165, 196–7
animals, 29, 192, 208
  chickens, 40, 43, 84, 89, 142
  donkey, 26, 27–8, 31
  goat, 26
  heifers, 142, 143, 144, 155
  milking cows, 155, 168
  pigs, 26, 43, 84, 88, 142, 153
  rabbits, 142
  sheep, 84
  veal, 142
Anspach, Donald F., 10, 226n21
anthropology, 5, 7
  affinity with oral history, 5
  community studies, 5
  fieldwork, 5
  the interview, 17
  transformation of, 5
  use of tape recorder, 17
Antonio, 48, 50, 52–3, 58, 64, 72, 92, 103, 146, 157–8, 164–5, 183, 186, 200, 202
  acquires truck, 140
  becomes secretary of Communist party, 179
  born, 45
  co-resides with Giovanni and Giulia, 144, 218–19
  drives dying father to hospital, 181
  entertains at Luigi's wedding, 194
  escapes bombardment during war, 59
  named for San Antonio, 47–8
  partnership with Michele, 164
  suckled by wetnurse, 46, 47
Appleby, Joyce, 14, 228n41
Argentina, 24–6
  Buenos Aires, 30
Aries, Phillip, 14, 228n39, n43
artisans, 12, 69
  see also tailoring
automobile
  Giacomo, 162, 167, 216
  Giacomo's desire for, 157–8
  Giacomo's first car (Fiat 500), 163
  Giacomo's second car (Fiat 124), 176, 184
  installment plan, 162
  Salvatore's, 145
  Tonino's truck, 144
autonomy, 14, 216, 224 search for, 223

Bane, Mary Jo, 223, 232n27, n28
Banfield, Edward, 11, 227n23, 230n9
baptism, 90, 203, 220
  of Bruno, 108
  of Caterina, 128
  of Concetta, 26
  of Luigi, 99–100

233

Index

DATE DUE

INTRA
ST. PETE
RET SEP 0 1 1987

BRODART, INC.

Cat. No. 23-221